ON CRITICAL PEDAGOGY

HENRY A. GIROUX

BLOOMSBURY

NEW YORK • LONDON • NEW DELHI • SYDNEY

Bloomsbury Academic
An imprint of Bloomsbury Publishing Inc

1385 Broadway
New York
NY 10018
USA

50 Bedford Square
London
WC1B 3DP
UK

www.bloomsbury.com

Bloomsbury is a registered trade mark of Bloomsbury Publishing Plc

First published in 201 by the Continuum International Publishing Group Inc
Reprinted 2012 (twice)
Reprinted by Bloomsbury Academic 2013, 2014

© Henry A. Giroux, 2011

Library of Congress Cataloging-in-Publication Data
A catalog record for this book is available from the Library of Congress.

ISBN: HB: 978-1-4411-6819-1
PB: 978-1-4411-1622-2
EPDF: 978-1-4411-6254-0
EPUB: 978-1-4411-9042-0

Printed and bound in the United States of America

Contents

Acknowledgments

For Susan.

I would also like to thank the Social Sciences and Humanities Research Council of Canada for their generous support in enabling me to finish this book.

Introduction

CHAPTER 1

Critical Pedagogy
in Dark Times

Some of the essays in this book were composed over 30 years ago, while the majority were written in the last decade — that the earlier essays remain relevant speaks to the ongoing attack on the very nature and condition of public and higher education in the United States. In recent years, there has been a resurgence of the logic and arguments that were first used against critical education in the 1970s and 1980s — today, ironically, they are put forth by their proponents in the name of "educational reform." Three decades ago, it was precisely the dismantling of education's critical capacity in conjunction with the emergence of a politics of authoritarianism that motivated my involvement in the field of education, and critical pedagogy in particular. What all the essays in this book have in common is the belief that education is fundamental to democracy and that no democratic society can survive without a formative culture shaped by pedagogical practices capable of creating the conditions for producing citizens who are critical, self-reflective, knowledgeable, and willing to make moral judgments and act in a socially responsible way. I recognized early on in my career that critical pedagogy as a moral and political practice does more than emphasize the importance of critical analysis and moral judgments. It also provides tools to unsettle commonsense assumptions, theorize matters of self and social agency, and engage the ever-changing demands and promises of a democratic polity.

Critical pedagogy takes as one of its central projects an attempt to be discerning and attentive to those places and practices in which social agency has been denied and produced. When I first began exploring and writing about critical pedagogy, I became aware that pedagogy might offer educators an important set of theoretical tools in support of the values of reason and freedom. During this time, I was teaching history to high school students. For me, critical pedagogy as theoretical and political practice became especially useful as a way to resist the increasingly prevalent approach to pedagogy that viewed it as merely a skill, technique, or disinterested method. Within this dominant educational paradigm, young people were at one time and are now once again shamelessly reduced to "cheerful robots" through modes of pedagogy that embrace an instrumental rationality in which matters of justice, values, ethics, and power are erased from any notion of teaching and learning. I rejected the mainstream assumption that treated pedagogy simply as a set of strategies and skills to use in order to teach prespecified subject matter. Critical pedagogy is not about an a priori method that simply can be applied regardless of context. It is the outcome of particular struggles and is always related to the specificity of particular contexts, students, communities, and available resources. It draws attention to the ways in which knowledge, power, desire, and experience are produced under specific basic conditions of learning and illuminates the role that pedagogy plays as part of a struggle over assigned meanings, modes of expression, and directions of desire, particularly as these bear on the formation of the multiple and ever-contradictory versions of the 'self' and its relationship to the larger society. My view of critical pedagogy developed out of a recognition that education was important not only for gainful employment but also for creating the formative culture of beliefs, practices, and social relations that enable individuals to wield power, learn how to govern, and nurture a democratic society that takes equality, justice, shared values, and freedom seriously. I began to see how pedagogy is central to politics in that it is involved in the construction of critical agents and provides the formative culture that is indispensable to a democratic society.

Wedded to a narrative of triumphalism and economic growth, education in the late 1970s and early 1980s was increasingly viewed less as a public good than as a private right. But there was more at stake in the emergent field of critical pedagogy than mapping the modes of economic and cultural domination that tied schools to new regimes of privatization, commodification, and consumerism. There was also an attempt to view schools as sites of struggle, to open up pedagogical forms to the possibility of resistance, and to connect teaching to the promise of self- and social change. As part of such an understanding, I attempted early on in my work to employ a notion of critical pedagogy that marshaled a language of critique and hope. While over the last three decades my understanding of the insights offered by critical pedagogy has expanded to spheres outside the classroom, the principles explored in my earlier work represent a crucial foundation. In order to address the struggles facing public and higher education today, I find it increasingly necessary to go back to these foundational principles as a starting point for explaining the value of a democratically informed notion of education and the importance of critical pedagogy.

The principles guiding my work on critical pedagogy are grounded in critique as a mode of analysis that interrogates texts, institutions, social relations, and ideologies as part of the script of official power. Put simply, critique focuses largely on how domination manifests as both a symbolic and an institutional force and the ways in which it impacts on all levels of society. For example, schools are often rightly criticized for becoming adjuncts of corporations or for modeling themselves on a culture of fear and security. Often this position goes no further than simply analyzing what is wrong with schools and in doing so makes it appear as if the problems portrayed are intractable. Domination in this mode of discourse appears to be sutured,

4

with little room to imagine any sense of either resistance or hope. While it is important to politicize the process of schooling and recognize the gritty sense of limits it faces within a capitalist society, what is also needed to supplement this view is an enobling, imaginative vision that takes us beyond the given and commonplace. Against the anti-democratic forces shaping public and higher education, there is a need to mobilize the imagination and develop a language of possibility in which any attempt to foreclose on hope could be effectively challenged. In this instance, the language of hope goes beyond acknowledging how power works as a mechanism of domination and offers up a vocabulary in which it becomes possible to imagine power working in the interest of justice, equality, and freedom. Examples of such a discourse emerge in my analyses of schools as democratic public spheres, teachers as public intellectuals, and students as potential democratic agents of individual and social change.

As part of the language of critique, I use critical pedagogy to examine the various ways in which classrooms too often function as modes of social, political, and cultural reproduction, particularly when the goals of education are defined through the promise of economic growth, job training, and mathematical utility. In the context of reproduction, pedagogy is largely reduced to a transmission model of teaching and limited to the propagation of a culture of conformity and the passive absorption of knowledge. Contrary to these ideas, I develop a theory of critical pedagogy that provides a range of critiques against a traditional pedagogy operating under the sway of technical mastery, instrumental logic, and various other fundamentalisms that acquire their authority by erasing any trace of subaltern histories, class struggles, and racial and gender inequalities and injustices.

As part of the language of hope and possibility, I develop a notion of critical pedagogy that addresses the democratic potential of engaging how experience, knowledge, and power are shaped in the classroom in different and often unequal contexts, and how teacher authority might be mobilized against dominant pedagogical practices as part of the practice of freedom. I stress pedagogical approaches that enable students to read texts differently as objects of interrogation rather than slavishly through a culture of pedagogical conformity that teaches unquestioning reverence. I also argue for developing a language for thinking critically about how culture deploys power and how pedagogy as a moral and political practice enables students to focus on the suffering of others. I develop a framework for engaging critical pedagogy as a theoretical resource and as a productive practice, and in doing so reject dominant notions of pedagogy as an a priori method, technique, or rationality that simply has to be implemented. Instead, I expand the meaning and theory of pedagogy as part of an ongoing individual and collective struggle over knowledge, desire, values, social relations, and, most important, modes of political agency. I develop the idea that critical pedagogy is central in drawing attention to questions regarding who has control over the conditions for the production of knowledge, values, and classroom practices. I also address the importance of recognizing the role critical pedagogy plays in acknowledging the different ways in which authority, experience, and power are produced under specific conditions of learning. I place great importance, as did Paulo Freire, Roger Simon, Joe Kincheloe, and others, on the productive and deliberative nature of pedagogy.

As part of a discourse of educated hope, critical pedagogy in my work functions as a lens for viewing public and higher education as important sites of struggle that are capable of providing students with alternative modes of teaching, social relations, and imagining rather than those that merely support the status quo. While recognizing the importance of public and higher education as potential democratic public spheres, I also present the case that educators at all levels of schooling should be addressed as public intellectuals willing to connect pedagogy with the problems of public life, a commitment to civic courage, and the demands of social responsibility. I understand pedagogy as immanently political, but not because I believe it is desirable to impose a particular ideology on teachers and students. On the contrary, I understand pedagogy as political because it is inherently productive and directive practice rather than neutral or objective. For me, pedagogy is part of an always unfinished project intent on developing a meaningful life for all students. Such a project becomes relevant to the degree that it provides the pedagogical conditions for students to appropriate the knowledge and skills necessary to address the limits of justice in democratic societies. As a responsible and self-reflective practice, critical pedagogy illuminates how classroom learning embodies selective values, is entangled with relations of power, entails judgments about what knowledge counts, legitimates specific social relations, defines agency in particular ways, and always presupposes a particular notion of the future. As a form of provocation and challenge, critical pedagogy attempts to take young people beyond the world they are familiar with and makes clear how classroom knowledge, values, desires, and social relations are always implicated in power.

Politics is central to any notion of pedagogy that takes as its primary project the necessity to provide conditions that expand the capacities of students to think critically and teach them how to take risks, act in a socially responsible way, and connect private issues with larger public considerations. What is more, critical pedagogy foregrounds a struggle over identities, modes of agency, and those maps of meaning that enable students to define who they are and how they relate to others. Though writing in another context, Stuart Hall is helpful in capturing how matters of agency and identity are central to any notion of pedagogy and political organization. He writes:

> How can we organize these huge, randomly varied, and diverse things we call human subjects into positions where they can recognize one another for long enough to act together, and thus to take up a position that one of these days they might live out and act through as an identity. Identity is at the end, not

6

the beginning, of the paradigm. Identity is what is at stake in any viable notion of political organization.[1]

Understood in these terms, critical pedagogy becomes a project that stresses the need for teachers and students to actively transform knowledge rather than simply consume it. At the same time, I believe it is crucial for educators not only to connect classroom knowledge to the experiences, histories, and resources that students bring to the classroom but also to link such knowledge to the goal of furthering their capacities to be critical agents who are responsive to moral and political problems of their time and recognize the importance of organized collective struggles.[2] At its most ambitious, the overarching narrative in this discourse is to educate students to lead a meaningful life, learn how to hold power and authority accountable, and develop the skills, knowledge, and courage to challenge commonsense assumptions while being willing to struggle for a more socially just world. In this view, it is necessary for critical pedagogy to be rooted in a project that is tied to the cultivation of an informed, critical citizenry capable of participating and governing in a democratic society. As such, it aims at enabling rather than subverting the potential of a democratic culture.

During the 1980s, I observed how the educational force of the wider culture had become more powerful (if not dangerous) in its role of educating young people to define themselves simply through the logic of commodification. In response, I expanded the notion of critical pedagogy to include sites other than schools. The growing prevalence of a variety of media — from traditional screen and print cultures to the digital world of the new media — necessitated a new language for understanding popular culture as a teaching machine, rather than simply as a source of entertainment or a place that objectively disseminates information. In response to the increasing influence of the broader culture in shaping people's perspectives and identities, I developed an analytic of *public pedagogy*, that is, a framework that illuminates the pedagogical practices at work in what C. Wright Mills once called the "cultural apparatus." What was clear to me at the time was that the cultural apparatus had been largely hijacked by the forces of neoliberalism, or what some theorists would call a new and more intense form of market fundamentalism. In this mode of public pedagogy, a new disciplinary apparatus developed at the institutional level through which the pedagogical possibilities for critical thought, analysis, dialogue, and action came under assault by a market-driven model of education. This became fully evident when many advocates of critical pedagogy and radical educational theory were fired from public schools and colleges. In addition, both liberal and conservative governments began to promote modes of pedagogy and educational goals that were largely about training future workers. Teachers and faculty were increasingly removed from exercising any vestige of real power in shaping the conditions under which they worked. Public school teachers were deskilled as one national political administration after another embraced a stripped down version of education, the central goal of which was to promote economic growth and global competitiveness, which entailed a much-narrowed form of pedagogy that focused on memorization, high-stakes testing, and helping students find a good fit within a wider market-oriented culture of commodification, standardization, and conformity. This model of education has continued to gain ground, despite its ill effects on students and teachers. Young people are now openly treated as customers and clients rather than a civic resource, while many poor youth are simply excluded from the benefits of a decent education through the implementation of zero-tolerance policies that treat them as criminals to be contained, punished, or placed under the jurisdiction of the criminal justice system.

Higher education more and more has been held hostage to market-driven modes of accountability as disciplines and programs are now largely rewarded to the degree that they contribute to economic profitability. Under this regime of economic Darwinism, higher education faculty are increasingly deprived of power and tenure-track jobs and are subjected to a relentless attack by right-wing religious and political fundamentalists who equate any critique of established power, history, and policy as tantamount to engaging in "un-American behavior." If the politics of economic growth, scientism, and technical rationality influenced public and higher education in the 1980s, a new and more vicious mode of ideology and teaching, which I call neoliberal pedagogy, has emerged and now dominates education at all levels of schooling. As a pedagogical practice, neoliberal pedagogy also pervades every aspect of the wider culture, stifling critical thought, reducing citizenship to the act of consuming, defining certain marginal populations as contaminated and disposable, and removing the discourse of democracy from any vestige of pedagogy both in and outside of schooling. The political sphere, like most educational sites, is increasingly driven by a culture of cruelty and a survival-of-the-fittest culture. I believe the threat to critical modes of education and democracy has never been greater than in the current historical moment.

Critical pedagogy has always been responsive to the deepest problems and conflicts of our time, and the essays in this book partake in that project. In what follows, I situate my work on critical pedagogy as part of a broader project that attempts to address the growing authoritarian threats posed by the current regime of market fundamentalism against youth, critical modes of education, and the ethos of democracy itself. In this way, the chapters in this book, while being written at different times, can be read as a complementary set of resources through which to imagine critical pedagogy — with its insistence on critical deliberation, careful judgment, and civic courage — as central to the cultivation of what John Dewey once called "democracy as a way of life." The chapters can also be read as interventions within the current historical conjuncture in which a renewed attention on pedagogy emerges out of the recognition that there is a real educational crisis in North America and a real need for developing a new theoretical, political, and pedagogical vocabulary for addressing the issue. In addition, these chapters can be used to rethink what democracy might mean at a time when public values, spheres, and identities are being eviscerated under a regime of economic Darwinism in which the "living dead" increasingly govern our educational apparatuses in public and higher education and also in the wider culture.[3] And, finally, these chapters collectively embody a politics of educated hope, responsive to the need to think beyond established narratives of power, prevailing "commonsense" approaches to educational policy and practice, a widening culture of punishment, and the banal script of using mathematical performance measures as benchmarks for academic success. We need to think otherwise as a condition for acting otherwise. Only a pedagogy that embraces the civic purpose of education and provides a vocabulary and set of practices that enlarge our humanity will contribute to increasing the possibility for public life and expanding shared spaces, values, and responsibilities. Only such a pedagogy can promote the modes of solidarity and collective action capable of defending the public good and the symbolic and institutional power relations necessary for a sustainable democracy.

With the growing influence of neoliberalism in the last 30 years, the United States has witnessed the emergence of modes of education that make human beings superfluous as political agents, close down democratic public spheres, disdain public values, and undermine the conditions for dissent. Within both institutions of schooling and the old and new media — with their expanding networks of knowledge production and circulation — we see the emergence and dominance of pedagogical models that fail to question and all too frequently embrace the economic Darwinism of neoliberalism. Neoliberal ideology emphasizes winning at all costs, even if it means a ruthless competitiveness, an almost rabid individualism, and a notion of agency largely constructed within a market-driven rationality that abstracts economics and markets from ethical considerations. Both President George W. Bush and President Barack Obama embraced models of education largely tied to the dictates of a narrow instrumental rationality and economic growth.[4] Both associated learning valuable knowledge and skills as part of a broader economic script that judges worth by what corporations need to increase their profits. President Obama continues to repeat the idea that education should be valued primarily for its ability to raise individual incomes and promote economic growth, with the consequence that pedagogy is tied to models of accountability driven by the need to "teach to the test." In this paradigm, students are educated primarily to acquire market-oriented skills in order to compete favorably in the global economy. This type of pedagogy celebrates rote learning, memorization, and high-stakes testing, while it "produces an atmosphere of student passivity and teacher routinization."[5] Rarely has President Obama mentioned the democratic goals of education or stressed that critical education is central to politics in that it provides the formative culture that produces engaged citizens and makes social action and democracy possible.

For too many educators, politicians, and corporate hedge fund managers, poor economic performance on the part of individuals is coded as a genetic and often racialized defect, while an unwillingness or inability to buy into a consumer culture is defined as a form of individual depravity.[6] Private endeavors now trump the public good across the full spectrum of political positions. Neoliberal public pedagogy strips education of its public values, critical content, and civic responsibilities as part of its broader goal of creating new subjects wedded to the logic of privatization, efficiency, flexibility, the accumulation of capital, and the destruction of the social state. Increasingly, the values that drive neoliberal pedagogies in the United States are also embodied in policies that attempt to shape diverse levels of public and higher education all over the globe. The script has become overly familiar and all too often is simply taken for granted, especially in Western countries. Shaping the neoliberal framing of public and higher education is a corporate-based ideology that embraces standardizing the curriculum, supports hierarchical management, and reduces all levels of education to job training sites. Marc Bousquet rightly argues that central to this notion of neoliberalism is a view of higher education that enshrines "more standardization! More managerial control! A teacher-proof curriculum! . . . a top-down control of curriculum [and] tenured management."[7] Significant numbers of faculty have been reduced to the status of part-time and temporary workers, comprising a new subaltern class of disempowered educators. In this view faculty become just another reserve army of cheap laborers, a force that can be eagerly exploited in order to raise the bottom line while disregarding the rights of academic labor and the quality of education that students deserve. There is no talk in this view of higher education about shared governance between faculty and administrators, educating students as critical citizens rather than as potential employees of Wal-Mart, or affirming faculty as scholars and public intellectuals who have a measure of both autonomy and power. Teachers in the public school system fare no better than university educators, as they are increasingly deskilled, reduced to either technicians or security guards, or both.

There is a general consensus among educators in North America that public and higher education are in a chronic state of crisis. As Stanley Aronowitz points out, "For some the main issue is whether schools are failing to transmit the general intellectual culture, even to the most able students. What is at stake in this critique is the fate of America as a civilization — particularly the condition of its democratic institutions and the citizens who are, in the final analysis, responsible for maintaining them."[8] Universities are now facing a growing set of challenges arising from drastic budget cuts, diminishing educational quality, the downsizing of faculty, the growth of military-funded research, and the revamping of the curriculum to fit the needs of the market.[9] Public schools are being devastated as tax revenues dry up. Thousands of teachers are being laid off, and vital programs are being slashed to the bone. It gets worse. Republican Party governors in Wisconsin, Ohio,

Florida, and other states are eliminating the bargaining rights of teachers' unions.

In the United States, many of the problems in higher education can be linked to low funding, the domination of universities by market mechanisms, public education's move towards privatization, the intrusion of the national security state, and the lack of faculty self-governance, all of which not only contradicts the culture and democratic value of higher education but also makes a mockery of the very meaning and mission of the university. Universities and colleges have been increasingly abandoned as democratic public spheres dedicated to providing a public service, expanding upon humankind's great intellectual and cultural achievements, and educating future generations to be able to confront the challenges of a global democracy. Meanwhile, public education has been under attack by the religious right and advocates of charter schools and privatization, and increasingly subject to disciplinary measures that prioritize a culture of conformity and punishment.

The crisis in education has crucial political, social, ethical, and spiritual consequences. At a time when market culture is aggressively colonizing everyday life and social forms increasingly lose their shape or disappear altogether, educational institutions seem to represent a reassuring permanence, as a slowly changing bulwark in a landscape of rapidly dissolving critical public spheres. But public and higher education in the United States and elsewhere are increasingly losing their civic character and commitment to public life as they become more closely aligned with corporate power and military values. Corporate leaders are now hired as university presidents; the shrinking ranks of tenure-line faculty are filled with contract labor; students are treated as customers; adjunct faculty are now hired through temp agencies; and learning is increasingly defined in instrumental terms. At the same time, critical knowledge is relegated to the dustbin of history, only retaining a vestige of support within impoverished and underfunded liberal arts programs that are themselves being downsized and marginalized within the larger institution.

Conscripting the university to serve as corporate power's apprentice, while reducing matters of university governance to an extension of corporate logic and interests, substantially weakens the possibility for higher education to function as a democratic public sphere, academics as engaged public intellectuals, and students as critical citizens. In a market-driven and militarized university, questions regarding how education might enable students to develop a keen sense of prophetic justice, promote the analytic skills necessary to hold power accountable, and provide the spiritual foundation through which they not only respect the rights of others but also, as Bill Moyers puts it, "claim their moral and political agency"[10] become increasingly irrelevant.[11] Public schools have fared even worse. They are subject to corporate modes of management, disciplinary measures, and commercial values that have stripped them of any semblance of democratic governance; teachers are reduced to a subaltern class of technicians; and students are positioned as mere recipients of the worst forms of banking education and, in the case of students marginalized by race and class, treated as disposable populations deserving of harsh punishments and disciplinary measures modeled after prisons.

If the commercialization, commodification, privatization, and militarization of public and higher education continue unabated, then education will become yet another casualty among a diminishing number of institutions capable of fostering critical inquiry, public debate, human acts of justice, and common deliberation. The calculating logic of an instrumentalized, corporatized, and privatized education does more than diminish the moral and political vision necessary to sustain a vibrant democracy and an engaged notion of social agency; it also undermines the development of public spaces where matters of dissent, public conscience, and social justice are valued and offered protection against the growing anti-democratic tendencies that are enveloping much of the United States and many other parts of the world.

Educating young people in the spirit of a critical democracy by providing them with the knowledge, passion, civic capacities, and social responsibility necessary to address the problems facing the nation and the globe means challenging those modes of schooling and pedagogy designed largely to promote economic gain, create consuming subjects, and substitute training for critical thinking and analysis. Such anti-democratic and anti-intellectual tendencies have intensified alongside the contemporary emergence of a number of diverse fundamentalisms, especially a market-based neoliberal rationality that exhibits a deep disdain, if not outright contempt, for both democracy and publically engaged teaching and scholarship. In such circumstances, it is not surprising that education in many parts of the world is held hostage to political and economic forces that wish to convert educational institutions into corporate establishments defined by a profit-oriented identity and mission.

Prominent educators and theorists such as Paulo Freire, Hannah Arendt, John Dewey, Cornelius Castoriadis, and C. Wright Mills have long believed and rightly argued that we should neither allow education to be modeled after the business world nor sit by while corporate power and influence undermine the relative autonomy of higher education by exercising control over its faculty, curricula, and students. All of these public intellectuals have in common a vision and project of rethinking what role education might play in providing students with the habits of mind and ways of acting that would enable them to identify and address the most acute challenges and dangers facing a world increasingly dominated by a mode of instrumental and technical thinking that is morally and spiritually bankrupt. All of these theorists offered a notion of the university as a bastion of democratic learning and meaningful social values, a notion that must be defended in discussions about what form should be taken by the relationship among corporations, the war industries, and higher education in the twenty-first century.

The major impetus of this book is to present the theoretical and practical elements of a critical pedagogy in which education has a responsibility not only to search for the truth regardless of where it may lead but also to educate students to make authority politically and morally accountable. Such an approach is informed by the assumption that public and higher education must strive to expand the pedagogical conditions necessary to sustain those modes of critical agency, dialogue, and social responsibility crucial to keeping democracies alive. Critical pedagogy within schools and the critical public pedagogy produced in broader cultural apparatuses are modes of intervention dedicated to creating those democratic public spheres where individuals can think critically, relate sympathetically to the problems of others, and intervene in the world in order to address major social problems. Although questions regarding whether educational institutions should serve strictly public rather than private interests no longer carry the weight of forceful criticism, as they did in the past, such questions are still crucial in addressing the reality of public and higher education and what it might mean to imagine the full participation of such institutions in public life as protectors and promoters of democratic values, especially at a time when the meaning and purpose of public and higher education are besieged by a phalanx of narrow economic and political interests.

All of the chapters in this book share the position that public and higher education may constitute one of the few public spheres left in which critical knowledge, values, and learning offer a glimpse of the promise of education for nurturing hope and a substantive democracy.[12] It may be the case that everyday life is increasingly organized around market principles, but confusing democracy with market relations hollows out the legacy of education, which is inherently moral, not commercial. Democracy places civic demands upon its citizens, and such demands point to the necessity of an education that is broad-based, critical, and supportive of meaningful citizen power, participation in self-governance, and democratic leadership. Only through such a critical educational culture can students learn how to become individual and social agents, rather than merely disengaged spectators, and become able not only to think otherwise but also to act upon civic commitments that "necessitate a reordering of basic power arrangements" fundamental to promoting the common good and producing a meaningful democracy.[13]

What all of the chapters in this book partake in is the aim of reclaiming public and higher education as sites of moral and political practice for which the purpose is both to introduce students to the great reservoir of diverse intellectual ideas and traditions and to engage those inherited bodies of knowledge thorough critical dialogue, analysis, and comprehension. Each chapter affirms the notion that education should be organized around a set of social experiences and ethical considerations through which students can rethink what Jacques Derrida once called the concepts of "the possible and the impossible"[14] and move toward what Jacques Rancière describes as loosening the coordinates of the sensible through a constant reexamination of the boundaries that distinguish the sensible from the subversive.[15] Both theorists express concern with how the boundaries of knowledge and everyday life are constructed in ways that seem unquestionable, which makes it all the more necessary not only to interrogate commonsense assumptions but also to ask what it means to question such assumptions and see beyond them. Critical pedagogy asserts that students can engage their own learning from a position of agency and in so doing can actively participate in narrating their identities through a culture of questioning that opens up a space of translation between the private and the public while changing the forms of self- and social recognition.

Another overarching theme of the book argues that central to any viable notion of critical pedagogy is enabling students to think critically while providing the conditions for students to recognize "how knowledge is related to the power of self-definition"[16] and to use the knowledge they gain both to critique the world in which they live and, when necessary, to intervene in socially responsible ways in order to change it. Critical pedagogy is about more than a struggle over assigned meanings, official knowledge, and established modes of authority: it is also about encouraging students to take risks, act on their sense of social responsibility, and engage the world as an object of both critical analysis and hopeful transformation. In this paradigm, pedagogy cannot be reduced only to learning critical skills or theoretical traditions but must also be infused with the possibility of using interpretation as a mode of intervention, as a potentially energizing practice that gets students to both think and act differently. I have always believed that critical pedagogy is not simply about the search for understanding and truth, because such a goal imposes limits on human agency, possibility, and politics. Critical pedagogy also takes seriously the educational imperative to encourage students to act on the knowledge, values, and social relations they acquire by being responsive to the deepest and most important problems of our times.

As a political and moral practice, education always presupposes a vision of the future in its introduction to, preparation for, and legitimation of particular forms of social life. Any meaningful consideration of educational theory and practice must confront the challenges arising from questions about whose future is affected by these forms. For what purposes and to what ends do certain forms endure and what promise or peril do they hold for future generations? How might we imagine different forms of social life that lead to a more democratic and just future? It is hoped that this book will make a small contribution in raising such questions, while purposefully engaging with the various struggles that produced them.

NOTES

1 Stuart Hall (1997), "Subjects in History: Making Diasporic Identities," in Wahneema Lubiano (ed.), *The House That Race Built*. New York: Pantheon, p. 291.

2 Chandra Mohanty (1989), "On Race and Voice: Challenges for Liberal Education in the 1990s," *Cultural Critique*, 14: 192.
3 I extend this concept of the living dead in Henry A. Giroux (2011), *Zombie Politics and Culture in the Age of Casino Capitalism*. New York: Peter Lang.
4 I take up Obama's educational failures in Henry A. Giroux (2010), *Politics After Hope: Obama and the Politics of Youth, Race, and Democracy*. Boulder: Paradigm Publishers.
5 Martha C. Nussbaum (2010), *Not For Profit: Why Democracy Needs the Humanities*. Princeton, NJ: Princeton University Press, p. 134.
6 Stanley Aronowitz (2008), *Against Schooling*. Boulder: Paradigm Publishers, p. 22.
7 Marc Bousquet (2009), "An Education President from Wal-Mart," *Chronicle of Higher Education*, July 23, 2009. Available online at: http://chronicle.com/blogPost/An-Education-President-From/7434. Accessed July 23, 2009.
8 Aronowitz, *Against Schooling*, pp. 16–17.
9 See Aronowitz, *Against Schooling*; Henry A. Giroux and Susan Searls Giroux (2004), *Take Back Higher Education*. New York: Palgrave; Henry A. Giroux (2008), *The University in Chains: Confronting the Military-Industrial-Academic Complex*. Boulder: Paradigm Publishers; John Wilson (2008), *Patriotic Correctness: Academic Freedom and Its Enemies*. Boulder: Paradigm Publishers; Christopher Newfield (2008), *Unmaking the Public University: The Forty Year Assault on the Middle Class*. Cambridge, MA: Harvard University Press; Mark Bousquet (2008), *How the University Works: Higher Education and the Low-Wage Nation*. New York: New York University Press; Frank Donoghue (2008), *The Last Professors: The Corporate University and the Fate of the Humanities*. New York: Fordham University Press; and Evan Watkins (2008), *Class Degrees: Smart Work, Managed Choice, and the Transformation of Higher Education*. New York: Fordham University Press.
10 Bill Moyers (2007), "A Time for Anger, a Call to Action," *CommonDreams.org*, February 7, 2007. Available online at: www.commondreams.org/views07/0322-24.htm . Accessed December 10, 2009.
11 I take up the issue of the increasing militarizing of the university in Giroux, *The University in Chains*.
12 On the relationship between education and hope, see Mark Coté, Richard J. F. Day, and Greig de Peuter (eds) (2007), *Utopian Pedagogy: Radical Experiments Against Neoliberal Globalization*. Toronto: University of Toronto Press; and Henry A. Giroux (2003), *Public Spaces/Private Lives: Democracy Beyond 9/11*. Boulder: Rowman and Littlefield.
13 Sheldon S. Wolin (2008), *Democracy, Inc.: Managed Democracy and the Specter of Inverted Totalitarianism*. Princeton, NJ: Princeton University Press, p. 43.
14 Jacques Derrida (2001), "The Future of the Profession or the Unconditional University," in Laurence Simmons and Heather Worth (eds), *Derrida Downunder*. Auckland: Dunmore Press, p. 245.
15 Fulvia Carnevale and John Kelsey (2007), "Art of the Possible: An Interview with Jacques Rancière," *Artforum*, March 2007, pp. 260–1.
16 Mohanty, "On Race and Voice," p. 192.

Pedagogy as Cultural Politics

CHAPTER 2

Schooling and the Culture of Positivism

Notes on the Death of History[1]

There is no neutral material of history. History is not a spectacle for us because it is our own living, our own violence and our own beliefs.[2]

John O'Neil

INTRODUCTION

One of the more fundamental questions raised by educators in recent years focuses on how public school classroom teachers might develop an orientation to curriculum development and implementation which acknowledges the important underlying ethical and normative dimensions that structure classroom decisions and experiences. The absence of such an orientation has been well noted.[3] For example, in different ways both phenomenological and neo-Marxist perspectives on educational thought and practice have pointed to the atheoretical, ahistorical, and unproblematic view of pedagogy that presently characterizes curriculum development, particularly in the social sciences.

Some phenomenological critics have charged that teaching practices are often rooted in "commonsense" assumptions that go relatively unchallenged by both teachers and students and serve to mask the social construction of different forms of knowledge. In this view the focus of criticism is on the classroom teacher who appears insensitive to the complex transmission of socially based definitions and expectations that function to reproduce and legitimize the dominant culture at the level of classroom instruction.[4] Teachers and other educational workers, in this case, often ignore questions concerning how they perceive their classrooms, how students make sense of what they are presented, and how knowledge is mediated between teachers (themselves) and students.

On the other hand, some neo-Marxist critics have attempted to explain how the politics of the dominant society is linked to the political character

19

of the classroom social encounter. In this perspective the focus shifts from an exclusive concern with how teachers and students construct knowledge to the ways in which the social order is legitimated and reproduced through the production and distribution of "acceptable" knowledge and classroom social processes.[5] Thus, neo-Marxist educators are not simply concerned with how teachers and students view knowledge; they are also concerned with the mechanisms of social control and how these mechanisms function to legitimate the beliefs and values underlying wider societal institutional arrangements.

Both views have led to a greater appreciation of the hermeneutic and political nature of public school pedagogy. Unfortunately, neither view has provided a thorough understanding of how the wider "culture of positivism," with its limited focus on objectivity, efficiency, and technique, is both embedded and reproduced in the form and content of public school curricula. While it is true that some phenomenologists have focused on the relationship between the social construction of classroom knowledge and the major tenets of positivism, they have generally ignored the forms and social practices involved in its transmission. On the other hand, while neo-Marxist critiques have emphasized the ideological underpinnings of classroom social practices, they have done so at the cost of providing an in-depth analysis of how specific forms of knowledge are produced, distributed, and legitimated in schools.[6]

While it is clear that the hermeneutic and political interests expressed by both groups must be used in a complementary fashion to analyze the interlocking beliefs and mechanisms that mediate between the wider culture of positivism and public school pedagogy, the conceptual foundation and distinct focus for such an analysis need to be further developed. This chapter attempts to contribute to that development by examining the culture of positivism and its relationship to classroom teaching through the lens of a recently focused social and educational problem, the alleged "loss of interest in history" among American students and the larger public. This issue provides a unique vehicle for such an analysis, because it presents a common denominator through which the connection between schools and the larger society might be clarified.

BEYOND THE DEATH OF HISTORY

Within the last decade a growing chorus of voices has pointed to the public's growing sense of the "irrelevance" of history. Some social critics have decried the trend while others have supported it. For instance, the historian David Donald believes that the "death of history" is related to the end of the "age of abundance." History, in Donald's view, can no longer provide an insightful perspective for the future. Voicing the despair of a dying age, Donald resigns himself to a universe that appears unmanageable, a sociopolitical universe that has nothing to learn from history. Thus, he writes:

20

The "lessons" taught by the American past are today not merely irrelevant but dangerous . . . Perhaps my most useful function would be to disenthrall [students] from the spell of history, to help them see the irrelevance of the past . . . [to] remind them to what a limited extent humans control their own destiny.[7]

Other critics, less pessimistic and more thoughtful, view the "death of history" as a crisis in historical consciousness itself, a crisis in the ability of the American people to remember those "lessons" of the past that illuminate the developmental preconditions of individual liberty and social freedom. These critics view the "crisis" in historical consciousness as a deplorable social phenomenon that buttresses the existing spiritual crisis of the seventies and points to a visionless and politically reactionary future. In their analyses the "irrelevance of history" argument contains conservative implications, implications that obscure the political nature of the problem: the notion that history has not become irrelevant, but rather that historical consciousness is being suppressed. To put it another way, history has been stripped of its critical and transcendent content and can no longer provide society with the historical insights necessary for the development of a collective critical consciousness. In this view the critical sense is inextricably rooted in the historical sense. In other words, modes of reasoning and interpretation develop a sharp critical sense to the degree that they pay attention to the flow of history. When lacking a sense of historical development, criticism is often blinded by the rule of social necessity that parades under the banner of so-called "natural laws." This assault on historical sensibility is no small matter. Herbert Marcuse claims that one consequence is a form of false consciousness, "the repression of society in the formation of concepts . . . a confinement of experience, a restriction of meaning."[8] In one sense, then, the call to ignore history represents an assault on thinking itself.

While it is true that both radicals and conservatives have often drawn upon history to sustain their respective points of view, this should not obscure the potentially subversive nature of history. Nor should it obscure the changing historical forces that sometimes rely upon "history" to legitimate existing power structures. Historical consciousness is acceptable to the prevailing dominant interest when it can be used to buttress the existing social order. It becomes dangerous when its truth content highlights contradictions in the given society. As one philosopher writes, "Remembrance of the past might give rise to dangerous insights, and the established society seems to be apprehensive of the subversive content of memory."[9]

The suppression of history has been accurately labeled by Russell Jacoby as a form of "social amnesia," and he says: "Social amnesia is a society's repression of its own past . . . memory driven out of mind by the social and economic dynamic of this society."[10] Jacoby's analysis is important because it situates the crisis in history in a specific sociohistorical context. If Jacoby is right, and I think he is, then the "crisis" in historical consciousness, at least its underlying ideological dimensions, can be explained in historical and political terms. This perspective can be put into sharper focus if we begin with an explanation of the changing nature of the mechanisms of social control over the last 60 years in the United States. To do this, we will have to turn briefly to the work of the late Italian theorist, Antonio Gramsci.

Gramsci was deeply concerned about what he saw as the changing modes of domination in the advanced industrial societies of the West. He claimed that with the rise of modern science and technology, social control was exercised less through the use of physical force (army, police, etc.) than through the distribution of an elaborate system of norms and imperatives. The latter were used to lend institutional authority a degree of unity and certainty and provide it with an apparent universality and legitimation. Gramsci called this form of control "ideological hegemony," a form of control which not only manipulated consciousness but also saturated and constituted the daily experiences that shaped one's behavior.[11] Hence, ideological hegemony referred to those systems of practices, meanings, and values that provided legitimacy to the dominant society's institutional arrangements and interest.

Gramsci's analysis is crucial to understanding how cultural hegemony is used by ruling elites to reproduce their economic and political power. It helps us to focus on the myths and social processes that characterize a specific form of common sense, particularly as it is distributed through different agencies of socialization such as schools, families, trade unions, work places, and other ideological state apparatuses.[12] Thus, the concept of cultural hegemony provides a theoretical foundation for examining the dialectical relationship between economic production and social and cultural reproduction.[13] At the core of this perspective is the recognition that advanced industrial societies such as the United States iniquitously distribute not only economic goods and services but also certain forms of cultural capital, i.e., "that system of meanings, abilities, language forms, and tastes that are directly and indirectly defined by dominant groups as socially legitimate."[14] This should not suggest that primary agencies of socialization in the United States simply mirror the dominant mode of economic production and function to process passive human beings into future occupational roles. This overdetermined view of socialization and human nature is both vulgar and mystifying. What is suggested is that the assumptions, beliefs, and social processes that occur in the primary agencies of socialization neither "mirror" wider societal interests nor are they autonomous from them. In other words, the correspondences and contradictions that mediate between institutions like schools and larger society exist in dialectical tension with each other and vary under specific historical conditions.[15]

It is within the parameters of the historically changing dialectical relationship between power and ideology that the social basis for the existing crisis in historical consciousness can be located. Moreover, it is also within this relationship that the role schooling plays in reproducing this crisis can be examined. Underlying the suppression of historical consciousness in the social sphere and the loss of interest in history in the sphere of schooling in the United States at the present time are the rise of science and technology and the subsequent growth of the culture of positivism. It is this historical development that will be briefly traced and analyzed before the role that public school pedagogy plays in reproducing the crisis in historical consciousness is examined.

With the development of science and new technology in the United States in the early part of the twentieth century, both the pattern of culture and the existing concept of progress changed considerably. Both of these changes set the foundation for the suppression of historical consciousness. As popular culture became more standardized in its attempt to reproduce not only goods but also the need to consume those goods, "industrialized" culture reached into new forms of communication to spread its message. Realms of popular culture, formerly limited to dance and dime store novels, were now expanded by almost all of the media of artistic expression.[16] The consolidation of culture by new technologies of mass communication, coupled with newly found social science disciplines such as social psychology and sociology, ushered in powerful new modes of administration in the public sphere.[17]

Twentieth-century capitalism gave rise to mass advertising and its attendant gospel of unending consumerism. All spheres of social existence were now informed, though far from entirely controlled, by the newly charged rationality of advanced industrial capitalism. Mass marketing, for example, drastically changed the realms of work and leisure and, as Stuart Ewen has pointed out, set the stage for the contestation and control over daily life.

> During the 1920s the stage was set by which the expanding diversity of corporate organization might do cultural battle with a population which was in need of, and demanding, social change. The stage was in the theatre of daily life, and it was within the intimacies of that reality — productive, cultural, social, psychological — that a corporate pièce-de-théâtre was being scripted.[18]

While industrialized culture was radically transforming daily life, scientific management was altering traditional patterns of work. For instance, the integration of skill and imagination that had once characterized craft production gave way to a fragmented work process in which conception was separated from both the execution and the experience of work. One result was a fragmented work process that reduced labor to a series of preordained and lifeless gestures.[19]

Accompanying changes in the workplace and the realm of leisure was a form of technocratic legitimation based on a positivist view of science and technology. This form of rationality defined itself through the alleged unalterable and productive effects the developing forces of technology and science were having on the foundations of twentieth-century progress. Whereas progress in the United States in the eighteenth and nineteenth centuries was linked to the development of moral self-improvement and self-discipline in the interest of building a better society, progress in the twentieth century was stripped of its concern with ameliorating the human condition and became applicable only to the realm of material and technical growth.[20] What was once considered humanly possible, a question involving values and human ends, was now reduced to the issue of what was technically possible. The application of scientific methodology to new forms of technology appeared as a social force generated by its own laws, laws governed by a rationality that appeared to exist above and beyond human control.[21]

Inherent in this notion of progress and its underlying technocratic rationality is the source of logic that denies the importance of historical consciousness. Moreover, this form of rationality serves to buttress the status quo by undermining the dialectic of human potential and will. As a mode of legitimation, this form of rationality has become the prevailing cultural hegemony. As the prevailing consciousness, it celebrates the continued enlargement of the comforts of life and the productivity of labor through increasing submission of the public to laws that govern the technical mastery of both human beings and nature. The price for increased productivity is the continued refinement and administration of not simply the forces of production but the constitutive nature of consciousness itself. For example, in spite of its own claims, positivist rationality contains a philosophy of history that "robs" history of its critical possibilities. Thomas McCarthy writes that this philosophy of history

> is based on the questionable thesis that human beings control their destinies to the degree to which social techniques are applied, and that human destiny is capable of being rationally guided to the extent of cybernetic control and the application of these techniques.[22]

RETHINKING THE CULTURE OF POSITIVISM

If critical consciousness, in part, represents an ability to think about the process as well as the genesis of various stages of reflection, then this notion of history contains few possibilities for its development as a critical and emancipatory force.

This form of rationality now represents an integral part of the social and political system of the United States and can be defined as the culture of positivism. If we are to understand its role in suppressing historical consciousness, the culture of positivism must be viewed through its wider function as a dominant ideology, powerfully communicated through various social agencies. The term "positivism" has gone through so many changes since it was first used by Saint-Simon and Comte that it is virtually impossible to narrow its meaning to a specific school of thought or a well-defined perspective. Thus, any discussion of positivism will be necessarily broad and devoid of clear-cut boundaries. However, we can speak of the culture of positivism as the legacy of positivistic thought, a legacy which includes those convictions, attitudes, techniques, and concepts that still exercise a powerful and pervasive influence on modern thought.[23]

"Culture of positivism," in this context, is used to make a distinction between a specific philosophic movement and *a form* of cultural hegemony. The distinction is important because it shifts the focus of debate about the tenets of positivism from the terrain of philosophy to the field of ideology. For our purposes it will be useful to indicate some of the main elements of "positivism." This will be followed by a short analysis of how the culture of positivism undermines any viable notion of critical historical consciousness.

The major assumptions that underlie the culture of positivism are drawn from the logic and method of inquiry associated with the natural sciences.[24] Based upon the logic of scientific methodology with its interest in explanation, prediction, and technical control, the principle of rationality in the natural sciences was seen as vastly superior to the hermeneutic principles underlying the speculative social sciences. Modes of rationality that relied upon or supported interpretative procedures rated little scientific status from those defending the assumptions and methods of the natural sciences. For instance, Theodore Abel echoed a sentiment about hermeneutic understanding that still retains its original force among many supporters of the culture of positivism.

> Primarily the operation of Verstehen (understanding human behavior) does two things: It relieves us of a sense of apprehension in connection with behavior that is unfamiliar or unexpected and it is a source of "hunches," which help us in the formulation of hypotheses. The operation of Verstehen does not, however, add to our store of knowledge, because it consists of the application of knowledge already validated by personal experience; nor does it serve as a means of verification. The probability of a connection can be ascertained only by means of objective, experimental, and statistical tests.[25]

Given the positivist emphasis on technical control and coordination, it is not surprising that the role of theory in this perspective functions as a foundation to boost scientific methodology. At the heart of this perspective is the assumption that theory plays a vital role in manipulating certain variables to either bring about a certain state of affairs, or to prevent its occurrence.[26] The basis for deciding what state of affairs is to be brought about, or the interests such state of affairs might serve, are not questions that are given much consideration. Thus, theory, as viewed here, becomes circumscribed within certain "methodological prohibitions."[27] It was August Comte who laid the foundation for the subordination of theory to the refinement of means when he insisted that theory must be "founded in the nature of things and the laws that govern them, not in the imaginary powers that the human mind attributes to itself, erroneously believing itself to be a free agent and the center of the universe."[28]

What is missing from Comte's perspective can be seen when it is instructively compared to the classical Greek notion of theory. In classical thought, theory was seen as a way men could free themselves from dogma and opinions in order to provide an orientation for ethical action.[29] In other words, theory was viewed as an extension of ethics and was linked to the search for truth and justice. The prevailing positivist consciousness has forgotten the function that theory once served. Under the prevailing dominant ideology, theory has been stripped of its concern with ends and ethics, and appears "unable to free itself from the ends set and given to science by the pre-given empirical reality."[30] The existing perspective on theory provides the background for examining another central tendency in the culture of positivism: the notion that knowledge is value-free.

Since theory functions in the interest of technical progress in the culture of positivism, the meaning of knowledge is limited to the realm of technical interests. In brief, the foundation for knowledge is drawn from two sources: "the empirical or natural sciences, and the formal disciplines such as logic and mathematics."[31] In this scheme knowledge consists of a realm of "objective facts" to be collected and arranged so they can be marshaled in the interest of empirical verification. Knowledge is relevant to the degree that it can be viewed "as description and explanation of objectified data, conceived — a priori — as cases of instances of possible laws."[32] Thus, knowledge becomes identified with scientific methodology and its orientation towards self-subsistent facts whose law-like connections can be grasped descriptively. Questions concerning the social construction of knowledge and the constitutive interests behind the selection, organization, and evaluation of "brute facts" are buried under the assumption that knowledge is objective and value-free. Information or "data" taken from the subjective world of intuition, insight, philosophy, and non-scientific theoretical frameworks is not acknowledged as being relevant. Values, then, appear as the nemeses of "facts," and are viewed at best as interesting, and at worst as irrational and subjective emotional responses.[33]

The central assumption by which the culture of positivism rationalizes its position on theory and knowledge is the notion of objectivity, the separation of values from knowledge and methodological inquiry alike. Not only are "facts" looked upon as objective, but the researcher himself is seen as engaging in value-free inquiry, far removed from the untidy world of beliefs and values. Thus, it appears that values, judgments, and normative-based inquiry are dismissed because they do not admit of either truth or falsity. It seems that empirical verification exacts a heavy price from those concerned about "the nature of truth."[34]

The severance of knowledge and research from value claims may appear to be admirable to some, but it hides more than it uncovers. Of course, this is not to suggest that challenging the value-neutrality claims of the culture of positivism is tantamount to supporting the use of bias, prejudice, and superstition in scientific inquiry. Instead, what is espoused is that the very notion of objectivity is based on the use of normative criteria established by communities of scholars and intellectual workers in any given field. The point is that intellectual inquiry and research free from values and norms are impossible to achieve. To separate values from facts, social inquiry from ethical considerations, is pointless. As Howard Zinn points out, it is like trying to draw a map that illustrates every detail on a chosen piece of terrain.[35] But this is not just a simple matter of intellectual error; it is an ethical failing as well. The notion that theory, facts, and inquiry can be objectively determined and used falls prey to a set of values that are both conservative and mystifying in their political orientation.

While it is impossible to provide a fully detailed critique of the assumptions that underlie the culture of positivism, it is appropriate to focus on how these assumptions undermine the development of a critical historical consciousness and further serve to diminish public communication and political action. Consequently, it is important to look briefly at how these assumptions function as part of the dominant ideology. Functioning both as an ideology and a productive force in the interest of a ruling elite, the culture of positivism cannot be viewed as simply a set of beliefs, smoothly functioning so as to rationalize the existing society. It is more than that. The point here is that the culture of positivism is not just a set of ideas, disseminated by the culture industry; it is also a material force, a set of material practices that are embedded in the routines and experiences of our daily lives.[36] In a sense, the daily rhythm of our lives is structured, in part, by the technical imperatives of a society that objectifies all it touches. This is not meant to suggest that there are no contradictions and challenges to the system. They exist, but all too often the contradictions result in challenges that lack a clear-cut political focus. Put another way, challenges to the system often function as a cathartic force rather than as a legitimate form of protest; fairly frequently they end up serving to maintain the very conditions and consciousness that spurred them in the first place. Within such a posture, there is little room for the development of an active, critical historical consciousness.

The present crisis in historical consciousness is linked to the American public's deepening commitment to an ever-expanding network of administrative systems and social control technologies. One consequence of this has been the removal of political decisions from public discourse by reducing these decisions to technical problems answerable to technical solutions. Underlying this crisis are the major assumptions of the culture of positivism, assumptions which abrogate the need for a viable theory of ideology, ethics, and political action.

Silent about its own ideology, the culture of positivism provides no conceptual insight into how oppression might mask itself in the language and lived experiences of daily life. "Imagining itself valuable only to the extent that it escapes history,"[37] this form of rationality prevents us from using historical consciousness as a vehicle to unmask existing forms of domination as they reproduce themselves through the "facts" and commonsense assumptions that structure our view and experience of the world. The flight from history is, in reality, the suppression of history. As Horkheimer writes, "Again and again in history, ideas have cast off swaddling clothes and struck out against social systems that bore them."[38] The logic of positivist thought suppresses the critical function of historical consciousness, for underlying all the major assumptions of the culture of positivism is a common theme: the denial of human action grounded in historical insight and committed to emancipation in all spheres of human activity. What is offered as a replacement "is a form of social engineering analogous to the applied physical sciences."[39] It is this very denial that represents the essence of the prevailing hegemonic ideology.

Instead of defining itself as a historically produced perspective, the culture of positivism asserts its superiority through its alleged suprahistorical and supracultural posture. Theory and method are held to be historically neutral. By maintaining a heavy silence about its own guiding interest in technical control, it falls prey to what Husserl once called the "fallacy of objectivism."[40] Unable to reflect on its own presuppositions, or to provide a model for critical reflection in general, it ends up uncritically supporting the status quo and rejecting history as a medium for political action.

As the fundamental dominant myth of our time, the positivist mode of rationality operates so as to undermine the value of history and the importance of historical consciousness in other significant ways. First, it fosters an undialectical and one-dimensional view of the world; second, it denies the world of politics and lacks a vision of the future; third, it denies the possibility that human beings can constitute their own reality and alter and change that reality in the face of domination.[41]

Wrapped in the logic of fragmentation and specialization, positivist rationality divorces the "fact" from its social and historical context and ends up glorifying scientific methodology at the expense of a more rational mode of thinking. Under these conditions the interdependence of knowledge, imagination, will, and creativity are lost in a reduction of all phenomena to the rule of the empirical formulation.

Rather than comprehending the world holistically as a network of interconnections, the American people are taught to approach problems as if they existed in isolation, detached from the social and political forces that give them meaning. The central failing of this mode of thinking is that it creates a form of tunnel vision in which only a small segment of social reality is open to examination. More important, it leaves unquestioned those economic, political, and social structures that shape our daily lives. Divorced from history, these structures appear to have acquired their present character naturally, rather than having been constructed by historically specific interests.

It seems clear that the mode of reasoning embedded in the culture of positivism cannot reflect upon meaning and value, or, for that matter, upon anything that cannot be verified in the empirical tradition. Since there is no room for human vision in this perspective, historical consciousness is stripped of its critical function and progress is limited to terms acceptable to the status quo. Yet, as Horkheimer points out, it is the contradiction between the existing society and the utopian promise of a better life that spurs an interest in both history and historical progress.[42] The suppression of mankind's longing for justice and a better world is the motive force that usurps the meaningfulness of history and a historical consciousness. This force is an inherent part of the logic of positivist rationality.

The culture of positivism rejects the future by celebrating the present. By substituting what is for what should be, it represses "ethics" as a category of life and reproduces the notion that society has a life of its own, independent of the will of human beings. The neutralization of ethics effectively underscores the value of historical consciousness as well as public discourse on important political issues. But instead, we are left with a mode of reasoning that makes it exceptionally difficult for human beings to struggle against the limitations of an oppressive society.[43]

Finally, inherent in this perspective is a passive model of humanity. The positivist view of knowledge, "facts," and ethics has neither use nor room for a historical reality in which humanity is able to constitute its own meanings, order its own experiences, or struggle against the forces that prevent it from doing so. Meaning, like "time and memory," becomes objectified in this tradition and is eliminated as a radical construct by being made to exist independently of human experience and intention. In a society that flattens contradictions and eliminates evaluative and intellectual conflict, the concept of historical consciousness appears as a disturbing irrationality. Marcuse puts it well:

> Recognition and relation to the past as present counteracts the functionalization of thought by and in the established reality. It militates against the closing of the universe of discourse and behavior; it renders possible the development of concepts which destabilize and transcend the closed universe by comprehending it as historical universe. Confronted with the given society as object of its reflection, critical thought becomes historical consciousness; as such it is essentially judgment.[44]

I have argued so far that the loss of interest in history in the public sphere can only be viewed within the context of existing sociopolitical arrangements, and that what has been described as a marginal problem by some social critics, in essence, represents a fundamental problem in which the dominant culture actively functions to suppress the development of a critical historical consciousness among the populace.[45] This is not meant to imply a conscious conspiracy on the part of an "invisible" ruling elite. The very existence, interests, and consciousness of the dominant class are deeply integrated into a belief system that legitimizes its rule. This suggests that existing institutional arrangements reproduce themselves, in part, through cultural hegemony in the form of a positivist worldview that becomes a self-delusion and leaves little room for an oppositional historical consciousness to develop in the society at large. In other words, the suppression of historical consciousness works itself out in the field of ideology. In part this is due to an underlying "self-perpetuating" logic that shapes the mechanisms and boundaries of the culture of positivism. This logic is situated in a structure of dominance and exists to meet the most fundamental needs of the existing power relations and their corresponding social formations.[46] It appears to be a logic that is believed by the oppressed and oppressors alike, those who benefit from it as well as those who do not.

DEPOLITICIZING EDUCATION THROUGH HISTORICAL AMNESIA

I now want to examine how the culture of positivism has influenced the process of schooling, particularly in relation to the way educators have defined the history "crisis" and its relationship to educational theory and practice at the classroom level. I will begin by analyzing how the nature of the loss of interest in history has been defined by leading members of the educational establishment.

Unlike critics such as Lasch and Marcuse, American educators have defined the "loss of interest" in history as an academic rather than political problem. For instance, the Organization of American Historians (OAH) published findings indicating that history was in a crisis and that the situation was "nationwide, affecting both secondary schools and higher education in every part of the country."[47] According to the OAH report, the value of history is being impugned by the growing assumption on the part of many educators that history is not a very practical subject. What is meant by practical appears problematic. For example, the Arizona Basic Goals Commission urged teachers to make history more practical: to place stress on "positive rather than negative aspects of the American past, eschew conflict as a theme, inculcate pride in the accomplishments of the nation and show the influence of rational, creative, and spiritual forces in shaping the nation's growth."[48]

For other educators, making history practical has meant reversing the growing divisions and specializations in history course offerings at all levels of education. This group would put back into the curriculum the broad-based history courses that were offered in the 1950s. In this perspective, the loss of interest in history among students has resulted from the fragmented perspective provided by specialized offerings in other disciplines. Warren L. Hickman sums this position up well when he writes:

> The utility of history is perspective, and that is in direct opposition to specialization at the undergraduate level. History's position in the curriculum, and its audience, have been eroded steadily as specialization, fragmentation, and proliferation of its offerings have increased.[49]

Both of these responses view the loss of interest in history as a purely academic problem. Severed from the socioeconomic context in which they operate, schools, in both of these views, appear to exist above and beyond the imperatives of power and ideology. Given this perspective, the erosion of interest in history is seen in isolation from the rest of society, and the "problem" is dealt with in technical rather than political terms, i.e., history can be rescued by restructuring academic courses in one way or another. These positions, in fact, represent part of the very problem they define. Collapsing the general into the particular results in severing isolated issues from larger public considerations, thus surrendering any sense of history, context, and politics. The loss of interest in history in schools is due less to the changes in course structure and offerings, though these have some effect, as much as it is due to the growing impact of the culture of positivism on the process of schooling itself, and in this particular case the social studies field. It is to this issue that we will now turn.

SOCIAL STUDIES AND THE CULTURE OF POSITIVISM

Classroom pedagogy in varying degrees is inextricably related to a number of social and political factors. Some of the more important include: the dominant societal rationality and its effect on curriculum thought and practice; the system of attitudes and values that govern how classroom teachers select, organize, and evaluate knowledge and classroom social relationships; and, finally, the way students perceive their classroom experiences and how they act on those perceptions. By focusing on these limited, but nonetheless important areas, we can flesh out the relationships among power, ideology, and critical pedagogy, particularly as applied to the social sciences.

As I have pointed out, within the United States the social sciences have been modeled largely against the prevailing assumptions and methods of the natural sciences.[50] In spite of recent attacks on this mainstream perspective, the idea of social science conceived after the model of the natural sciences exerts a strong influence on contemporary educational thought and practice. Historically, the curriculum field, in general, has increasingly endeavored to become a science. That is, it has sought to develop a rationality based on objectivity, consistency, "hard data," and replicability. As Walter Feinberg writes, "The social scientists and policy makers who laboured in the field of education in this century were born under the star of Darwin, and . . . this influence was to have a profound impact upon the direction of educational theory."[51]

Moreover, in the 1970s, as financial aid to education has decreased and radical critics have dwindled in number, the positivist orientation to schooling appears to be stronger than ever. Calls for accountability in education, coupled with the back-to-basics and systems management approaches to education, have strengthened rather than weakened the traditional positivist paradigm in the curriculum field. As William Pinar and others have pointed out, the field is presently dominated by traditionalists and conceptual-empiricists, and while both groups view curriculum in different ways, neither group steps outside of the positivist or technocratic worldview.[52]

These two groups must be viewed in something other than merely descriptive, categorical terms. Both the assumptions they hold and the modes of inquiry they pursue are based upon a worldview that shapes their respective educational perspectives. Moreover, these worldviews precede and channel their work and influence the development of public school curricula.[53] This suggests that, whether adherents to these positions realize it or not, their theoretical frameworks are inherently valuative and political; thus, they share a relationship to the wider social order. Thomas Popkewitz captures the essence of this when he writes:

> [E]ducational theory is a form of political affirmation. The selection and organization of pedagogical activities give emphasis to certain people, events and things. Educational theory is potent because its language has prescriptive qualities. A theory "guides" individuals to reconsider their personal world in light of more abstract concepts, generalizations and principles. These more abstract categories are not neutral; they give emphasis to certain institutional relationships as good, reasonable and legitimate. Visions of society, interests to be favored and courses of action to be followed are sustained in history.[54]

One way of looking at the political and valuative nature of educational thought and practice is through what Thomas Kuhn has called a "paradigm." A paradigm refers to the shared images, assumptions, and practices that characterize a community of scholars in a given field. In any specific field one can find different paradigms; thus, it is reasonable to conclude that any field of study is usually marked by competing intellectual and normative perspectives. As Kuhn has written: "A paradigm governs, in the first instance, not a subject matter but a group of practitioners."[55]

The concept of paradigm is important not merely because it guides practitioners in their work; it also illustrates that paradigms are related to the nexus of social and political values in the larger society. That is, the genesis, development, and effects of a given paradigm have to be measured against wider social and cultural commitments. In a simple sense, a paradigm might be viewed as in opposition or in support of the dominant ideology, but it cannot be judged independently of it. Educational workers in public education are not only born into a specific historical context; they embody its history in varying ways both as a state of consciousness and as sedimented experience, as a felt reality. To what degree they critically mediate that history and its attendant ideology is another issue. Thus, educational practitioners can be viewed as not only products of history but producers of history as well. And it is this dynamic process of socialization that links them and the schools in which they work to the larger society.[56] Finally, it is important to stress that acknowledging the social and cultural basis of the character of different modes of pedagogy is important but incomplete. This approach must be supplemented by analyzing the assumptions embedded in a given educational paradigm against larger social and political interests. Questions that arise out of this type of analysis might take the following form: What interest do these assumptions serve? What are their latent consequences? What are the material and intellectual forces that sustain these assumptions and their corresponding paradigm?

Both the traditionalists and conceptual-empiricists in the curriculum field share the basic assumptions of the culture of positivism. Furthermore, these assumptions shape their view of social science knowledge and classroom pedagogy as well as classroom evaluation and research. In brief, both groups support a form of positivist rationality in which it is assumed: (1) the natural sciences provide the "deductive-nomological" model of explanation for the concepts and techniques proper for social science; (2) social science ought to aim at the discovery of lawlike propositions about human behavior which are empirically testable; (3) social science modes of inquiry can and ought to be objective; (4) the relationship between theory and practice in the social science domain is primarily a technical one, i.e., social science knowledge can be used to predict how a course of action can best be realized; (5) social science procedures of verification and falsification must rely upon scientific techniques and "hard data," which lead to results that are value-free and intersubjectively applicable.[57]

At the core of this social science paradigm is a preoccupation with the instrumental use of knowledge. That is, knowledge is prized for its control value — its use in mastering all dimensions of the classroom environment. In this perspective, technical rationality eschews notions of meaning that cannot be quantified and objectified. This becomes clear when we examine the relationship between theory and practice in the culture of positivism as it affects the curriculum field in general. For instance, traditionalists in the curriculum field like Robert Zais, Glen Nass, and John McNeil, whose influence on public school pedagogy is considerable, view theory as secondary to meeting the existing needs and demands of social practitioners. In this case, theoretical formulations used in the shaping of curriculum development, design, and evaluation are guided by assumptions that bend to the dictates or exigencies of administrators and teachers in the "real" world of public school education. In this perspective, the "iron link" between knowledge and practical needs dissolves theory into utility.[58]

While the traditionalists may be viewed as atheoretical, the conceptual-empiricists acknowledge the importance of theory in curriculum work, but limit its meaning and importance by subordinating it to technical interests. The conceptual-empiricists have developed an approach to curriculum which "celebrates" rigorous and systematic research. Theory is used to generate and accumulate "hard data" and knowledge. Theory, in this sense, is linked to forms of explanation that are subject only to the criteria of empirical verification or refutation. Theory, as used in this paradigm, capitalizes upon one type of experience. As Habermas writes: "Only the controlled observation of physical behavior, which is set up in an isolated field under reproducible conditions by subjects interchangeable at will, seems to permit intersubjectively valid judgments of perceptions."[59]

Central to this form of rationality in the curriculum field is the notion of objective neutrality. Guided by the search for reliability, consistency, and quantitative predictions, positivist educational practice excludes the role of values, feelings, and subjectively defined meanings in its paradigm. Normative criteria are either dismissed as forms of bias or seen as subjective data that contribute little to the goals of schooling. Criticism of this sort is often couched in calls for more precise methods of pedagogy. W. James Popham, a leading spokesman for systems analysis methods, illustrates this position when he writes:

> I believe that those who discourage educators from precisely explicating their educational objectives are often permitting, if not promoting, the same kind of unclear thinking that has led to the generally abysmal quality of education in this country.[60]

More guarded critics such as George Beauchamp acknowledge that normative-based curriculum theories have their place in the field, but, true to the spirit of his own view, he reminds us that "we" need to "grow up in the use of conventional modes of research in curriculum before we can hope to have the ingenuity to develop new ones."[61] In both Popham's and Beauchamp's arguments, the underlying notion of the superiority of efficiency and control as educational goals are accepted as given and then pointed to as a rationale for curriculum models that enshrine them as guiding principles. The circularity of the argument can best be gauged by the nature of the ideology that it thinly camouflages.

Missing from this form of educational rationality is the complex interplay among knowledge, power, and ideology. The sources of this failing can be traced to the confusion between objectivity and objectivism, a confusion which once identified lays bare the conservative ideological underpinnings of the positivist educational paradigm. If objectivity in classroom teaching refers to the attempt to be scrupulously careful about minimizing biases, false beliefs, and discriminating behavior in rationalizing and developing pedagogical thought and practice, then this is a laudable notion that should govern our work. By contrast, objectivism refers to an orientation that is atemporal and ahistorical in nature. In this orientation, "fact" becomes the foundation for all forms of knowledge, and values and intentionality lose their political potency by being abstracted from the notion of meaning. When objectivism replaces objectivity, the result, as Bernstein points out, "is not an innocent mistaken epistemological doctrine."[62] It becomes a potent form of ideology that smothers the tug of conscience and blinds its adherents to the ideological nature of their own frame of reference.

Objectivism is the cornerstone of the culture of positivism in public education. Adulating "facts" and empirically based discourse, positivist rationality provides no basis for acknowledging its own historically contingent character. As such, it represents not only an assault on critical thinking; it also grounds itself in the politics of "what is." As Gouldner points out, "It is the tacit affirmation that 'what is,' the status quo, is basically sound."[63] Assuming that problems are basically technocratic in nature, it elevates methodology to the status of a truth and sets aside questions about moral purposes as matters of individual opinion. Buried beneath this "end of ideology" thesis is a form of positivist pedagogy that tacitly supports deeply conservative views about human nature, society, knowledge, and social action.

Objectivism suggests more than a false expression of neutrality. In essence, it tacitly represents a denial of ethical values. Its commitment to rigorous techniques, mathematical expression, and law-like regularities supports not only *one* form of scientific inquiry but social formations that are inherently repressive and elitist as well. Its elimination of "ideology" works in the service of the ideology of social engineers. By denying the relevance of certain norms in guiding and shaping how we ought to live with each other, it tacitly supports principles of hierarchy and control. Built into its objective quest for certainty is not simply the elimination of intellectual and valuative conflict, but the suppression of free will, intentionality, and collective struggle. Clearly, such interests can move beyond the culture of positivism only to the degree that they are able to make a distinction between emancipatory political practice and technological administrative control.

Unfortunately, "methodology madness" is rampant in public school pedagogy and has resulted in a form of curricular design and implementation that *substitutes* technological control for democratic processes and goals. For instance, Fenwick W. English, a former superintendent of schools and curriculum designer, provides a model for curriculum design in which technique and schooling become synonymous. Echoing the principles of the scientific management movement of the 1920s, English states that there are three primary developments in curriculum design. These are worth quoting in full.

> The first is to establish the mission of the school system in terms that are assessable and replicable. The second is to effectively and efficiently configure the resources of the system to accomplish the mission. The third is to use feedback obtained to make adjustments in order to keep the mission within agreed-upon costs.[64]

In perspectives such as this, unfortunately pervasive in the curriculum field, manipulation takes the place of learning, and any attempt at intersubjective understanding is substituted for a science of educational technology in which "choices exist only when they make the systems more rational, efficient, and controllable."[65] In a critical sense, the Achilles heel of the culture of positivism in public school pedagogy is its refusal to acknowledge its own ideology as well as the relationship between knowledge and social control. The claims to objectivism and certainty are themselves ideological and can be most clearly revealed in the prevailing view of school knowledge and classroom social relationships.

The way knowledge is viewed and used in public school classrooms, particularly at the elementary through secondary levels, rests on a number of assumptions that reveal its positivist ideological underpinnings. In other words, the way classroom teachers view knowledge, the way knowledge is mediated through specific classroom methodologies, and the way students are taught to view knowledge all structure classroom experiences in a manner that is consistent with the principles of positivism.

In this view, knowledge is objective, "bounded and 'out there.'"[66] Classroom knowledge is often treated as an external body of information, the production of which appears to be independent of human beings. From this perspective, objective knowledge is viewed as independent of time and place; it becomes universalized, ahistorical knowledge. Moreover, it is expressed in a language that is basically technical and allegedly value-free. This language is instrumental and defines knowledge in terms that are empirically verifiable and suited to finding the best possible means for goals that go unquestioned.[67] Knowledge, then, becomes not only countable and measurable; it also becomes impersonal. Teaching in this pedagogical paradigm is usually discipline-based and treats subject matter in a compartmentalized and atomized fashion.[68]

Another important point concerning knowledge in this view is that it takes on the appearance of being context-free. That is, knowledge is divorced from the political and cultural traditions that give it meaning. And in this sense, it can be viewed as technical knowledge, the knowledge of instrumentality.[69] Stanley Aronowitz points out that this form of empiricist reasoning is one in which "reality is dissolved into object-hood,"[70] and results in students being so overwhelmed by the world of "facts" that they have "enormous difficulty making the jump to concepts which controvert appearances."[71]

By resigning itself to the registering of "facts," the positivist view of knowledge not only represents a false mode of reasoning that undermines reflective thinking; it is also a form of legitimation that obscures the relationship between "valued" knowledge and the constellation of economic, political, and social interests that such knowledge supports. This is clearly revealed in a number of important studies that have analyzed how knowledge is presented in elementary and secondary social studies textbooks.[72]

For example, Jean Anyon found, in her analysis of the content of elementary social studies textbooks, that the "knowledge which 'counts' as social studies knowledge will tend to be that knowledge which provides formal justification for, and legitimation of, prevailing institutional arrangements, and forms of conduct and beliefs."[73] In addition to pointing out that social studies textbooks provide a systematic exposure to selected aspects of the dominant culture, she found that material in the texts about dominant institutional arrangements was presented in a way that eschewed social conflict, social injustice, and institutional violence. Instead, social harmony and social consensus were the pivotal concepts that described American society. Quoting Fox and Hess, she points out that in a study of 58 elementary social studies textbooks used in eight states, the United States political system was described in one-dimensional consensual terms. "People in the textbooks are pictured as easily getting together, discussing their differences and rationally arriving at decisions . . . [moreover,] everyone accepts the decisions."[74] These textbooks present a problematic assumption as an unquestioned truth: conflict and dissent among different social groups are presented as inherently bad. Not only is American society abstracted from the dictates of class and power in the consensus view of history, but students are viewed as value receiving and value transmitting persons.[75] There is no room in consensus history for intellectual, moral, and political conflict. Such a view would have to treat people as *value creating* agents. While it is true that some of the newer elementary and secondary texts discuss controversial issues more often, "social conflict" is still avoided.[76]

Popkewitz has argued cogently that many of the social studies curriculum projects that came out of the discipline-based curriculum movements of the 1960s did more to impede critical inquiry than to promote it. Based on fundamentally flawed assumptions about theory, values, knowledge, and instructional techniques in social studies curricular design and implementation, these projects "ignored the multiplicity of perspectives found in any one discipline."[77] With the social nature of conflict and skepticism removed from these projects, ideas appear as inert and ahistorical, reified categories whose underlying ideology is only matched by the tunnel vision they produce.

Human intentionality and problem solving in these texts are either ignored or stripped of any viable, critical edge. For example, in one set of texts pioneered under the inquiry method, comparative analysis exercises are undercut by the use of socially constructed biases built into definitional terms that distort the subjects to be compared. In analyzing the political systems of the United States and the Soviet Union, the United States is labeled as a "democratic system" and the Soviet Union as a "totalitarian state."[78] Needless to say, the uncriticized and simplistic dichotomy revealed in categories such as these represents nothing other than an updated version of the vulgar "democracy" versus "communism" dichotomy that characterized so much of the old social studies of the 1950s and early 1960s. While the labels have changed, the underlying typifications have not. What is new is not necessarily better. The "alleged" innovative discipline-centered social studies curriculum of the last 15 years has based its reputation on its claim to promote critical inquiry. Instead, this approach appears to have created "new forms of mystification which make the social world seem mechanistic and predeterministic."[79]

A more critical view of knowledge would define it as a social construction linked to human intentionality and behavior. But if this view of knowledge is to be translated into a meaningful pedagogical principle, the concept of knowledge as a social construct will have to be linked to the notion of power. On one level this means that classroom knowledge can be used in the interest of either emancipation or domination. It can be critically used and analyzed in order to break through mystifications and modes of false reasoning.[80] Or it can be used unreflectively to legitimize specific sociopolitical interests by appearing to be value-free and beyond criticism. If the interface between knowledge, power, and ideology is to be understood, knowledge will have to be defined not only as a set of meanings generated by human actors, but also as a communicative act embedded in specific forms of social relationships. The principles that govern the selection, organization, and control of classroom knowledge have important consequences for the type of classroom encounter in which such knowledge will be distributed.

The notion of "objectified" knowledge as it operates in the classroom obscures the interplay of meaning and intentionality as the foundation for all forms of knowledge. Absent from this perspective is a critical awareness of the varying theoretical perspectives, assumptions, and methodologies which underlie the construction and distribution of knowledge.[81] Unfortunately, the notion of "objectified" knowledge represents more than a conceptual problem; it also plays a decisive role in shaping classroom experiences. Thus, one is apt to find classroom situations in which "objective" information is "impartially" relayed to "able" students willing to "learn" it. Within this pedagogical framework, what is deemed "legitimate" public school knowledge is often matched by models of socialization that reproduce authoritarian modes of communication. Regardless of how a pedagogy is defined, whether in traditional or progressive terms, if it fails to encourage self-reflection and communicative interaction, it ends up providing students with the illusion rather than the substance of choice; moreover, it ends up promoting manipulation and denying critical reflection.[82] Alternative forms of pedagogy, such as those developed by Paulo Freire, not only emphasize the interpretive dimensions of knowing; they also highlight the insight that any progressive notion of learning must be accompanied by pedagogical relationships marked by dialogue, questioning, and communication.[83] This view of knowledge stresses structuring classroom encounters that *synthesize and demonstrate* the relationships among meaning, critical thinking, and democratized classroom encounters.

The role that teachers play in the schooling process is not a mechanistic one. To the degree that they are aware of the hidden assumptions that underlie the nature of the knowledge they use and the pedagogical practices they implement, classroom teachers will be able to minimize the worst dimensions of the culture of positivism. More specifically, under certain circumstances teachers can work to strip away the unexamined reality that hides behind the objectivism and fetishism of "facts" in positivist pedagogy. In doing so, the fixed essences, the invariant structures, and the common-sense knowledge that provide the foundation for much of existing public school pedagogy can be shown for what they are: social constructs that serve to mystify rather than illuminate reality.

But at the present time, it appears that the vast majority of public school teachers have yet to step beyond the taken-for-granted assumptions that shape their view of pedagogy and structure their educational experiences. Mass culture, teacher-training institutions, and the power of the state all play a powerful role in pressuring teachers to give unquestioning support to the basic assumptions of the wider dominant culture. Maxine Greene captures part of this dynamic when she writes:

> It is not that teachers consciously mystify or deliberately concoct the positive images that deflect critical thought. It is not even that they themselves are necessarily sanguine about the health of the society. Often submerged in the bureaucracies for which they work, they simply accede to what is taken-for-granted. Identifying themselves as spokespersons for or representatives of the system in its local manifestations, they avoid interrogation and critique. They transmit, often tacitly, benign or neutral versions of the social reality. They may, deliberately or not, adopt these to accommodate to what they perceive to be the class origins or the capacities of their students, but, whether they are moving those young people towards assembly lines or administrative offices, they are likely to present the world around as given, probably unchangeable and predefined.[84]

For many students, the categories that shape their learning experience and mediate their relationship between the school and the larger society have little to do with the value of critical thinking and social commitment. In this case, the *objectification* of the students themselves by the positivist pedagogical model leaves students with little reason to generate their own meanings, to capitalize on their own cultural capital, or to participate in evaluating their own classroom experiences. The principles of order, control, and certainty in positivist pedagogy appear inherently opposed to such an approach.

In the objectified forms of communication that characterize positivist public school pedagogy, it is difficult for students to perceive the socially constructed basis of classroom knowledge. The arbitrary division between objective and subjective knowledge tends to remain undetected by students and teachers alike. The results are not inconsequential. Thus, though the routines and practices of classroom teachers and the perceptions and behavior of their students are sedimented in varying layers of meaning, questions concerning how these layers of meaning are mediated and in whose interest they function are given little attention in the learning and research paradigms that dominate public school pedagogy at the present time. The behavioral and management approaches to such pedagogy, particularly at the level of middle and secondary education, reduce learning to a set of practices that neither defines nor responds critically to the basic normative categories that shape day-to-day classroom methods and evaluation procedures. As C. A. Bowers writes, "the classroom can become a precarious place indeed, particularly when neither the teacher nor the student is fully aware of the hidden cultural messages being communicated and reinforced."[85]

The objectification of meaning results in the objectification of thought itself, a posture that the culture of positivism reproduces and celebrates in both the wider society and in public schools. In the public schools, prevailing research procedures in the curriculum field capitalize upon as well as reproduce the most basic assumptions of the positivist paradigm. For instance, methodological elegance in educational research appears to rate higher than its overall purpose or its truth value. The consequences are not lost on schools. As one critic points out:

> Educational research has social and political ramifications which are as important as the tests of reliability. First, people tacitly accept institutional assumptions, some of which are denied by school professionals themselves. Achievement, intelligence and "use of time" are accepted as useful variables for stating problems about schools and these categories provide the basis for research. Inquiry enables researchers to see how school categories relate, but it does not test assumptions or implications underlying the school categories. For example, there is no question about the nature of the tasks at which children spend their time. Research conclusions are conceived within parameters provided by school administrators. Second, researchers accept social myths as moral prescriptions. Social class, social occupation (engineer or machinist) or divorce are accepted as information which should be used in decision making. These assumptions maintain a moral quality and criteria which may justify social inequality. Third, the research orientation tacitly directs people to consider school failure as caused by those who happen to come to its classes. Social and educational assumptions are unscrutinized.[86]

It does not seem unreasonable to conclude at this point that critical thinking as a mode of reasoning appears to be in eclipse in both the wider society and the sphere of public school education. Aronowitz has written that critical thought has lost its contemplative character and "has been debased to the level of technical intelligence, subordinate to meeting operational problems."[87] What does this have to do with the suppression of historical consciousness? This becomes more clear when we analyze the relationships among critical thinking, historical consciousness, and the notion of emancipation.

If we think of emancipation as praxis, as both an understanding as well as a form of action designed to overthrow structures of domination, we can begin to illuminate the interplay among historical consciousness, critical thinking, and emancipatory behavior. At the level of understanding, critical thinking represents the ability to step beyond commonsense assumptions and to be able to evaluate them in terms of their genesis, development, and purpose. In short, critical thinking cannot be viewed simply as a form of progressive reasoning; it must be seen as a fundamental political act. In this perspective, critical thinking becomes a mode of reasoning that, as Merleau-Ponty points out, represents the realization that "I am able," meaning that one can use individual capacities and collective possibilities "to go beyond the created structures in order to create others."[88] Critical thinking as a political act means that human beings must emerge from their own "submersion and acquire the ability to intvervene in reality as it is unveiled."[89] Not only does this indicate that they must act with others to intervene in the shaping of history, it also means that they must "escape" from their own history; i.e., that which society has made of them. As Sartre writes, "you become what you are in the context of what others have made of you."[90] This is a crucial point, and one that links praxis and historical consciousness. For we must turn to history in order to understand the traditions that have shaped our individual biographies and intersubjective relationships with other human beings. This critical attentiveness to one's own history represents an important element in examining the socially constructed sources underlying one's formative processes. To become aware of the processes of historical self-formation indicates an important beginning in breaking through the taken-for-granted assumptions that legitimize existing institutional arrangements.[91] Therefore, critical thinking demands a form of hermeneutic understanding that is historically grounded. Similarly, it must be stressed that the capacity for a historically grounded critique is inseparable from those conditions that foster collective communication and critical dialogue. In this case, such conditions take as a starting point the need to delegitimize the culture of positivism and the socioeconomic structure it supports.

CONCLUSION

Schools play a crucial, though far from mechanistic, role in reproducing the culture of positivism. While schools function so as to mediate the social, political, and economic tensions of the wider society, they do so in a complex and contradictory fashion. This is an essential point. Schools operate in accordance, either implicitly or explicitly, with their established roles in society. But they do so in terms not entirely determined by the larger society. Diverse institutional restraints, different school cultures, varied regional and community forces, different social formations, and a host of other factors lend varying degrees of autonomy and complexity to the school setting. All of these factors must be analyzed and taken into account if the mechanisms of domination and social control in day-to-day school life are to be understood.[92]

Moreover, the assumptions and methods that characterize schooling are themselves representations of the historical process. But the mechanisms of social control that characterize school life are not simply the factual manifestations of the culture of positivism. They also represent a historical condition that has functioned to transform human needs as well as buttress dominant social and political institutions. Put another way, the prevailing mode of technocratic rationality that permeates both the schools and the larger society has not just been tacked on to the existing social order. It has developed historically over the last century and with particular intensity in the last fifty years; consequently, it deeply saturates our collective experiences, practices, and routines. Thus, to overcome the culture of positivism means that social studies educators will have to do more than exchange one set of principles of social organization for another. They will have to construct alternative social formations and worldviews that affect both the consciousness as well as the deep vital structure of needs in their students.[93]

Unfortunately, classroom teachers and curriculum developers, in general, have been unaware of the historical nature of their own fields. This is not meant to suggest that they should be blamed for either the present failings in public education or the suppression of historical consciousness and critical thinking in the schools. It simply means that the pervasiveness of the culture of positivism and its attendant commonsense assumptions exert a powerful mode of influence on the process of schooling. Moreover, this analysis does not suggest that there is little that teachers can do to change the nature of schooling and the present structure of society. Teachers at all levels of schooling represent a potentially powerful force for social change. But one thing should be clear: the present crisis in history, in essence, is not an academic problem but a political problem. It is a problem that speaks to a form of technological domination that goes far beyond the schools and permeates every sphere of our social existence. There is a lesson to be learned here. What classroom teachers can and must do is work in their respective roles to develop pedagogical theories and methods that link self-reflection and understanding with a commitment to change the nature of the larger society. There are a number of strategies that teachers at all levels of schooling can use in their classrooms. In general terms, they can question the commonsense assumptions that shape their own lives as well as those assumptions that influence and legitimize existing forms of public school classroom knowledge, teaching styles, and evaluation. In adopting such a critical stance while concomitantly reconstructing new educational theories and practices, classroom teachers can help to raise the political consciousness of themselves, their fellow teachers, and their students.[94]

In more specific terms, social studies teachers can treat as problematic those socially constructed assumptions that underlie the concerns of curriculum, classroom social relationships, and classroom evaluation. They can make these issues problematic by raising fundamental questions such as: What counts as social studies knowledge? How is this knowledge produced and legitimized? Whose interests does this knowledge serve? Who has access to this knowledge? How is this knowledge distributed and reproduced in the classroom? What kinds of classroom social relationships serve to parallel and reproduce the social relations of production in the wider society? How do the prevailing methods of evaluation serve to legitimize existing forms of knowledge? What are the contradictions that exist between the ideology embodied in existing forms of social studies knowledge and the objective social reality?

Similarly, questions such as these, which focus on the production, distribution, and evaluation of classroom knowledge and social relationships, should be related to the principles and practices that characterize institutional arrangements in the larger society. Moreover, these questions should be analyzed before social studies teachers structure their classroom experiences. In other words, these are important initial questions that should provide the foundation for educational theory and practice. It is important to recognize that these questions can become an important force in helping teachers identify, understand, and generate those pivotal social processes needed to encourage students to become active participants in the search for knowledge and meaning, a search designed to foster rather than suppress critical thinking and social action.

While it is true that such action will not in and of itself change the nature of existing society, it will set the foundation for producing generations of students who might. As indicated, an important step in that direction can begin by linking the process of classroom pedagogy to wider structural processes. To do so will enable educators to develop a better understanding of the political nature of schooling and the role they might play in shaping it. The relationship between the wider culture of positivism and the process of schooling is, in essence, a relationship between ideology and social control. The dynamic at work in this relationship is complex and diverse. To begin to understand that dynamic is to understand that history is not dead; it is waiting to be seized. Marcuse has stated elegantly what it means to "remember history."

> All reification is forgetting . . . Forgetting past suffering and past joy alienates life under a repressive reality principle. In contrast, remembrance is frustrated: joy is overshadowed by pain. Inexorably so? The horizon of history is still open. If the remembrance of things past would become a motive power in the struggle for changing the world, the struggle would be waged for a revolution hitherto suppressed in the previous historical revolutions.[95]

The culture of positivism has undermined the critical nature of pedagogy, reduced education to a narrow focus on mathematical utility, weakened the democratic purpose of schooling, and undermined the role of educators as engaged and critical public intellectuals. Given the importance of education in providing the formative culture necessary for students to develop the capacities for connecting reason and freedom, ethics and knowledge, and learning to social change, educators must reclaim schooling as an emancipatory project deeply rooted in the project of deepening and expanding the possibilities of critical thought, agency, and democracy itself. Such a task is about both reclaiming the Enlightenment emphasis on freedom, reason, and educated hope as well as engaging education as a crucial site of struggle, one that cannot be frozen in the empty, depoliticizing rationality that drives an oppressive culture of positivism.

NOTES

1 Originally published as Henry A. Giroux (1979), "Schooling and the Culture of Positivism," *Educational Theory*, 29, (4): 263–84.

2 John O'Neil (1978), "Merleau-Ponty's Criticism of Marxist Scientism," *Canadian Journal of Political and Social Theory*, 2, (1): 45.

3 Michael W. Apple (1971), "The Hidden Curriculum and the Nature of Conflict," *Interchange* 2, (4): 22–70; C. A. Bowers (1976), "Curriculum and Our Technocracy Culture: The Problem of Reform," *Teachers College Record*, 78, (1): 53–67; Thomas S. Popkewitz (1977), "The Latent Values of the Discipline Centered Curriculum," *Theory and Research in Social Education*, 5, (1): 41–61; Henry A. Giroux and Anthony N. Penna (1979), "Social Education in the Classroom: The Dynamics of the Hidden Curriculum," *Theory and Research in Education*, 7, (1): 21–42; Henry A. Giroux (1979), "Toward a New Sociology of Education," *Educational Leadership*, 37, (3): 249–52.

4 Michael F. D. Young (ed.) (1976), *Knowledge and Control*. London: Collier-Macmillan.

5 Samuel Bowles and Herbert Gintis (1976), *Schooling in Capitalist America*. New York: Basic Books; Pierre Bourdieu and Jean-Claude Passeron (1977), *Reproduction in Education, Society, and Culture*. London: Sage Publications.

6 Rachel Sharp (1978), "The Sociology of the Curriculum: A Marxist Critique of the Work of Basil Bernstein, Pierre Bourdieu, and Michael Young," unpublished manuscript; Mandan Samp (1978), *Marxism and Education*. London: Routledge and Kegan Paul.

7 David Donald, quoted in Christopher Lasch (1978), *The Culture of Narcissism*. New York: W. W. Norton, p. xiv.

8 Herbert Marcuse (1964), *One Dimensional Man*. Boston: Beacon Press, p. 208.

9 Ibid., p. 98.

10 Russell Jacoby (1975), *Social Amnesia*. Boston: Beacon Press, p. 4.

11 Antonio Gramsci (1971), *Selections from Prison Notebooks*, trans. by Quinton Hoare and Goeffrey Smith. New York: International Publishers, 1971.

12 Louis Althusser (1971), *Lenin and Philosophy*. New York: Monthly Review Press, pp. 127–86.

13 Michael W. Apple (1978), "The New Sociology of Education: Analyzing Cultural and Economic Reproduction," *Harvard Educational Review*, 48, (4): 495–503; Basil Bernstein (1977), *Class, Codes and Control*, vol. 3, 2nd edn. London and Boston: Routledge and Kegan Paul.

14 Apple, "The New Sociology of Education," p. 496.

15 Paul Willis (1977), *Learning to Labour: How Working Class Kids Get Working Class Jobs*. Westmead: Saxon House.

16 Theodore W. Adorno (1967), *Prisms*. London: Nevill Spearman.

17 Hans Magnus Enzenberger (1974), *The Consciousness Industry*. New York: Seabury Press; Trent Schroyer (1973), *The Critique of Domination*. Boston: Beacon Press; David Noble (1977), *America by Design*. New York: Knopf; Christopher Lasch (1978), *Haven in a Heartless World*. New York: Basic Books.

18 Stuart Ewen (1976), *Captains of Consciousness*. New York: McGraw-Hill, p. 202.

19 Harry Braverman (1974), *Labor and Monopoly Capital*. New York: Monthly Review Press; Ewen, *Captains of Consciousness*, p. 195.

20 Herbert Marcuse (1965), "Remarks on a Redefinition of Culture," *Daedalus*, 271: 190–207.

21 Thomas McCarthy (1978), *The Critical Theory of Jurgen Habermas*. Cambridge, MA: The MIT Press, p. 37.

22 Ibid., p. 11.

23 Mihailo Markovic (1974), *From Affluence to Praxis*. Ann Arbor: University of Michigan Press; Richard Bernstein (1976), *The Restructuring of Social and Political Theory*. Philadelphia: University of Pennsylvania Press.

24 Fred R. Dallmayr and Thomas McCarthy (eds) (1977), *Understanding and Social Inquiry*. Notre Dame, IN: University of Notre Dame Press, p. 285.

25 Theodore Abel (1971), "The Operation Called Verstehen," *The American Journal of Sociology*, 54: 211–18.

26 Brian Fay (1975), *Social Theory and Political Practice*. London: George Allen and Unwin, p. 39.

27 Jurgen Habermas (1971), *Knowledge and Human Interest*. Boston: Beacon Press, p. 304.

28 Gertrud Lenzer (1975), *August Comte and Positivism*. New York: Harper and Row, p. xxxix.

29 Hannah Arendt (1958), *The Human Condition*. Chicago: University of Chicago Press, 1958.

30 Herbert Marcuse (1978), "On Science and Phenomenology," in Andrew Arato and Hike Gebhardt (eds), *The Essential Frankfurt Reader*. New York: Urizen Books, pp. 466–76.

31 Richard Bernstein, *The Restructuring of Social and Political Theory*, p. 5.

32 Karl-Otto Apel (1977), "The A Priori of Communication and the Foundation of the Humanities," in Fred R. Dallmayr and Thomas McCarthy (eds), *Understanding and Social Inquiry*. Notre Dame: University of Notre Dame Press, p. 293.

33 Jurgen Habermas (1970), *Toward a Rational Society*, trans. Jeremy Shapiro. Boston: Beacon Press, pp. 81–122.

34 Elliot G. Mishler (1979), "Meaning in Context: Is There Any Other Kind?" *Harvard Educational Review*, 49, (1): 1–19.

35 Howard Zinn (1970), *The Politics of History*. Boston: Beacon Press, pp. 10–11.

36 Raymond Williams (1977), *Marxism and Literature*. New York: Oxford University Press.

37 Alvin W. Gouldner (1976), *The Dialectic of Ideology and Technology*. New York: Seabury Press, p. 50.

38 Max Horkheimer (1974), *Eclipse of Reason*. New York: Seabury Press, p. 178.

39 Fay, *Social Theory and Political Practice*, p. 27.

40 Edmund Husserl (1966), *Phenomenology and the Crisis of Philosophy*. New York: Harper.

41 Schroyer, *The Critique of Domination*, p. 213.

42 Horkheimer, *Eclipse of Reason*, p. 73.

43 Habermas, *Toward A Rational Society*, p. 113.

44 Marcuse, *One Dimensional Man*, p. 99.

45 Marcuse, *One Dimensional Man*; Jacoby, *Social Amnesia*.

46 Nicos Poulantzas (1973), *Political Power and Social Classes*, trans. by Timothy O'Hagen. London: New Left Books.

47 Richard S. Kirkendall (1975), "The Status of History in the Schools," *The Journal of American History*, 62, (2): 557–8.

48 Kirkendall, "The Status of History in the Schools," p. 465.

49 Warren L. Hickman (1977), "The Erosion of History," *Social Education*, 43, (1): 22.

50 Richard Bernstein, *The Restructuring of Social and Political Theory*; Mishler, "Meaning in Context."

51 Michael Quinn Patton (1975), *Alternative Evaluation Research Design*, North Dakota Study Group on Evaluation Monograph. Grand Forks: University of North Dakota Press, p. 41.

52 William Pinar (1978), "The Reconceptualization of Curriculum Studies," *Journal of Curriculum Studies*, 10, (3): 205–14.

53 James McDonald (1975), "Curriculum and Human Interests," in William F. Pinar (ed.), *Curriculum Theorizing*. Berkeley: McCutchan, p. 289.

54 Thomas S. Popkewitz (1978), "Educational Research: Values and Visions of a Social Order," *Theory and Research in Social Education*, 11, (9): 28.

55 Thomas S. Kuhn (1970), *The Structure of Scientific Revolutions*. Chicago: University of Chicago Press, p. 80.

56 Alfred Schutz and Thomas Luckmann (1973), *The Structure of the Life-World*. Evanston, IL: Northwestern University Press.

57 Marcuse, *One Dimensional Man*, p. 172; Trent Schroyer (1990), "Toward a Critical Theory of Advanced Industrial Society," in Hans Peter Dreitzel (ed.), *Recent Sociology No. 2*. New York: Macmillan, pp. 210–34.

58 William F. Pinar (1978), "Notes on the Curriculum Field 1978," *Educational Researcher*, 7, (8): 5–12.

59 T. W. Adorno, H. Albert, R. Dahrendorf, J. Habermas, H. Pilot, and K. R. Popper (1976), *The Positivist Dispute in German Sociology*. New York: Harper and Row, p. 135.

60 W. James Popham (1970), "Probing the Validity of Arguments against Behavioral Goals," in Robert J. Kibler, Larry Lee Barker, David T. Miles (eds), *Behavioral Objectives and Instruction*. Boston: Allyn and Bacon, p. 116.

61 George Beauchamp (February1978), "A Hard Look at Curriculum," *Educational Leadership*, 35, (5): 409.

62 Richard Bernstein, *The Restructuring of Social and Political Theory*, p. 112.

63 Gouldner, *The Dialectic of Ideology and Technology*, p. 50.

64 Fenwick W. English (1979), "Management Practice as a Key to Curriculum Leadership," *Educational Leadership*, 36, (6): 408–9.

65 Popkewitz, "Educational Research," p. 32.

66 Peter Woods (1979), *The Divided School*. London and Boston: Routledge and Kegan Paul, p. 137.

67 John Friedman (1978), "The Epistemology of Social Practice: A Critique of Objective Knowledge," *Theory and Society*, 6, (1): 75–92.

68 An interesting lament on this subject can be found in Frank R. Harrison (1978), "The Humanistic Lesson of Solzhenitzen and Proposition 13," *Chronicle of Higher Education*, 32.

69 Michael W. Apple (1979), "The Production of Knowledge and the Production of Deviance Schools." Speech given at Sociology of Knowledge Conference in Birmingham, England. January 2–4, 1979.

70 Stanley Aronowitz (1973), *False Promises*. New York: McGraw-Hill, p. 270.

71 Ibid.

72 Thomas E. Fox and Robert D. Hess (1972), "An Analysis of Social Conflict in Social Studies Textbooks," Final Report, Project No. 1-1-116, United States Department of Health, Education, and Welfare; Popkewitz, "Discipline Centered Curriculum"; Jean Anyon (1978), "Elementary Social Studies Textbooks and Legitimating Knowledge," *Theory and Research in Social Education*, 6, (3): 40–55.

73 Anyon, "Elementary Social Studies Textbooks," p. 40.

74 Ibid., p. 43.

75 Alvin W. Gouldner (1970), *The Coming Crisis in Western Sociology*. New York: Basic Books, p. 193.

76 Anyon, "Elementary Social Studies Textbooks," p. 44.

77 Popkewitz, "Educational Research," p. 44.

78 Edwin Fenton (ed.) (1968), *Holt Social Studies Curriculum*. New York: Holt, Rinehart and Winston.

79 Popkewitz, "Discipline Centered Curriculum," p. 58.

80 Maxine Greene (1978), *Landscapes of Learning*. New York: Teachers College Press.
81 Ration, *Alternative Evaluation*, p. 22.
82 Rachel Sharp and Anthony Green (1975), *Education and Social Control*. London: Routledge and Kegan Paul.
83 Paulo Freire (1973), *Pedagogy of the Oppressed*. New York: Seabury Press.
84 Greene, *Landscapes of Learning*, p. 56.
85 Bowers, "Curriculum and Our Technocracy Culture."
86 Popkewitz, "Educational Research," pp. 27–8; also see J. Karabel and H. Halsey (eds) (1977), "Educational Research: A Review and an Interpretation," in *Power and Ideology*. New York: Oxford University Press, pp. 1–88; Ulf P. Lundgren and Stern Pettersson (eds) (1979), *Code, Context and Curriculum Processes*. Stockholm: Stockholm Institute of Education, pp. 5–29.
87 Aronowitz, *False Promises*, p. 278.
88 M. Merleau-Ponty (1967), *The Structure of Behavior*. Boston: Beacon Press, p. 175.
89 Freire, *Pedagogy of the Oppressed*, pp. 100–1; Henry A. Giroux (1980), "Beyond the Limits of Radical Educational Reform," *Journal of Curriculum Theorizing*, 2, (1): 20–46.
90 Jean-Paul Sartre (1977), *Sartre by Himself*, trans. Michael Seaver. New York: Urizen Books, p. 54.
91 Henry A. Giroux and Anthony N. Penna (1979), "Social Education in the Classroom," *Theory and Research in Social Education*, 7: 21–42.
92 Willis, *Learning to Labour*; Williams, *Marxism and Literature*. Other penetrating critiques of the correspondence theory as a truncated view of "manipulation" theory can be found in Richard Lichtman (1975), "Marx's Theory of Ideology," *Socialist Revolution*, 23: 45–76. Also see Daniel Ben-Horin (1977), "Television without Tears: An Outline of a Socialist Approach to Popular Television," *Socialist Review*, 35: 7–35.
93 Agnes Heller (1974), *Theory of Need in Marx*. London: Allen and Busby.
94 Henry A. Giroux (1978), "Writing and Critical Thinking in the Social Studies," *Curriculum Inquiry*, 8, (4): 291–310; Richard J. Bates (1978), "The New Sociology of Education: Directions for Theory and Research," *New Zealand Journal of Educational Studies*, 13, (1): 3–22.
95 Herbert Marcuse (1978), *The Aesthetic Dimension*. Boston: Beacon Press, p. 73.

CHAPTER 3

Rethinking Cultural Politics and Radical Pedagogy

In the Work of Antonio Gramsci[1]

INTRODUCTION

More than seventy years after his death, the Italian Marxist, Antonio Gramsci, still looms large as one of the great political theorists of the twentieth century. Refusing to separate culture from systemic relations of power, or politics from the production of knowledge and identities, Gramsci redefined how politics bore down on everyday life through the force of its pedagogical practices, relations, and discourses. This position is in stark contrast to a growing and insistent number of progressive theorists who abstract politics from culture and political struggle from pedagogical practices. In opposition to Gramsci, such theorists privilege a materialist politics that ignores the ways in which cultural formations have become one of the chief means through which individuals engage and comprehend the material circumstances and forces that shape their lives. In a strange twist of politics, many progressives and left intellectuals now view culture as ornamental, a burden on class-based politics, or identical with a much maligned identity politics.[2]

Gramsci's work both challenges this position and provides a theoretical framework for understanding how class is always lived through the modalities of race and gender.[3] Moreover, it provides an important political corrective to those social theories that fail to acknowledge how pedagogical politics work in shaping and articulating the divide between diverse institutional and cultural formations. According to Gramsci, social theory should expand the meaning of the political by being self-conscious about the multiple ways pedagogy works to inform its own cultural practices, legitimates its motivating questions, and secures particular modes of authority. It should also be self-reflective about how it privileges particular "institutional frameworks and disciplinary rules by which its research imperatives are formed."[4] Gramsci's work presents a much-needed challenge to this position. According to Gramsci, culture needed to be addressed as part of a new political configuration and set of historical conditions that had emerged in the beginning of the twentieth century in the advanced industrial societies of the West. Critical intellectuals could not address the material machineries of power, the institutional arrangements of capitalism, and the changing politics of class formation without being attentive to how common sense and consent were being constructed within new public spheres marked by an expanding application of the dynamics and politics of specific, yet shifting, pedagogical practices. Such an understanding not only required a new attentiveness to "culture in its political role and consequences,"[5] but foregrounded the issue of how alternative cultural spheres might be transformed into sites of struggle and resistance animated by a new group of subaltern intellectuals.

While the context for taking up Gramsci's work is radically different from the historical context in which his politics and theories developed, Gramsci's views on the relationships among culture, pedagogy, and power provide an important theoretical resource for addressing the challenge currently facing public and higher education in the United States. I want to analyze the importance of Gramsci's work, especially his work on education, by first outlining the nature of the current right-wing attempt to subordinate public and higher education to the needs of capital — reconfiguring the purpose and meaning of education from a public to a private good — and the central role that cultural politics plays in spearheading such an assault. In addition, I want to analyze the attempt on the part of right-wing theorists such as E. D. Hirsch to appropriate Gramsci's views on education for a conservative educational project. Finally, I will conclude by analyzing the implications Gramsci's work might have for defending education as a public good and cultural pedagogy as central to any discourse of radical politics.

DEMOCRACY AND EDUCATION UNDER SIEGE

As the United States moves into the next millennium, questions of culture have become central to understanding how politics and power reorganize practices that have a profound effect on the social and economic forces that regulate everyday life. The politics of culture can be seen not only in the ways that symbolic resources and knowledge have replaced traditional skills as the main productive force, but also in the role that culture now plays as the main pedagogical force to secure the authority and interests of dominant groups. Media technologies have redefined the power of particular groups to construct a representational politics that plays a crucial role shaping self and group identities as well as determining and marking off different conceptions of community and belonging. The notion that culture has become "a crucial site and weapon of power"[6] has not been lost on conservatives and the growing forces of the new right.

Beginning with Reagan and Bush in the 1980s and culminating with the Gingrich-Republican revolution in the 1990s and the election of George W. Bush in 2000 and 2004, conservatives have taken control over an ever-growing electronic media industry and new global communication systems

— acknowledging that politics has taken on an important pedagogical function in the information age.[7] Recognizing the political value of defining culture as both a site of struggle and a sphere of education becomes central to social and political change, and conservatives have easily outmaneuvered progressives in the ongoing battle over control of the conditions for the production of knowledge, values, identities, desires, and those social practices central to winning the consent of diverse segments of the American public. Utilizing the power of the established press, new media, and the Internet as a site of cultural politics, conservatives have used their massive financial resources and foundations to gain control of various segments of the culture industry.[8] Conservative foundations and groups have also played a pivotal role in educating a new generation of public intellectuals in order to wage a relentless battle against all facets of democratic life; bearing the brunt of this vicious attack are groups disadvantaged by virtue of their race, age, gender, class, and lack of citizenship. With profound irony, conservative forces have appropriated Antonio Gramsci's insight that "every relationship of 'hegemony' is necessarily an educational relationship."[9] In doing so, they have reasserted the role of culture as an educational force for social and economic reproduction and have waged an intense ideological battle both within various cultural sites such as the media and over important cultural sites such as public schools, the arts, and higher education.

The effects of the current assault on democracy by the right can be seen in the dismantling of state supports for immigrants, people of color, and working people. More specifically, it is evident in the passage of retrograde social policies that promote deindustrialization, downsizing, and free market reforms, which in the case of welfare reform legislation will prohibit over 3.5 million children from receiving any type of government assistance, adding more children to the ranks of over 15.5 million children already living in poverty in the United States.[10] As conservative policies move away from a politics of social investment to one of social containment, state services are hollowed out and reduced to their more repressive functions — discipline, control, and surveillance.[11] This is evident not only in states such as California and Florida, which spend more to incarcerate people than to educate their college-age populations, but also in the disproportionate number of African American males throughout the country who are being incarcerated or placed under the control of the criminal justice system.[12] The aftermath of this battle against democracy and social and economic justice can also be seen in a resurgent racism, marked by anti-immigrant legislation passed in Arizona in 2010, the dismantling of affirmative action, and the re-emergence of racist ideologies attempting to prove that differences in intelligence are both racially distinctive and genetically determined.[13] The resurgent racism is also evident in the modes of public pedagogy found on talk radio, Fox News, and a host of other right-wing media that dominate the cultural politics with a resurgent vitriol, especially since the election of Barack Obama in 2008. In this instance, racially coded attacks on criminals, the underclass, and welfare mothers are legitimated, in part, through a politically invigorated rhetoric of Social Darwinism that scapegoats people of color while simultaneously blaming them for the social problems that result in their exploitation, suffering, and oppression.[14]

As part of this broader assault on democracy, public education has become one of the most contested public spheres in political life at the turn of the century. More than any other institution, public schools serve as a dangerous reminder of both the promise and the shortcomings of the social, political, and economic forces that shape society. Embodying the contradictions of the larger society, public schools provide a critical referent for measuring the degree to which American society fulfills its obligation to provide all students with the knowledge and skills necessary for critical citizenship and the possibilities of democratic public life. As sites that reflect the nation's alleged commitment to the legacy of democracy, schools offer both a challenge and a threat to attempts by conservatives and liberals alike to remove the language of choice from the discourse of democracy and to diminish citizenship to a largely privatized affair in which civic responsibilities are reduced to the act of consuming. A euphemism for privatization, "choice" relieves schools of the pretense of serving the public good. No longer institutions designed to benefit all members of the community, they are refashioned in market terms designed to serve the narrow interests of individual consumers and national economic policies.

Dismissing the role that schools might play as democratic public spheres, conservatives have redefined the meaning and purpose of schooling in accordance with the interest of global capitalism. As financial support for public schools dries up, conservatives increasingly attempt to harness all educational institutions to corporate control through calls for privatization, vouchers, and so-called choice programs. Rewriting the tradition of schooling as a public good, conservatives abstract questions of equity from excellence and subsume the political mission of schooling within the ideology and logic of the market. Similarly, conservatives have waged a relentless attack on teacher unions, called for the return of authoritarian teaching approaches, and endorsed learning by drill and rote memorization. In this scenario, public education is replaced by the call for privately funded educational institutions that can safely ignore civil rights, exclude students who are disenfranchised by class or race, and conveniently blur the lines between religion and the state.

Given the prevailing attack on education, we are witnessing both the elimination of public school as a potential site for expanding the public good and the realignment of the mission of higher education within the discourse and ideology of the corporate world.[15] Within this perspective, higher education is aggressively shorn of its utopian impulses. Undermined as a repository of critical thinking, writing, teaching, and learning, universities are refashioned to meet the interests of commerce and regulation. Within the current onslaught against non-commodified public spheres, the mission of the university becomes instrumental; it is redesigned largely to serve corporate interests whose aim is to restructure higher education along the lines of global capitalism. In specific terms, this means privileging instrumental over substantive knowledge, shifting power away from faculty to administrations, and corporatizing the culture of the university. As the college curriculum is stripped of those subjects (typically in the humanities) that do not translate immediately into market considerations, programs are downsized and reduced to service programs for business. In this case, not only does instrumental knowledge replace substantive knowledge as the basis for research, writing, and teaching, but the university intellectual is reduced to low-level technocrat whose role is to manage and legitimate the downsizing, knowledge production, and labor practices that characterize the institutional power and culture of the corporatized and vocationalized university.

The defining principle of the current right-wing attack against higher education and public schooling is the dismantling of all public spheres that refuse to be defined strictly by the instrumental logic of the market. As such, the battle waged over education must be understood as part of a much broader struggle for democratic public life, the political function of culture, the role of intellectuals, and the importance of pedagogy as a hegemonic technology in various aspects of daily life. At stake here is the issue of how we "think" politics in Gramscian terms, that is, how we create a new culture through a reformulation of the meaning of cultural politics, intellectual engagement, and pedagogical change.[16] In short, how do we reassert the primacy of a non-dogmatic, progressive politics by analyzing how culture as a force for resistance is related to power, education, and agency? This project suggests the need to understand how culture shapes the everyday lives of people: how culture constitutes a defining principle for understanding how struggles over meaning, identity, social practices, and institutional machineries of power can be waged while inserting the pedagogical back into the political and expanding the pedagogical by recognizing the "educational force of our whole social and cultural experience [as one] that actively and profoundly teaches."[17]

Gramsci's legacy is important for progressives because he provides a wide-ranging and insightful analysis of how education functions as part of a wider set of political discourses and social relations aimed at promoting ideological and structural change. But in spite of Gramsci's politics and intentions, his work has also been used by conservatives to legitimate a profoundly reactionary view of education and the processes of learning and persuasion. In opposition to such an appropriation, I want to analyze in detail how Gramsci's work has been used by Harold Entwistle in his *Antonio Gramsci: Conservative Schooling for Radical Politics* and more recently by E. D. Hirsch in his book, *The Schools We Need*, to push a deeply conservative educational agenda. While recognizing that Gramsci's writings on education represent a problematic legacy for progressives, I want to argue in opposition to Entwistle and Hirsch that Gramsci's work, when read within the appropriate historical context and in relation to Gramsci's revolutionary project, provides an invaluable theoretical service for helping educators rethink the political nature of educational work and the role it might play in the struggle for expanding and developing the relationship between learning and democratic social change, on the one hand, and committed intellectual practice and political struggle on the other.[18]

APPROPRIATING GRAMSCI

Although the work of Entwistle and Hirsch is separated by a decade, they share similar views about the value of a conservative approach to schooling.[19] Not only do both authors legitimate schools as agents of social and economic reproduction, they advocate classroom practices based on learning a common culture, rigid disciplinary rules, an authoritarian pedagogy, and standardized curricula. At the same time, it is important to note that Entwistle provides a far more serious engagement with Gramsci's work and makes some valuable contributions both in his critiques of some progressive forms of political education and in his suggestions for rethinking the politics of adult education. While Hirsch's work on Gramsci was inspired by Entwistle, he attempts to reappropriate Entwistle in the service of a right-wing conservatism that blames educational progressives in the United States for the decline of teaching and learning in the public schools. Hirsch's "discovery" that Gramsci is in actuality a poster boy for conservative thought combines the bad faith of misrepresentation with the reductionism of an ideological fervor that seems to make a mockery of political sense and historical accuracy.[20] While the nature of the political appropriation of Gramsci's work by a diverse body of radical educators may be open to interpretation, it certainly stretches the bounds of plausibility when Hirsch aligns Gramsci with contemporary, right-wing educational theorists such as Charles Sykes. Not only does such an appropriation represent a form of theoretical disingenuousness and political opportunism, but it is also an affront to everything that Gramsci stood for as a Marxist revolutionary.

Entwistle and Hirsch share a view of schooling that stands in sharp contrast to the radical educational theories of their time; yet, they appropriate from Gramsci's work a rationale for conservative pedagogical practices as part of their attempt to redefine the relationship between schooling and society, on the one hand, and intellectuals and their social responsibilities on the other. Although Entwistle's book, *Antonio Gramsci: Conservative Schooling for Radical Politics*, provides a more extensive reading of Gramsci, E. D. Hirsch applies the implications of such a conservative interpretation directly to matters affecting teaching and learning in the United States. Moreover, Hirsch draws upon the work of Gramsci in addition to his conservative contemporaries in a spurious effort to produce what he calls a "pragmatic" and bipartisan, rather than "ideological" and conservative, agenda for educational reform. In what follows, I will critically engage how both authors appropriate Gramsci as well as analyze the implications of their work for a theory of schooling and pedagogy.

Harold Entwistle's book represents one of the first comprehensive analyses of the relevance of Gramsci's writings for educational theory and practice. Providing his own detailed interpretation of Gramsci's writings on schooling, Entwistle rejects as misguided the way Gramsci's work has been previously interpreted and excoriates "new sociologists of education" as well as other radical educational theorists who rose to prominence in the 1970s and 1980s in England. After resurrecting the "real" Gramsci, Entwistle proceeds to dismiss those "radical" critics who have allegedly misinterpreted Gramsci's work. The remainder of Entwistle's book focuses on the relevance of Gramsci's writings for adult education, ending with the "remarkable" conclusion that the lesson to be learned from Gramsci's work is that schools do not provide the setting for "a radical, counterhegemonic education."[21]

Entwistle's reading of Gramsci's work portrays him as a "stern" taskmaster whose views on discipline, knowledge, and hegemony render him more compatible with Karl Popper and Jacques Barzun (both of whom are referred to positively) than the likes of Karl Marx, Paulo Freire or, for that matter, even John Dewey. If we are to take Entwistle's version of Gramsci seriously as a model for socialist education, then we will have to accept the claim that Gramsci supported unproblematically a deference to authority, the rote memorizing of facts, and a subservience to imposed standards as core pedagogical principles for a theory and practice of schooling. Needless to say, such a claim is hardly consistent with Gramsci's call for an educational practice and project aimed at generating "more and more organic intellectuals from the children of the peasantry and the proletariat."[22]

The conservative literary theorist, E. D. Hirsch, mentioned earlier, echoes a similar argument. Hirsch describes Gramsci's work as a critical response to Giovanni Gentile's educational reforms, enacted under Benito Mussolini in the 1920s — reforms that emphasized "emotion," "feeling," and the "most immediate needs of the child." The failure of these reforms, according to Hirsch, served as proof of the inadequacy of what he incorrectly terms the central tenets of critical educational theory. In opposition to the alleged failure of this form of "progressive" pedagogy, Hirsch argues that Gramsci offers a rationale for conservative methods such as "phonics and memorization of the multiplication table," claiming that they are necessary for "the oppressed classes to learn how to read, write, and communicate — and to gain enough traditional knowledge to understand the worlds of nature and culture surrounding them."[23]

What Hirsch and Entwistle fail to acknowledge in their selective readings of Gramsci is that his concern with "facts" and intellectual rigor makes sense only as a rightly argued critique of inane methodologies that separate facts from values, learning from understanding, and emotion from the intellect. As David Forgacs points out in the introduction to An Antonio Gramsci Reader,

Gramsci "begins not from the point of view of the teacher but from that of the learner, and he emphasizes that the learning process is a movement toward self-knowledge, self-mastery, and thus liberation. Education is not a matter of handing out 'encyclopedic knowledge' but of developing and disciplining the awareness which the learner already possesses."[24] Gramsci's emphasis on intellectual rigor and discipline can only be understood as part of a broader concern for students to develop a critical understanding of how the past informs the present in order that they could liberate themselves from the ideologies and commonsense assumptions that formed the core beliefs of the dominant order. Gramsci was quite clear on the distinction between learning facts that enlarged one's perception of the larger social order and simply gathering information. Even in his earlier writings, Gramsci understood the relationship between a pedagogy of rote memorization and the conservative nature of the culture it served to legitimate. For instance, in 1916 he wrote:

> We must break the habit of thinking that culture is encyclopedic knowledge whereby man [sic] is viewed as a mere container in which to pour and conserve empirical data or brute disconnected facts which he will have to subsequently pigeonhole in his brain as in the columns of a dictionary so as to be able to eventually respond to the varied stimuli of the external world. This form of culture is truly harmful, especially to the proletariat. It only serves to create misfits, people who believe themselves superior to the rest of humanity because they have accumulated in their memory a certain quantity of facts and dates which they cough up at every opportunity to almost raise a barrier between themselves and others.[25]

Hirsch ignores Gramsci's critique of encyclopedic knowledge and in doing so argues that

> romantic anti-intellectualism and developmentalism [critical thinking and critical social theory], as Gramsci understood, are luxuries of the merchant class that the poor cannot afford ... Today, the Enlightenment view of the value of knowledge is the only view we can afford. When the eighteenth-century Encyclopedists attempted to systematize human knowledge in a set of books, they were placing their hope for progress in the ever-growing experience of human kind.[26]

For Hirsch, the production of knowledge by the middle class is only paved with good intentions. It seems unimaginable for Hirsch to engage critically the relationship between knowledge and power or ideology and politics. To address how culture and power combined to produce knowledge that often legitimates not the general interests but particular racial, class, and gendered interests would work against his general educational program: to teach children a core knowledge base of "facts." For Hirsch the most distinguishing mark of encyclopedic knowledge is its use for inculcating mental discipline; moreover, the primary purpose of education is not only to transmit such knowledge but to prevent it from being undermined by forms of "anti-intellectualism" in the American educational community whose legacy Hirsch argues extends from "home economics and shop in the 1920s to all forms of critical thinking and problem solving skills in the 1990s."[27]

For Gramsci, the production of knowledge and its reception and transformation were historical, dialectical, and critical. Gramsci rejected mere factuality and demanded that schooling be "formative, while being instructive." The pedagogical task entailed, in part, "mitigating and rendering more fertile the dogmatic approach which must inevitably characterize these first few years."[28] Such a task was not easy and demanded, on the one hand, the necessity "to place limits on libertarian ideologies," while, on the other hand, it was necessary to recognize that "the elements of struggle against the mechanical and Jesuitical school have become unhealthily exaggerated."[29] Underlying Gramsci's pedagogy is an educational principle in which a comfortable humanism is replaced by a hard-headed radicalism, not a radicalism that falsely separates necessity and spontaneity, discipline and the acquisition of basic skills from imagination, but, instead, one that integrates them.

In contrast, Entwistle and Hirsch interpret Gramsci's view of schooling as one that surrenders pedagogy to dull routine, and in doing so imply that such a pedagogy can be and should be maintained at the expense of the spirit. The interconnections between discipline and critical thinking in Gramsci's view of schooling only lend support to a conservative notion of pedagogy if the concept of physical discipline and self-control is abstracted from his emphasis on the importance of developing a counterhegemonic project, one "which demands the formation of a militant, self-conscious proletariat that will fight unyieldingly for its right to govern itself."[30] In other words, Gramsci's claim that "it will always be an effort to learn physical self-discipline and self-control, the pupil, has, in effect, to undergo psyche-physical training"[31] gets seriously distorted unless understood within the context of Gramsci's other remarks on learning and intellectual development. Gramsci stressed this view not only in his early writing in 1916 but just as forcefully in the *Notebooks*. In the latter he writes: "Many people have to be persuaded that studying too is a job, and a very tiring one with its own particular apprenticeship involving muscles and nerves as well as *intellect*" (my emphasis).[32]

For Gramsci, there was a dynamic tension between self-discipline and critical understanding. Consequently, what in fact often appears like a paradox in Gramsci's work on education is in reality a nuanced and dialectical endorsement of a critical and disciplined educational practice informed by a notion of radical pedagogical authority. Distinguishing between classroom authority that works in the service of critical agency and authority that is used to promote conformity and allegiance to the state, Gramsci provides a political referent for criticizing schools that he claims are merely a bourgeois affair. According to Gramsci, any pedagogical practice has to be examined and implemented within a broader understanding of what the purpose of schooling might become and how such a view of political education articulates with a wider democratic project. Schools, in this instance, are seen as central and formative sites for the production of political identities, the struggle over culture, and for educating organic intellectuals. In "Men or Machines," Gramsci argues that acquiring political power must be matched with the "problem of winning intellectual power."[33] If the school is to offer students of the working class and other subaltern groups the knowledge and skills necessary for political leadership, they cannot be simply, as Hirsch, in particular, would have it, boot camps for the intellectually malleable. Gramsci is quite clear on this issue:

> A school which does not mortgage the child's future, a school that does not force the child's will, his intelligence and growing awareness to run along the tracks to a predetermined station. A school of freedom and free initiative, not a school of slavery and mechanical precision. The children of proletarians too should have all possibilities open to them; they should be able to develop their own individuality in the optimal way, and hence in the most productive way for both themselves and society.[34]

For Gramsci, any analysis of education can only be understood in relation to existing social and cultural formations and the power relations these imply. Gramsci emphasized that schooling constitutes only one form of political education within a broader network of experience, history, and collective struggle. Given Gramsci's view of political education, it is difficult to reduce his view of teaching and learning to a form of positivist reductionism in which a particular methodology such as rote learning is endorsed without questioning whether such pedagogical practices are implicated in or offer resistance to the mechanisms of consent, common sense, and dominant social relations.

Hirsch enlists Gramsci not only to justify authoritarian classroom relations in which students are deprived of the basic right to address disturbing, urgent questions but also to foster a sense that the point of view of the learner is irrelevant. For both Hirsch and Entwistle, schools are dysfunctional not because they oppress students from subaltern groups but because the legacy of progressive education emphasizes "'project oriented,' 'hands-on,' 'critical thinking' and so-called 'democratic education'" rather than a core curriculum of facts and information.[35] Hirsch, in particular, endorses a reductive view of information accumulation in which the critical relationship between culture and power remains largely unexamined, except as a pretext to urge working-class and subaltern groups to master the dominant culture as a way of reproducing the social order. Hirsch makes this point quite clearly:

The oppressed class should be taught to master the tools of power and authority — the ability to read, write, and communicate — and to gain enough traditional knowledge to understand the worlds of nature and culture surrounding them. Children, particularly the children of the poor, should not be encouraged to flourish "naturally," which would keep them ignorant and make them slaves of emotion. They should learn the value of hard work, gain the knowledge that leads to understanding, and master the traditional culture in order to command its rhetoric, as Gramsci himself had learned to do.[36]

The implication here is that any recourse to teaching working-class children about the specificities of their histories, experiences, and cultural memories would simply result in a form of pedagogical infantilism. More importantly, Hirsch misses a central concern that runs throughout Gramsci's work — skills are not universal, and must be addressed within the context that educators, not to mention students, both intervene in and attempt to change. Similarly, Hirsch assumes that the poor performance of working-class students results from intellectual sloth and has nothing to do with underfunded schools, a diminished tax base, and urban politics. On the contrary, for Hirsch, overcrowded classrooms, inadequate classroom resources, and broken down school buildings play no role in whether working-class kids and other subaltern groups do well in schools. The real enemy of student learning, according to Hirsch, is the critical legacy of progressivism and its failure to endorse rote learning, a core curriculum, and uniform teaching rather than the force of racial and class bias, poor working conditions for teachers, or poverty.[37]

Of course, while Gramsci was deeply concerned with students learning "facts" and specific forms of knowledge, he did not advocate that the context of such learning was irrelevant. For Gramsci, learning had to be rigorous but meaningful, subject-based but related to practical activities. Appropriating Marx's "Theses on Feuerbach" (the educator must be educated), Gramsci believed that "the relationship between teacher and pupil is active and reciprocal so that every teacher is always a pupil and every pupil a teacher."[38] By arguing that the teacher–student relationship leaves no room for elitism or sterile pedantry, Gramsci introduces an important principle into the structuring of classroom social relations. The concept of the teacher as a learner suggests that teachers must help students critically appropriate their own histories, but also look critically at their own role as public intellectuals located within specific cultural formations and relations of power. In this instance, Gramsci not only argues implicitly against forms of authoritarian teaching; he sharply criticizes the assumption that knowledge should be treated unproblematically — beyond the dynamics of interrogation, criticism, and political engagement. Gramsci had no interest in allowing schools to produce a culture that served repressive authority and state power, nor did he have any interest in supporting teachers and intellectuals who were reduced to what he called "experts in legitimation."[39]

By ignoring how the imposition of meanings and values distributed in schools are dialectically related to the mechanisms of economic and political control in the dominant society, both Entwistle and Hirsch depoliticize the relationship between power and culture, but Hirsch is especially vehement in normalizing the hegemonic role that schools play in defining what is legitimate knowledge and social practice. For Hirsch, this position translates into a call for a common national curriculum that emphasizes the acquisition of core knowledge and standardized testing.[40] Hirsch has no conception that such a position is at odds with the counterhegemonic project posed by Gramsci — cultural pedagogy as a means to create organic intellectuals whose task is to identify the social interests behind power; challenge traditional understandings of culture, power and politics; and share such knowledge as the basis for organizing diverse forms of class struggle in order to create a socialist society. Class struggle or the goal of socialism couldn't be more removed from Hirsch's politics.

Rather than acknowledge the need to revalue the "disrespected identities and the cultural products of maligned groups,"[41] Hirsch wants to "save" underprivileged kids by stripping them of their identities and histories and assimilating them into the dominant culture. Curriculum in these terms provides the legitimation for forms of middle-class cultural capital that serve as an institutionally sanctioned bunker against learning and living with differences.[42] Hirsch argues that while teaching multiculturalism may have some value, it ultimately is disruptive to subaltern students because it is approached through "amateur psychological efforts [that] fail because [they result] in lies to children about their achievements . . . and lead to further erosion of their self-esteem."[43] It appears not to occur to Hirsch that schools may actually systematize failing students through racially motivated models of teaching, tracking, and evaluation. Should we assume that curricular knowledge that represents middle-class cultural capital as the referent against which the narratives of history, identity, and social experience should be judged is unproblematically uplifting for working-class kids? Or that the warehousing and tracking often built into school curricula to the disadvantage of racial, class, and gender minorities work to their advantage? This position is not merely naive; it is a construct of reactionary politics parading as common sense, and is completely at odds with Gramsci's view of the role that education should play in liberating subaltern groups.

In opposition to Gramsci, neither Entwistle nor Hirsch provide a critical language to deconstruct the basis of privileges that are accorded to the dominant culture. There is no attempt to interrogate culture as the shared and lived principles of life, characteristic of different groups and classes as these emerge within unequal relations of power and struggle. Nor do Entwistle and Hirsch critically engage how questions of power, history, and race, gender, and class privilege work to codify specific ideological educational practices as merely the accumulation of disinterested knowledge "that can be exchanged on the world market for upward mobility."[44] In effect, they de-emphasize unequally valued cultural styles and the ways in which dominant pedagogical practices work to disparage the multiple languages, histories, and experiences at work in a multicultural society.

Hirsch, in particular, ends up legitimating a homogenizing cultural discourse that institutionalizes various policing techniques to safeguard the interests and power of dominant groups. In the end, both Entwistle and Hirsch support a view of culture and knowledge as monolithic: the product of a single, durable history and vision at odds with the notion and politics of difference. The cultural politics at work in this view of education maintains an ominous ideological silence regarding the validity and importance of the experiences of women, blacks, and other groups excluded from the narrative of mainstream history and culture. Thus there emerges no critical under-standing of Gramsci's focus on culture as a field of struggle or of competing interests through which dominant and subordinate groups live out and make sense of their given circumstances and conditions of life within incommen-surate hierarchies of power and possibility.

Entwistle and Hirsch do more than offer an unenlightened and reductive reading of culture; they appropriate the Gramscian position that schools are agencies of social and cultural reproduction and in doing so defend this position rather than criticize it. Rather than understood as a storehouse of immutable facts, behaviors, and practices, culture is inextricably related to the outcomes of struggle over the complex and often contradictory processes of learning, persuasion, agency, and leadership. Culture is about the produc-tion and legitimation of particular ways of life transmitted in schools through the overt and hidden curricula so as to legitimate the cultural capital of dominant groups while marginalizing the voices of the subaltern. If power is related to culture in the discourses of Entwistle and Hirsch, the outcome is a notion of culture cleansed of its own complicity in furthering social relations and pedagogical practices that reproduce the worst dimensions of schooling. For example, missing from this analysis is any understanding of the increasing corporatism and its effects on schools; poverty, racism, and gender bias and the ways in which these forces structure the school curricula; the distribution of financial resources between schools; or the organization of the teaching labor force. While Hirsch's reading of Gramsci is much more reductive than Entwistle's extensive analysis, both theorists share a conserva-tive ideological project in their reading of the role of intellectuals and the purpose of schooling. In both cases, Entwistle and Hirsch represent different versions of the same ideology, one that is deeply committed to expunging democracy of its critical and emancipatory possibilities. In what follows, I want to conclude by pointing to aspects of Gramsci's work that might be use-ful for developing some important theoretical principles for a critical theory of schooling and pedagogy.

THINKING LIKE GRAMSCI: RECLAIMING
THE STRUGGLE OVER SCHOOLING

Given the current assault on schooling and public life more generally, it is imperative that progressive educators develop a language of critique and possibility along with new strategies for understanding and intervention in order to reclaim and reinvigorate the struggle to sustain public schooling as a central feature of democratic life. Gramsci's work is enormously helpful in this regard because it forcefully reminds us that any attempt to articulate the nature and purpose of schooling must be addressed as part of a broader comprehensive politics of social change. Schooling, in Gramsci's terms, was always part of some larger ensemble "of relationships headed and moved by authority and power."[45] Hence, the struggle over schooling must be inextricably linked to the struggle against abusive state power, on the one hand, and the battle for "creating more equitable and just public spheres within and outside of educational institutions"[46] on the other. Gramsci also makes clear that pedagogy is the outcome of struggles over both the relations of meaning and institutional relations of power and that such struggles cannot be abstracted from the construction of national identity and what it means to be an active citizen. In this context, the pedagogical is inextricably grounded in a notion of hegemony, struggle, and political education articulated through a normative position and project aimed at overcoming the stark inequalities and forms of oppression suffered by subaltern groups. The theoretical and ideological contours of Gramsci's project offer no immediate solutions to the context and content of the problems faced by American educators. Nor can Gramsci's work simply be appropriated outside of his own history and the challenges it posed. What his vast writings do provide are opportunities for raising questions about what it means to learn from Gramsci at a time that demands theoretical rigor, moral courage, and political boldness.

Gramsci's analysis of the political and social role of culture in establishing and reproducing the power of the modern state represents a crucial theoretical sphere for progressive educators. Central to Gramsci's analysis is not only the important recognition of culture as a terrain of consent and struggle, but also the political imperative to analyze how diverse groups make meaning of their lives within a variety of cultural sites and social practices in relation to and not outside of the material contexts of everyday life. For Gramsci, the politics of culture was inseparable from a politics that provided the pedagogical conditions for educators to think critically about how knowledge is produced, taken up, and transformed as a force for social change and collective struggle. The practical relevance of Gramsci's work on culture and pedagogy can be made more clear by commenting further on two issues: the role of basic education and the relevance of Gramsci's call for pedagogical practices that instill young children with an appreciation for self-discipline and an array of intellectual skills. While it is crucial to recognize Gramsci's call for treating various levels of schooling as sites of struggle, it is equally imperative to recognize that education for Gramsci was fundamental to preparing young people and adults with the knowledge and skills that would enable them to be able to govern and not just be governed and, equally important, to be able use civil society as a public enclave from which to organize their moral and political energies as acts of resistance and struggle. While Gramsci did not believe that state-sponsored schools alone would provide the conditions for radical change, he did suggest they had a role to play in nourishing the tension between the democratic principles of civil society and the dominating principles of capitalism and corporate power. The project of liberal education for Gramsci was wedded to the fundamental socialist principle of educating the complete person, rather than the traditional concern with educating specialists, technocrats, and other professional experts. Gramsci was insistent that critical intellectuals had to use their education in order both to know more than their enemies and to make such knowledge consequential by bringing it to bear in all those sites of everyday life where the struggle for and against the powerful was being waged. While Gramsci's work is neither transparent nor merely transportable to different historical and political contexts, it seems reasonable within the current historical conjuncture to argue that education for Gramsci was deeply implicated in the project of furthering economic and political democracy, and that such a project is especially important today for articulating a progressive, if not radical, defense of the purpose of public and higher education. In the broadest sense, this would offer progressives a theoretical rationale for challenging the existing movement on the part of corporate culture in its various manifestations to define public and higher education as a private rather than public good. The purpose of such an education would also serve to challenge the dominant society's increasing pressure to use the liberal arts to assert the primacy of citizen rights over consumer rights and democratic values over commercial values.

Gramsci's emphasis on the importance of culture and pedagogy in shaping a social subject rather than an adaptive, depoliticized consuming subject provided the context for his insistence on the importance of skills, rigor, discipline, and hard work. For instance, his often cited call for teaching young children skills cannot be read, as I previously argued, as simply legitimating a conservative pedagogy. Gramsci recognized that children within the "new" Italian reforms, which argued that children should simply discover truths for themselves, were being deprived of basic skills that would enable them to read, write, struggle over complex problems as well as prepare themselves to use such skills to expand their capacities as critical intellectuals and citizens. For Gramsci, pedagogical approaches that refused to deal with such issues often reneged on using their authority self-consciously in the interests of providing the skills and discipline necessary for young children to assume the role of critical or organic intellectuals. Gramsci rightly understood that those pedagogies that both focused on the alleged natural development of the child and devalued firm classroom authority as antithetical to good teaching simply offered a rationale for Mussolini's educational clerks to conceal their own authority while simultaneously employing it to limit the intellectual and political capacities, especially of working-class students, to learn those skills necessary for resistance, opposition, and, more important, civic struggle. What Hirsch misses in Gramsci's analysis is that rather than being a call for a depoliticized justification of rote learning, it is an attempt to analyze the context both for teaching young children the skills they will need to be active citizens and for calling into question any pedagogy that refuses to name the political interests that shapes its own project.

For Gramsci, skills, discipline, and rigor were not in and of themselves valuable; they were meaningful when seen as part of a broader project and performative politics, one that embraced authority in the service of social change and culture as the terrain in which such authority became both the object of autocritique and the basis for social analysis and struggle. Hence, Gramsci's emphasis on culture as a medium of politics and power is important for progressive educators because it challenges theories of social and cultural reproduction that overemphasize power as a force of domination. Gramsci is extremely sensitive to the productive nature of power as a complex and often contradictory site of domination, struggle, and resistance. Long before Foucault, Gramsci interrogates how culture is deployed, represented, addressed, and taken up in order to understand how power works to produce not merely forms of domination but also complicity and dissent. Gramsci's dialectical analysis of culture and power provides an important theoretical model for linking cultural politics and the discourse of critique to a language of hope, struggle, and possibility. Of course, Gramsci doesn't provide, nor should we expect him to offer, a blueprint for such a struggle, but his view of leadership and his theory of intellectuals offer a powerful challenge to those conservative ideologues and theoreticians who currently either reduce the function of intellectuals to their technical expertise or privilege them unproblematically as the cultural guardians and servants of oppressive state power.

Gramsci's theory of hegemony as a form of cultural pedagogy is also invaluable as an element of critical educational thought. By emphasizing the pedagogical force of culture, Gramsci expands the sphere of the political by pointing to those diverse spaces and spheres in which cultural practices are deployed, lived, and mobilized in the service of knowledge, power and authority. For Gramsci, learning and politics were inextricably related and took place not merely in schools but in a vast array of public sites. While Gramsci could not anticipate the full extent of the ways in which knowledge and power would be configured within the postmodern technologies that emerged in the age of the high-speed computer and other electronic media, he did recognize the political and pedagogical significance of popular culture and the need to take it seriously in reconstructing and mapping the relations between everyday life and the formations of power. Clearly, Gramsci's recognition that the study of everyday life and popular culture needed to be incorporated strategically and performatively as part of a struggle for power and leadership is as relevant today as it was in his own time. This is especially true for challenging and transforming the modernist curriculum, steeped in its celebration of the traditional Western canon, and its refusal to address subordinated forms of knowledge. If critical educators are to make a case for the context-specific nature of pedagogy — a pedagogy that not only negotiates difference, but takes seriously the imperative to make knowledge meaningful in order that it might become critical and transformative — it is crucial that educators expand curricula to include those elements of popular culture that play a powerful role in shaping the desires, needs, and identities of students. This is not to suggest that students ignore the Western-oriented curriculum or dispense with print culture as much as to redefine the relationship between knowledge and power, and how the latter is used to mobilize desire, shape identities, and secure particular forms of authority. It is not enough for students to simply be literate in the print culture of the humanities or in the subordinated histories of oppressed groups. Critical education demands that teachers and students must also learn how to read critically the new technological and visual cultures that exercise a powerful pedagogical influence over their lives as well as their conception of what it means to be a social subject engaged in acts of responsible citizenship. In addition, they must master the tools of these technologies, whether they be computer programming, video production, or magazine production, in order to create alternative public spheres actively engaged in shaping what Gramsci referred to as a new and oppositional culture.

The questions that Gramsci raises about education, culture, and political struggle also have important ramifications for theorizing about educators as public intellectuals and how such intellectuals might challenge the institutional and cultural terrains through which dominant authority is secured and state power legitimated. Marcia Landy is on target in arguing that one of Gramsci's most important contributions to political change is the recognition that "study of intellectuals and their production is synonymous with the study of political power."[47] Gramsci's concern with the formation and responsibility of intellectuals stems from the recognition that they are central not only to fostering critical consciousness, demystifying dominant social relations, and disrupting common sense, but also for situating political education in the context of a more comprehensive project aimed at the liberation of the oppressed as historical agents within the framework of a revolutionary culture.

According to Gramsci, political education demanded that such intellectuals could not be neutral, nor could they ignore the most pressing social and political problems of their times. For Gramsci, the new intellectuals have little to do with the traditional humanist project of speaking for a universal culture or abstracting culture from the workings of power, history, and struggle in the name of an arid professionalism. As a cultural critic, the Gramscian intellectual refuses to define culture merely as a refined aesthetic of taste and civility. On the contrary, the task of Gramscian intellectuals was to provide modes of leadership that bridged the gap between criticism and politics, theory and action, and traditional educational institutions and everyday life. For Gramsci, the role of the engaged intellectual was a matter of moral compassion and practical politics aimed at addressing the gap between theory and practice. This suggests that such intellectuals become what Gramsci calls "permanent persuaders and not just orators,"[48] and that such persuasion takes place not merely in the isolated and safe confines of the universities but in those spheres and public cultures of daily life in which subordinated groups bear the weight of the mechanisms of coercion and domination. Clearly, Gramsci's discourse on the education and political function of "organic" intellectuals provides an important theoretical discourse for questioning the meaning and function of public and higher education at a time when the latter are not only selling their curricula, space, and buildings to corporations but undermining even the humanist understanding of the intellectual as a purveyor of art and culture, now seen as merely ornamental next to the role of the intellectual as servant of corporate interests.

Gramsci's work does more than challenge the reduction of intellectuals to corporate clerks; it also broadens the meaning and role of intellectuals in terms of their social functions and individual capabilities. Changes in the mass media, modes of production, and socioeconomic needs of the state enlarged the role that intellectuals played in exercising authority, producing knowledge, and securing consent. For Gramsci, intellectuals played a crucial political and pedagogical role in integrating thought and action for subaltern groups as part of a broader project to assert the primacy of political education far beyond the limited circle of party hacks or university academics. Moreover, Gramsci is not just suggesting that marginal groups generate their own intellectuals; he is also broadening the conditions for the production of knowledge and the range of sites through which learning for self-determination can occur. This is an important issue because it legitimates the call for progressives to create their own public intellectuals and counter-public spheres both within and outside of traditional sites of learning as part of a broader effort to expand the sources of resistance and the dynamics of democratic struggle.

Finally, Gramsci's radical theory of political education provides an ethical language for grounding intellectual work in a project that not only demands commitment and risk, but also recognizes the ethical imperative to bear witness to collective suffering and to provide a referent for translating such a recognition into social engagement. This suggests that intellectuals must be self-critical in order to address the nature of their own locations, self-interests, and privileges. Moreover, they must be in constant dialogue with those with whom they deploy their authority as teachers, researchers, theorists, and planners in order to expose and transform those cruelties and oppressive conditions through which individuals and groups are constructed and differentiated. For Gramsci, critical intellectuals must begin by acknowledging their engagement with the "density, complexity, and historical-semantic value of culture," an engagement that grounds them in the power-making possibilities of politics.[49] At the current historical conjuncture, Gramsci's work serves as a reminder that "democracy requires a certain kind of citizen . . . citizens who feel responsible for something more than their own well-feathered little corner; citizens who want to participate in society's affairs, who insist on it; citizens with backbones; citizens who hold their ideas about democracy at the deepest level."[50] Education in this context becomes central to principled leadership, agency, and the ongoing task of keeping the idea of justice alive while struggling collectively on many fronts to restructure society in the interest of expanding the possibilities of democracy. Gramsci's readings of culture, political education, the role and responsibility of intellectuals, and the necessity to struggle in the interests of equality and justice are crucial starting points for progressives to rethink and address the current assault on public schooling and the basic foundations of democracy itself.

NOTES

1 Originally published as Henry A. Giroux (1999), "Rethinking Cultural Politics and Radical Pedagogy in the Work of Antonio Gramsci," *Educational Theory*, 49, (1): 19.

2 For example, see Todd Gitlin (1995), *The Twilight of Common Dreams*. New York: Metropolitan Books; Richard Rorty (1998), "The Dark Side of the Academic Left," *Chronicle of Higher Education*, April 3, 1998: B4–6.

3 For a critique of the tendency of theorists such as Todd Gitlin to pit class politics against identity and cultural politics, see Robin D. G. Kelley (1998), *Yo' Mama's Disfunktional: Fighting the Culture Wars in Urban America*. Boston: Beacon Press, especially chapter 4, "Looking Extremely Backward: Why the Enlightenment Will Only Lead Us into the Dark," pp. 102–24.

4 John Frow and Meghan Morris cited in Lawrence Grossberg (1977), *Bringing It All Back Home: Essays on Cultural Studies*. Durham, NC: Duke University Press, p. 268.

5 Terry Cochran (1994), "Culture in its Sociohistorical Dimension," *Boundary 2*, 21, (2): 157.

6 Lawrence Grossberg (1996), "Toward a Genealogy of the State of Cultural Studies," in Cary Nelson and Dilip Parameshwar Gaonkar (eds), *Disciplinarity and Dissent in Cultural Studies*. New York: Routledge, p. 142.

7 See, for example, Herbert I. Schiller (1989), *Culture Inc.: The Corporate Takeover of Public Expression*. New York: Oxford University Press; Erik Barnouw (ed.) (1997), *Conglomerates and the Media*. New York: Free Press.

8 Henry A. Giroux (1995), "Talking Heads: Public Intellectuals and Radio Pedagogy," *Art Papers*, July/August: 17–21.

9 Antonio Gramsci (1971), *Selections from the Prison Notebooks*, trans. and ed. by Quintin Hoare and Geoffrey Nowell Smith. New York: International Publishers, p. 350.

10 Children's Defense Fund (2010), "Millions More Children Living in Poverty," *ChildrensDefenseFund.org*, September 16. Available online at: www.childrens defense.org/newsroom/cdf-in-the-news/press-releases/2010/millions-more-children-living-in-poverty.html . Accessed September 19, 2010.

11 This issue is taken up brilliantly in Stanley Aronowitz (1996), *The Death and Rebirth of American Radicalism*. New York: Routledge.

12 On this issue, see Michael Tonry (1995), *Malign Neglect: Race, Crime, and*

Punishment in America. New York: Oxford University Press; James G. Miller (1996), *Search and Destroy: African-American Males in the Criminal Justice System.* New York: Cambridge University Press; Fox Butterfield (1997), "Crime Keeps on Falling, but Prisons Keep on Filling," *New York Times,* September 28, 1997, Section 4: 1.

13 In this case, I am referring specifically to the widely popularized work of Charles Murray and Richard J. Herrnstein. See Charles Murray and Richard J. Herrnstein (1994), *The Bell Curve.* New York: Free Press. For three important critical responses to Murray and Herrnstein, see Russell Jacoby and Naomi Glauberman (eds) (1995), *The Bell Curve Debate.* New York: Random House; Joe L. Kincheloe, Shirley Steinberg, and Aaron D. Gresson III (eds) (1996), *Measured Lies: The Bell Curved Examined.* New York: St. Martin's Press; Claude Fisher, Michael Hout, Martin Sanchez Jankowski, Samuel Lucas, Ann Swidler, and Kim Voss (1996), *Inequality by Design: Cracking the Bell Curve Myth.* Princeton, NJ: Princeton University Press.

14 See, for example, Kofi Buenor Hadjor (1995), *Another America: The Politics of Race and Blame.* Boston: South End Press; Andrew Hacker (1995), *Two Nations: Black and White, Separate, Hostile and Unequal.* New York: Scribner; Manning Marable (1995), *Beyond Black and White.* London: Verso.

15 For some excellent recent sources on the corporatization of the university, see Evan Watkins (1989), *Work Time: English Departments and the Circulation of Cultural Value.* Stanford: Stanford University Press; Stanley Aronowitz and William DiFazio (1994), *The Jobless Future.* Minneapolis: University of Minnesota Press, especially chapter 8, "A Taxonomy of Teacher Work," pp. 226–63; Cary Nelson (ed.) (1997), *Will Teach for Food: Academic Labor in Crisis.* Minneapolis: University of Minnesota Press.

16 The notion of thinking in Gramscian terms comes from Paul Bove (1994), "Foreword," in Marcia Landy, *Film, Politics, and Gramsci.* Minneapolis: University of Minnesota Press, p. xvi.

17 Raymond Williams (1967), *Communications.* New York: Barnes & Noble, p. 15.

18 Joseph Buttigieg is on target in arguing that while Gramsci's writings are fragmentary, there is nothing unclear about his views regarding "the relation between the theoretical work of intellectuals and political praxis." See Joseph Buttigieg (1991), "After Gramsci," *The Journal of the Midwest Modern Language Association,* 24, (1): 93.

19 Harold Entwistle (1989), *Antonio Gramsci: Conservative Schooling for Radical Politics.* Boston: Routledge and Kegan Paul; E. D. Hirsch, Jr. (1996), *The Schools We Need.* New York: Doubleday.

20 There are a number of instances in Hirsch's book where he misrepresents the work of critical theorists in education. For instance, he completely misreads the work of the French sociologist Pierre Bourdieu by claiming that his analysis of "cultural capital" is important because it provides the basis for working-class kids to succeed in schools. Of course, cultural capital for Bourdieu was a class-specific category based on the Marxist notion of exchange value and used to illuminate how middle-class cultural capital is used in schools to legitimate forms of class inequality. See Walter Feinberg's analysis of Hirsch's distortion of Bourdieu's work in Walter Feinberg (1997), "Educational Manifestos and the New Fundamentalism," *Educational Researcher,* 26, (8): 27–35.

21 Entwistle, *Antonio Gramsci,* p. 177.

22 Douglas Holly (1980), "Antonio Gramsci: Conservative Schooling for Radical Politics," *British Journal of the Sociology of Education,* 1, (3): 319.

23 Hirsch, *The Schools We Need,* p. 7.

24 David Forgacs, "Working-Class Education and Culture: Introduction," in David Forgacs (ed.), *An Antonio Gramsci Reader.* New York: Shocken, p. 54.

25 Antonio Gramsci, "Socialism and Culture," in Paul Piccone and Pedro Cavalcante

(eds), *History, Philosophy, and Culture in the Young Gramsci*. St. Louis, MO: Telos Press, pp. 20–1.

26 Hirsch, *The Schools We Need*, p. 113.
27 Ibid.
28 Gramsci, *Selections from the Prison Notebooks*, p. 30.
29 Ibid., pp. 32–3.
30 Jerome Karabel (1976), "Revolutionary Contradictions: Antonio Gramsci and the Problem of Intellectuals," *Politics and Society*, 6: 172.
31 Gramsci, *Selections from the Prison Notebooks*, p. 42.
32 Ibid.
33 Antonio Gramsci, "Men or Machines," in David Forgacs (ed.), *An Antonio Gramsci Reader*. New York: Shocken, p. 62.
34 Ibid., p. 64.
35 Hirsch, *The Schools We Need*, p. 7.
36 Ibid.
37 For an analysis of schools within a broader political, cultural, and economic context, see Henry A. Giroux (1997), *Pedagogy and the Politics of Hope*. Boulder: Westview Press.
38 Gramsci, *Selections from the Prison Notebooks*, p. 350.
39 Gramsci, cited in Edward Said (1983), *The World, the Text, and the Critic*. Cambridge, MA: Harvard University Press, p. 172.
40 For in-depth analyses of the work of E. D. Hirsch, see Stanley Aronowitz and Henry A. Giroux (1988), "Schooling, Culture, and Literacy in the Age of Broken Dreams: A Review of Bloom and Hirsch," *Harvard Educational Review*, 58, (2): 171–94; Barbara Hernstein Smith (1990), "Cult-Lit: Hirsch, Literacy and the National Culture," *The South Atlantic Quarterly*, 89, (1): 69–88; Walter Feinberg (1997), "Educational Manifestos and the New Fundamentalism," *Educational Researcher*, 26, (8): 27–35.
41 Nancy Fraser (1995), "'From Redistribution to Recognition?' Dilemmas of Justice in a 'Post-Socialist' Age," *New Left Review*, 212: 71.
42 Stuart Hall (1997), "Subjects in History: Making Diasporic Identities," in Wahneema Lubiano (ed.), *The House that Race Built*. New York: Pantheon, p. 297.
43 Hirsch, *The Schools We Need*, pp. 103–4.
44 Chandra Talpade Mohanty (1989–1990), "On Race and Voice: Challenge for Liberal Education in the 1990s," *Cultural Critique*, 14: 184.
45 Said, *The World, the Text, and the Critic*, p. 169.
46 Mohanty, "On Race and Voice," p. 192.
47 Marcia Landy (1994), *Film, Politics, and Gramsci*. Minneapolis: University of Minnesota Press, p. 26.
48 Gramsci cited in Cochran, "Culture in its Sociohistorical Dimension," p. 153.
49 On Gramsci's contribution to this issue, see Edward Said (1983), *The World, the Text, and the Critic*. Cambridge, MA: Harvard University Press, p. 171.
50 Paul Berman (1997), "The Philosopher-King is Mortal," *New York Times Magazine*, May 11, 1997, 37.

CHAPTER 4

The Promise of Critical Pedagogy in the Age of Globalization

Towards a Pedagogy of Democratization

Neither modernity nor democracy has reached the end of its potential development. That is why I prefer the term "democratization," which stresses the dynamic aspect of a still-unfinished process, to the term "democracy," which reinforces the illusion that we can give a definitive formula for it.

Samir Amin[1]

BEYOND THE MODERN/POSTMODERN DIVIDE

All over the world, the forces of neoliberalism are on the march, dismantling the historically guaranteed social provisions provided by the welfare state, defining profit-making and market freedoms as the essence of democracy, while diminishing civil liberties as part of the alleged "war" against terrorism. Secure in its dystopian vision, as Margaret Thatcher once put it, that there are no alternatives, neoliberalism eliminates issues of contingency, struggle, and social agency by celebrating the inevitability of economic laws in which the ethical ideal of intervening in the world gives way to the idea that we "have no choice but to adapt both our hopes and our abilities to the new global market."[2] Coupled with an ever-expanding culture of fear, market freedoms seem securely grounded in a defense of national security and a defense of property.

Educators and other cultural workers need a new political and pedagogical language for addressing the changing contexts and issues facing a world in which capital draws upon an unprecedented convergence of resources — financial, cultural, political, economic, scientific, military, and technological — to exercise powerful and diverse forms of hegemony. If educators are to counter global capitalism's increased ability to substitute the traditional reach of politics for the ever transnational reach of power, it is crucial to develop educational approaches that reject a collapse of the distinction between market liberties and civil liberties, a market economy and a market society.

This suggests developing forms of critical pedagogy capable of appropriating from a variety of radical theories — feminism, postmodernism, critical theory, post-structuralism, neo-Marxism, etc. — those progressive elements that might be useful in both challenging neoliberalism on many fronts while resurrecting a militant democratic socialism that provides the basis for imagining a life beyond the "dream world" of capitalism. More specifically, this suggests, on the one hand, resurrecting the blemished traditions of Enlightenment thought that affirmed issues of freedom, equality, liberty, self-determination, and civic agency. On the other hand, critical theory's engagement with Enlightenment thought must be expanded through those postmodern discourses that problematize modernity's universal project of citizenship, its narrow understanding of domination, its obsession with order, and its refusal to expand both the meaning of the political and the sites in which political struggles and possibilities might occur.

CULTURAL POLITICS MATTERS

Against the growing separation between a postmodern cultural politics and modernist material politics — defined primarily over the issue of what constitutes "real" politics — educators need to avoid the modern/postmodern divide that suggests that we can do either culture or economics but that we cannot do both.[3] Cultural politics matters because it is the pedagogical site on which identities are formed; subject positions are made available; social agency is enacted; and cultural forms both reflect and deploy power through their modes of ownership and mode of public pedagogy. Critical theorists from Marcuse to Adorno have always recognized that the most important forms of domination are not simply economic but also cultural and that the pedagogical force of the culture with its emphasis on belief and persuasion is a crucial element of how we both think about politics and enact forms resistance and social transformation. If radical cultural politics in its various postmodern and poststructuralist forms deepened our understanding of the political value of ambivalence and how culture works within a wider variety of spaces and sites, critical theory politicized its meaning and refused to collapse such an understanding into either the exclusive study of texts or the narrow engagement with the polysemic nature of language. Drawing on the insights of each tradition, the issue that becomes primary is not how culture cancels out material relations of power, or how an emphasis on discourse and cultural representations overrides the materiality of politics, but how each works through and on the other within and across specific historical contexts and social formations.

AFFIRMING MODERNITY'S DEMOCRATIC LEGACY

At the same time, modernity's ongoing project of democracy is not something that can be dismissed against the postmodern infatuation with irony, simulacra, or the alleged death of the subject. Critical theory's engagement with modernity and democracy must be rethought and reformulated but only if taken up through the postmodern assertion that democracy is never finished and must be viewed primarily as a process of democratization. Post-colonial theorist Samir Amin echoes this call by arguing that educators should consider addressing the project of a more realized democracy as part of an ongoing process of democratization. According to Amin, democratization "stresses the dynamic aspect of a still-unfinished process" while rejecting notions of democracy that are given a definitive formula.[4]

The search for a new politics and a new critical language that crosses the critical theory/postmodern divide must reinvigorate the relationships among democracy, ethics, and political agency by expanding the meaning of the pedagogical as a political practice while at the same time making the political more pedagogical. In the first instance, it is crucial to recognize that pedagogy has less to do with the language of technique and methodology than it does with issues of politics and power. Pedagogy is a moral and political practice that is always implicated in power relations and must be understood as a cultural politics that offers both a particular version and vision of civic life, the future, and how we might construct representations of ourselves, others, and our physical and social environment. As Roger Simon observes:

> As an introduction to, preparation for, and legitimation of particular forms of social life, education always presupposes a vision of the future. In this respect a curriculum and its supporting pedagogy are a version of our own dreams for ourselves, our children, and our communities. But such dreams are never neutral; they are always someone's dreams and to the degree that they are implicated in organizing the future for others they always have a moral and political dimension. It is in this respect that any discussion of pedagogy must begin with a discussion of educational practice as a form of cultural politics, as a particular way in which a sense of identity, place, worth, and above all value is informed by practices which organize knowledge and meaning.[5]

An oppositional cultural politics can take many forms, but given the current assault by neoliberalism on all aspects of democratic public life, it seems imperative that educators revitalize the struggles to create conditions in which learning would be linked to social change in a wide variety of social sites, and pedagogy would take on the task of regenerating both a renewed sense of social and political agency and a critical subversion of dominant power itself. Under such circumstances, agency becomes the site through which power is not transcended but reworked, replayed, and restaged in productive ways. Central to my argument is the assumption that politics is not only about power, but also, as Cornelius Castoriadis points out, "has to do with political judgements and value choices,"[6] indicating that questions of civic education and critical pedagogy (learning how to become a skilled citizen) are central to the struggle over political agency and democracy. In this instance, critical pedagogy emphasizes critical reflexivity, bridging the gap between learning and everyday life, understanding the connection between power and knowledge, and extending democratic rights and identities by using the resources of history. However, among many educators and social theorists, there is a widespread refusal to recognize that this form of education is not only the foundation for expanding and enabling political agency, but also that it takes place across a wide variety of public spheres mediated through the very force of culture itself.

One of the central tasks of any viable critical pedagogy would be to make visible alternative models of radical democratic relations in a wide variety of sites. These spaces can make the pedagogical more political by raising fundamental questions such as: What is the relationship between social justice and the distribution of public resources and goods? What are the conditions, knowledge, and skills that are a prerequisite for political agency and social change? At the very least, such a project involves understanding and critically engaging dominant public transcripts and values within a broader set of historical and institutional contexts. Making the political more pedagogical in this instance suggests producing modes of knowledge and social practices that not only affirm oppositional cultural work but offer opportunities to mobilize instances of collective outrage, if not collective action. Such mobilization opposes glaring material inequities and the growing cynical belief that today's culture of investment and finance makes it *impossible* to address many of the major social problems facing both the United States and the larger world. Most importantly, such work points to the links among civic education, critical pedagogy, and modes of oppositional political agency that are pivotal to elucidating a politics that promotes autonomy and social change.

At the very least, critical pedagogy proposes that education is a form of political intervention in the world and is capable of creating the possibilities for social transformation, a theme I take up later in this chapter. Rather than viewing teaching as technical practice, radical pedagogy in the broadest terms is a moral and political practice premised on the assumption that learning is not about processing received knowledge but about actually transforming it as part of a more expansive struggle for individual rights and social justice. This implies that any viable notion of pedagogy and resistance should illustrate how knowledge, values, desire, and social relations are always implicated in relations of power, and how such an understanding can be used pedagogically and politically by students to further expand and deepen the imperatives of economic and political democracy. The fundamental challenge facing educators within the current age of neoliberalism is to provide the conditions for students to address how knowledge is related to the power of both self-definition and social agency. Central to such a challenge is providing students with the skills, knowledge, and authority they need to inquire and act upon what it means to live in a substantive democracy, to recognize anti-democratic forms of power, and to fight deeply rooted injustices in a society and world founded on systemic economic, racial, and gender inequalities.

THE RESPONSIBILITY OF TEACHERS
AS PUBLIC INTELLECTUALS

I believe that educators and other cultural workers bear an enormous responsibility in terms of opposing neoliberalism by bringing democratic political culture back to life. This is not meant to suggest that before neoliberalism's current onslaught on all things public that liberal democratic culture encouraged widespread critical thinking and inclusive debate — an argument that allows any appeal to democracy to be dismissed as nostalgic. While liberal democracy offers an important discourse around issues of "rights, freedoms, participation, self-rule, and citizenship," it has been mediated historically through the "damaged and burdened tradition" of racial and gender exclusions, economic injustice, and a formalistic, ritualized democracy that substituted the swindle for the promise of democratic participation.[7] At the same time, liberal and republican traditions of Western democratic thought have given rise to forms of social and political criticism that at least contained a "referent" for addressing the deep gap between the promise of a radical democracy and the existing reality. With the rise of neoliberalism, referents for imagining even a weak democracy, or for that matter understanding the tensions between capitalism and democracy, which animated political discourse for the first half of the twentieth century, appear to be overwhelmed by market discourses, identities, and practices, on the one hand, or a corrosive cynicism on the other. Democracy has now been reduced to a metaphor for the alleged "free" market. It is not that a genuine democratic public space once existed in some ideal form and has now been corrupted by the values of the market, but that these democratic public spheres, even in limited forms, seem to no longer be animating concepts for making visible the contradiction and tension between the reality of existing democracy and the promise of a more fully realized, substantive democracy.

Part of the challenge of linking critical pedagogy with the process of democratization suggests constructing new locations of struggle, vocabularies, and subject positions that allow people in a wide variety of public spheres to become more than they are now, to question what it is they have become within existing institutional and social formations and to give some thought to what it might mean to transform existing relations of subordination and oppression. But if such a task is to become meaningful, critical theory's concern with the universal project of modernity must be forged with a deeper understanding of a postmodern notion of difference and how the latter can expand and deepen the democratic project of modernity. Chantal Mouffe captures this concern well in her claim:

> What we need is a hegemony of democratic values, and this requires a multiplication of democratic practices, institutionalizing them into ever more diverse social relations, so that a multiplicity of subject-positions can be formed through a democratic matrix. It is in this way — and not by trying to provide it

73

with a rational foundation — that we will be able not only to defend democracy but also to deepen it.[8]

CRITICAL PEDAGOGY AS A PROJECT OF INTERVENTION

In what follows, I want highlight some pedagogical, though provisional, principles that offer a language of both critique and possibility for referencing pedagogy as a moral and political practice that is informed by a politics and project that takes a position against the scourge of neoliberalism but does not stand still, that points to the possibility of a politics of democratic struggle without underwriting a politics with guarantees. If educators are to revitalize the language of civic education as part of a broader discourse of political agency and critical citizenship in a global world, they will have to consider grounding such a pedagogy in a defense of militant utopian thinking in which any viable notion of the political takes up the primacy of pedagogy as part of a broader attempt to revitalize the conditions for individual and social agency while simultaneously addressing the most basic problems facing the prospects for social justice and global democracy. This suggests addressing critical pedagogy as a project informed by a political vision while being conscious of the diverse ways such a vision gets mediated in different contexts. Such a project also suggests recasting the relationship between the pedagogical and political as a project that is indeterminate, open to constant revision, and constantly in dialogue with its own assumptions. The concept of the project in this sense speaks to the directive nature of pedagogy, the recognition that any pedagogical practice presupposes some notion of the future, prioritizes some forms of identification over others, and upholds selective modes of social relations. At the same time, the normative nature of such a pedagogy does not offer guarantees as much as it recognizes that its own position is grounded in modes of authority, values, and ethical considerations that must be constantly debated for the ways in which they both open up and close down democratic relations, values, and identities. Central to both keeping any notion of critical pedagogy alive and challenging things is the recognition that it must address real social needs, be imbued with a passion for democracy, and provide the conditions for expanding democratic forms of political and social agency.

CRITICAL PEDAGOGY AS A MATTER OF CONTEXT, ETHICS, AND POLITICS

In opposition to the increasingly dominant views of education and cultural politics, I want to argue for a transformative pedagogy — rooted in the project of resurgent democracy — one that relentlessly questions the kinds of labor, practices, and forms of production that are enacted in public and higher education. Such an analysis should be both relational and contextual, as well as self-reflective and theoretically rigorous. By relational, I mean that the current crisis of schooling must be understood in relation to the broader assault that is being waged against all aspects of democratic public life. As Jeffrey Williams has recently pointed out, "the current restructuring of higher education is only one facet of the restructuring of civic life in the US whereby previously assured public entitlements such as healthcare, welfare, and social security have evaporated or been 'privatized,' so no solution can be separated from a larger vision of what it means to enfranchise citizens or our republic."[9] But as important as such articulations are in understanding the challenges that public and higher education face in the current historical conjuncture, they do not go far enough. Any critical comprehension of those wider forces that shape public and higher education must also be supplemented by an attentiveness to the conditional nature of pedagogy itself. This suggests that pedagogy can never be treated as a fixed set of principles and practices that can be applied indiscriminately across a variety of pedagogical sites. Pedagogy must always be contextually defined, allowing it to respond specifically to the conditions, formations, and problems that arise in various sites in which education takes place. Rather than treating pedagogy as a commodity, progressive educators need to engage their teaching as a theoretical resource that is both shaped by and responsive to the very problems that arise in the in-between space/places/contexts that connect classrooms with the experiences of everyday life. Under such circumstances, educators can address the meaning and purpose that schools might play in their relationship to the demands of the broader society while simultaneously being sensitive to the distinctive nature of the issues educators address within the shifting contexts in which they interact with a diverse body of students, texts, and institutional formations.

Critical pedagogy locates discursive practices in a broader set of interrelations, but it analyzes and gives meaning to such relations by defining them within particular contexts constructed through the operations of power as articulated through the interaction among texts, teachers, and students. Questions of articulation and contexts need to be foregrounded as a matter of both ethics and politics. Ethically, critical pedagogy requires an ongoing indictment "of those forms of truth-seeking which imagined themselves to be eternally and placelessly valid."[10] Put simply, educators need to cast a critical eye on those forms of knowledge and social relations that define them through a conceptual purity and political innocence that not only cloud how they come into being but also ignore that the alleged neutrality on which they stand is already grounded in ethico-political choices. Thomas Keenan rightly argues that ethics on the pedagogical front demands an openness to the other, a willingness to engage a "politics of possibility" through a continual critical engagement with texts, images, events, and other registers of meaning as they are transformed into public pedagogies.[11] One consequence of linking pedagogy to the specificity of place is that it foregrounds the need for educators to rethink the cultural and political baggage they bring to each educational encounter; it also highlights the necessity of making educators ethically and politically accountable for the stories they produce, the claims they make upon public memory, and the images of the future they deem legitimate. Pedagogy is never innocent and if it is to be understood and problematized as a form of academic labor, educators must not only critically question and register their own subjective involvement in how and what they teach, they must also resist all calls to depoliticize pedagogy through appeals to either scientific objectivity or ideological dogmatism. Far from being disinterested or ideologically frozen, critical pedagogy is concerned about the articulation of knowledge to social effects and succeeds to the degree to which educators encourage critical reflection and moral and civic agency rather than simply mold them. Crucial to this position is the necessity for critical educators to be attentive to the ethical dimensions of their own practice.

CRITICAL PEDAGOGY AND THE PROMISE OF DEMOCRATIZATION

But as an act of intervention, critical pedagogy, as I mentioned above, needs to be grounded in a project that not only problematizes its own location, mechanisms of transmission, and effects, but also functions as part of a larger project to contest various forms of domination and to help students think more critically about how existing social, political, and economic arrangements might be better suited to address the promise of a radical democracy as an anticipatory rather than messianic goal. The late Jacques Derrida suggested that the social function of intellectuals as well as any viable notion of education should be grounded in a vibrant politics that makes the promise of democracy a matter of concrete urgency. For Derrida, making visible a "democracy" that is to come as opposed to that which presents itself in its name provides a referent for both criticizing everywhere what parades as democracy — "the current state of all so-called democracy" — and for critically assessing the conditions and possibilities for democratic transformation.[12] Derrida sees the promise of democracy as the proper articulation of a political ethics and by implication suggests that when higher education is engaged and articulated through the project of democratic social transformation it can function as a vital public sphere for critical learning, ethical deliberation, and civic engagement. Moreover, the utopian dimension of pedagogy articulated through the project of radical democracy offers the possibility of resistance to the increasing depoliticization of the citizenry, provides a language to challenge the politics of accommodation that connects education to the logic of privatization, refuses to define the citizen as simply a consuming subject, and actively opposes the view of teaching as market-driven practice and learning and a form of training. Utopian in this sense is not an antidote to politics, a nostalgic yearning for a better time or for some "inconceivably alternative future." It is rather an "attempt to find a bridge between the present and future in those forces within the present which are potentially able to transform it."[13]

In opposition to dominant forms of education and pedagogy that simply reinvent the future in the interest of a present in which ethical principles are scorned and the essence of democracy is reduced to the imperatives of the bottom line, critical pedagogy must address the challenge of providing students with the competencies they need to cultivate the capacity for critical judgment, thoughtfully connect politics to social responsibility, and expand their own sense of agency in order to curb the excesses of dominant power, revitalize a sense of public commitment, and expand democratic relations. Animated by a sense of critique and possibility, critical pedagogy at its best attempts to provoke students to deliberate, resist, and cultivate a range of capacities that enable them to move beyond the world they already know without insisting on a fixed set of meanings.

Against the current onslaught to privatize public schools and vocationalize higher education, educators need to defend public and higher education as a resource vital to the democratic and civic life of the nation. Central to such a task is the challenge of academics, cultural workers, and labor organizers to find ways to join together in broad-based social movements and oppose the transformation of public schools and higher education into commercial spheres, to resist what Bill Readings has called a consumer-oriented corporation more concerned about accounting than accountability.[14] The crisis of public schooling and higher education — while having different registers — needs to be analyzed in terms of wider configurations of economic, political, and social forces that exacerbate tensions between those who value such institutions as public goods and those advocates of neoliberalism who see market culture as a master design for all human affairs. The threat corporate power poses can be seen in the ongoing attempts by neoliberals and other hyper capitalists to subject all forms of public life, including public and higher education, to the dictates of the market while simultaneously working to empty democracy itself of any vestige of ethical, political, and social considerations. What educators must challenge is the attempt on the part of neoliberals to either define democracy exclusively as a liability or enervate its substantive ideals by reducing it to the imperatives and freedoms of the marketplace. This requires that educators consider the political and pedagogical importance of struggling over the meaning and definition of democracy and situate such a debate within an expansive notion of human rights, social provisions, civil liberties, equity, and economic justice. What must be challenged at all costs is the increasingly dominant view propagated by neoliberal gurus such as Milton Friedman that profit-making is the essence of democracy and accumulating material goods is the essence of the good life.

BEYOND THE PEDAGOGY OF DESKILLING

Defending public and higher education as vital democratic spheres is necessary to develop and nourish the proper balance between public values and commercial power, between identities founded on democratic principles and identities steeped in forms of competitive, self-interested individualism that celebrate selfishness, profit-making, and greed. Educators also must reconsider the critical roles educators might take up within public and higher education so as to enable them to oppose those approaches to schooling that corporatize and bureaucratize the teaching process. A critical pedagogy should, in part, be premised on the assumption that educators vigorously resist any attempt on the part of liberals and conservatives to reduce their role in schools to that of either technicians or corporate pawns. Instead, progressive educators might redefine their roles as engaged public intellectuals capable of teaching students the language of critique and possibility as a precondition for social agency. Such a redefinition of purpose, meaning, and politics suggests that educators critically interrogate the fundamental link between knowledge and power, pedagogical practices and social consequences, and authority and civic responsibility.

By redefining the purpose and meaning of schooling as part of a broader attempt to struggle for a radical democratic social order, progressive educators can begin to vigorously challenge a number of dominant assumptions and policies currently structuring public and higher education, including but not limited to: ongoing attempts by corporate culture to define educators as multinational operatives; escalating efforts by colleges and universities to deny students the loans, resources, and public support they need to have access to a quality education; the mounting influence of corporate interests in pressuring universities to reward forms of scholarship that generate corporate profits; increasing attempts to deny women and students of color access to higher education through the reversal of affirmative action policies, the raising of tuition costs, and a growing emphasis on classroom pedagogies designed to create marketable products and active consumers. Rather than providing students with an opportunity to learn how to shape and govern public life, education is increasingly being vocationalized, reduced to a commodity that provides privileges for a few students and industrial training for the service sector for the rest, especially those who are marginalized by reason of their class and race.

Increasingly, the corporatization of education functions so as to cancel out the democratic values, impulses, and practices of a civil society by either devaluing or absorbing them within the logic of the market. Educators need a critical language to address these challenges to public and higher education. But they also need to join with other groups outside of the spheres of public and higher education in order to create a national movement that links the defense of non-commodified education with a broader struggle to deepen the imperatives of democratic public life. The quality of educational reform can, in part, be gauged by the caliber of public discourse concerning the role that education plays in furthering not the market-driven agenda of corporate interests, but the imperatives of critical agency, social justice, and an operational democracy. In this capacity, educators need to develop a language of possibility for raising critical questions about both the aim of schooling and the purpose and meaning of what and how educators teach. In doing so, pedagogy draws attention to engaging classroom practice as a moral and political consideration animated by a fierce sense of commitment to expanding the range of individual capacities that enable students to become critical agents capable of linking knowledge, responsibility, and democratic social transformation.

Approaching pedagogy as a critical and political practice suggests that educators refuse all attempts to reduce classroom teaching exclusively to matters of technique and method. In opposition to such approaches, educators can highlight the performative character of education as an act of intervention in the world — focusing on the work that pedagogy does as a deliberate attempt to influence how and what knowledge and experiences are produced within particular sets of classroom relations. Within this perspective, critical pedagogy foregrounds the diverse conditions under which authority, knowledge, values, and subject positions are produced and interact within unequal relations of power; it also problematizes the ideologically laden and often contradictory roles and social functions that educators assume within the classroom. Pedagogy in this view can also be reclaimed as a form of academic labor that bridges the gap between individual considerations and public concerns, affirms bonds of sociality and reciprocity, interrogates the relationship between individual freedom and privatized notions of the good life, and asserts the social obligations and collective structures necessary to support a vibrant democracy.

CLASSROOM AUTHORITY AND PEDAGOGY
AS THE OUTCOME OF STRUGGLES

The question of what educators teach is inseparable from what it means to locate oneself in public discourses and invest in public commitments. Implicit in this argument is the assumption that the responsibility of critical educators cannot be separated from the consequences of the subject positions they have been assigned, the knowledge they produce, the social relations they legitimate, and the ideologies they disseminate to students. Educational work at its best represents a response to questions and issues posed by the tensions and contradictions of the broader society; it is an attempt to understand and intervene in specific problems that emanate from those sites that people concretely inhabit and in which they actually live out their lives and everyday existence. Teaching in this sense becomes performative and contextual, and it highlights considerations of power, politics, and ethics fundamental to any form of teacher–student–text interaction. As I mentioned previously, this suggests the importance of addressing education in political and ethical terms. By drawing attention to pedagogy's productive character, critical educators can highlight pedagogy as the outcome of specific deliberations and struggles that need to be addressed in terms of the "material and historical specificities of (its) enactments"[15] and in doing so reject the conservative notion that pedagogy can be theorized as either an a priori set of prescriptions or as a commodity to be exchanged in any context.

It is crucial to reiterate that any pedagogy that is alive to its own democratic implications is always cautious of its need for closure; it self-consciously resists totalizing certainties and answers. Refusing the pull of dogmatism and imperious authority, progressive educators must at the same time grasp the complexity and contradictions that inform the conditions under which they produce and disseminate knowledge. Recognizing that pedagogy is the outgrowth of struggles that are historically specific, as are the problems that govern the questions and issues that guide what and how we teach, should not suggest that educators renounce their authority. On the contrary, it is precisely by recognizing that teaching is always an act of intervention inextricably mediated through particular forms of authority that teachers *can* offer students — for whatever use they wish to make of them — a variety of analytic tools, diverse historical traditions, and a wide ranging knowledge of dominant and subaltern cultures and how they influence each other. This is a far cry from suggesting that critical pedagogy either define itself within the grip of a self-righteous mode of authority or completely remove itself from any sense of commitment whatsoever. Neither authoritarianism nor nihilism serves any viable notion of critical pedagogy. On the contrary, at stake here is the need to insist on modes of authority that are directive but not imperious, linking knowledge to power in the service of self-production, and encouraging students to go beyond the world they already know to expand their range of human possibilities. Robert Miklitsch rightly argues that teacher authority and institutional positioning are pivotal considerations for analyzing the politics of teaching and the ethical responsibilities that define both the project and the articulation of pedagogy to particular effects. He writes:

> I want to argue . . . that teachers must begin from the pedagogic subject-position to which they have been assigned. If the latter position is not necessarily one of mastery (in either sense of the word), it nonetheless remains one of authority. In other words, to attempt absolutely to renounce the pedagogic subject-position — from whatever motivation, liberal or otherwise — is not only to accede to a "bad" egalitarian logic, it is to evade our responsibility as teachers. And that responsibility — which needless to say, is an implicitly political one — involves recognizing those structures (social, cultural, economic, and so forth) that both enable and constrain out activities.[16]

Academics must deliberate, make decisions, take positions, and in doing so recognize that authority "is the very condition for intellectual work" and pedagogical interventions.[17] Miklitsch suggests above that teacher authority cannot be merely renounced as an act of domination, but should be addressed dialectically and deployed strategically so as to enable students to become witnesses to the material and cultural relations of power that often prevent them and others from speaking and acting in particular ways.

Authority in this perspective is not simply on the side of oppression, but is used to intervene and shape the space of teaching and learning to provide students with a range of possibilities for challenging a society's commonsense assumptions, and for analyzing the interface between their own everyday lives and those broader social formations that bear down on them. Authority, at best, becomes both a referent for legitimating a commitment to a particular vision of pedagogy and a critical referent for a kind of autocritique. It demands consideration of how authority functions within specific relations of power regarding its own promise to provide students with a public space where they can learn, debate, and engage critical traditions in order to imagine otherwise and develop discourses that are crucial for defending vital social institutions as a public good.

Educators need to rethink the tension between the pedagogical and the performative by asking how the performative functions pedagogically. While pedagogy can be understood performatively as an event where many things can happen in the service of learning, it is crucial to stress the importance of democratic classroom relations that encourage dialogue, deliberation, and the power of students to raise questions. Moreover, such relations don't signal a retreat from teacher authority as much as they suggest using authority reflexively to provide the conditions for students to exercise intellectual rigor, theoretical competence, and informed judgments. Thus students can think critically about the knowledge they gain and what it means to act on such knowledge in order to expand their sense of agency as part of a broader project of increasing both "the scope of their freedoms" and "the operations of democracy."[18] What students learn and how they learn should amplify what it means to experience democracy from a position of possibility, affirmation, and critical engagement. In part, this suggests that progressive educators develop pedagogical practices that open up the terrain of the political while simultaneously encouraging students to "think better about how arrangements might be otherwise."[19]

At its best, critical pedagogy must be interdisciplinary and radically contextual, engage the complex relationships between power and knowledge, critically address the institutional constraints under which teaching takes place, and focus on how students can engage the imperatives of critical social citizenship. Once again, critical pedagogy must be self-reflexive about its aims and practices, conscious of its ongoing project of democratic transformation, but also openly committed to a politics that does not offer any guarantees. But refusing dogmatism does not suggest that educators descend into a laissez-faire pluralism or an appeal to methodologies designed to "teach the conflicts." On the contrary, it suggests that in order to make the pedagogical more political, educators afford students with diverse opportunities to understand and experience how politics, power, commitment, and responsibility work on and through them both within and outside of schools. This in turn enables students to locate themselves within an interrelated confluence of ideological and material forces as critical agents who can both influence such forces and simultaneously be held responsible for their own views and actions. Within this perspective, relations between institutional forms and pedagogical practices are acknowledged as complex, open, and contradictory — though always situated within unequal relations of power.[20]

MAKING THE PEDAGOGICAL MORE MEANINGFUL

I also want to stress the importance of addressing in any viable theory of critical pedagogy the role that affect and emotion play in the formation of individual identities and social collectivities. Any viable approach to critical pedagogy suggests taking seriously those maps of meaning, affective invest-ments, and sedimented desires that enable students to connect their own lives and everyday experiences to what they learn. Pedagogy in this sense becomes more than a mere transfer of received knowledge, an inscription of a unified and static identity, or a rigid methodology; it presupposes that students are moved by their passions and motivated, in part, by the affective investments they bring to the learning process. This suggests, as Paulo Freire points out, the need for a theory of pedagogy willing to develop a "critical comprehension of the value of sentiments, emotions, and desire as part of the learning process."[21] Not only do students need to understand the ideological, economic, and political interests that shape the nature of their educational experiences, they must also address the strong emotional investments they may bring to such beliefs. For Shoshana Felman, this suggests that educators take seriously the role of desire in both ignorance and learning.

> Teaching has to deal not so much with lack of knowledge as with resistances to knowledge. Ignorance, suggests Jacques Lacan, is a "passion." Inasmuch as tra-ditional pedagogy postulated a desire for knowledge, an analytically informed pedagogy has to reckon with the passion for ignorance.[22]

Felman elaborates further on the productive nature of ignorance, arguing: "Ignorance is nothing other than a desire to ignore: its nature is less cognitive than performative . . . it is not a simple lack of information but the incapacity — or the refusal — to acknowledge one's own implication in the informa-tion."[23] If students are to move beyond the issue of understanding on to an engagement with the deeper affective investments that make them complicit with oppressive ideologies, they must be positioned to address and formulate strategies of transformation through which their individualized beliefs and affective investments can be articulated with broader public discourses that extend the imperatives of democratic public life. An unsettling pedagogy in this instance would engage student identities and resistances from unex-pected vantage points and articulate how they connect to existing material relations of power. At stake here is not only a pedagogical practice that recalls how knowledge, identifications, and subject positions are produced, unfolded, and remembered but also how they become part of an ongoing process, more strategic so to speak, of mediating and challenging existing relations of power.

CONCLUSION

In the current historical conjuncture, the concept of the social is being refigured and displaced as a constitutive category for making democracy operational and critical agency essential for social and political transformation. In this instance, the notion of the social and the public are not being erased as much as they are being reconstructed under circumstances in which public forums for serious debate, including public education, are being eroded. Within the ongoing logic of neoliberalism, teaching and learning are removed from the discourse of democracy and civic culture and defined in often narrow instrumental and methodological terms. Increasingly stripped of its civic function, education becomes merely a matter of training and removed from any notion of power, critique, or imaginative inquiry. Divorced from the imperatives of a democratic society, pedagogy is reduced to a matter of taste, individual choice, and job training. Pedagogy as a mode of witnessing, a public engagement in which students learn to be attentive and responsible to the memories and narratives of others, disappears within a corporate-driven notion of learning in which the logic of market devalues the opportunity for students to make connections with others through social relations which foster a mix of compassion, ethics, and hope. The crisis of the social is further amplified by the withdrawal of the state as a guardian of the public trust and its growing lack of investment in those sectors of social life that promote the public good. With the supreme court ruling that now makes vouchers constitutional, a deeply conservative government once again will be given full reign to renege on the responsibility of government to provide every child with a education that affirms public life, embraces the need for critical citizens, and supports the truism that political agency is central to the possibility of democratic life.

The greatest threat to our children does not come from lowered standards, the absence of privatized choice schemes, or the lack of rigid testing measures. On the contrary, it comes from a society that refuses to view children as a social investment and instead consigns 15.5 million children to live in poverty, reduces critical learning to massive testing programs, promotes policies that eliminate most crucial health and public services, and defines masculinity through the degrading celebration of a gun culture, extreme sports, and the spectacles of violence that permeate corporate-controlled media industries. Students are not at risk because of the absence of market incentives in the schools. Children and young adults are under siege in both public and higher education because far too many schools have increasingly become institutional breeding grounds for commercialism, racism, social intolerance, sexism, and homophobia.[24] We live in a society in which a culture of punishment and intolerance has replaced a culture of social responsibility and compassion. Within such a climate of harsh discipline and disdain, it is easier for states such as California to set aside more financial resources to build prisons than to support higher education. Within this context, the project(s) of critical pedagogy need to be taken up both inside and outside of public and higher education. Pedagogy is a public practice largely defined within a range of cultural apparatuses extending from television networks to print media to the internet, cell phones, and other forms of screen culture. As a central element of a broad-based cultural politics, critical pedagogy, in its various forms, when linked to the ongoing project of democratization can provide opportunities for educators and other cultural workers to redefine and transform the connections among language, desire, meaning, everyday life, and material relations of power as part of a broader social movement to reclaim the promise and possibilities of a democratic public life.

NOTES

1 Samir Amin (2001), "Imperialization and Globalization," *Monthly Review*, June: 12.
2 Stanley Aronowitz (1998), "Introduction," in Paulo Freire, *Pedagogy of Freedom*. Lanham: Rowman and Littlefield, p. 7.
3 I take this issue up in great detail in Henry A. Giroux (1999), *Impure Acts: The Practical Politics of Cultural Studies*. New York: Routledge; and Henry A. Giroux (2001), *Public Spaces, Private Lives: Beyond the Culture of Cynicism*. Lanham: Rowman and Littlefield.
4 Amin, "Imperialization and Globalization," 12.
5 Roger Simon (1987), "Empowerment as a Pedagogy of Possibility," *Language Arts*, 64 (4): 372.
6 Cornelius Castoriadis (1996), "Institutions and Autonomy," in Peter Osborne (ed.), *A Critical Sense*. New York: Routledge, p. 8.
7 John Brenkman (2000), "Extreme Criticism," in Judith Butler, John Guillory, and Kendall Thomas (eds), *What's Left of Theory?* New York: Routledge, p. 123.
8 Chantal Mouffe (1988), "Radical Democracy: Modern or Postmodern," in Andrew Ross (ed.), *Universal Abandon*. Minneapolis: University of Minnesota Press, p. 18.
9 Jeffrey Williams (1999), "Brave New University," *College English*, 61, (6): 749.
10 Paul Gilroy (2000), *Against Race*. Cambridge, MA: Harvard University Press, p. 69.
11 For a brilliant discussion of the ethics and politics of deconstruction, see Thomas Keenan (1997), *Fables of Responsibility: Aberrations and Predicaments in Ethics and Politics*. Stanford: Stanford University Press, p. 2.
12 Jacques Derrida (2000), "Intellectual Courage: An Interview," trans. Peter Krapp, *Culture Machine*, 2: 9.
13 Terry Eagleton (2000), *The Idea of Culture*. Malden, MA: Basil Blackwell, p. 22.
14 Bill Readings (1997), *The University in Ruins*. Cambridge, MA: Harvard University Press, pp. 11, 18.
15 Bruce Horner (2000), "Politics, Pedagogy, and the Profession of Composition: Confronting Commodification and the Contingencies of Power," *Journal of Advanced Composition*, 20, (1): 141.
16 Robert Miklitsch (1990), "The Politics of Teaching Literature: The 'Pedagogical Effect,'" *College Literature*, 17, (2/3): 93.
17 This expression comes from John Michael (2000), *Anxious Intellects: Academic*

Professionals, Public Intellectuals, and Enlightenment Values. Durham, NC: Duke University Press, p. 2.

18 Cornel West (1991), "The New Cultural Politics of Difference," in Russell Ferguson, Martha Gever, Trinh T. Minh-Ha, and Cornel West (eds), *Out There.* Cambridge, MA: MIT Press, p. 35.

19 Jodi Dean (2000), "The Interface of Political Theory and Cultural Studies," in Jodi Dean (ed.), *Cultural Studies and Political Theory.* Ithaca, NY: Cornell University Press, p. 3.

20 Alan O'Shea (1998), "A Special Relationship? Cultural Studies, Academia and Pedagogy," *Cultural Studies,* 12, (4): 513–27.

21 Paulo Freire (1999), *Pedagogy of Freedom.* Lanham: Rowman and Littlefield, p. 48.

22 Shoshana Felman (1987), *Jacques Lacan and the Adventure of Insight: Psychoanalysis in Contemporary Culture.* Cambridge, MA: Harvard University Press, p. 79. For an extensive analysis of the relationship among schooling, literacy, and desire, see Ursula A. Kelly (1997), *Schooling Desire: Literacy, Cultural Politics, and Pedagogy.* New York: Routledge; Sharon Todd (1997), *Learning Desire: Perspectives on Pedagogy, Culture, and the Unsaid.* New York: Routledge.

23 Shoshana Felman (1987), *Jacques Lacan and the Adventure of Insight: Psychoanalysis in Contemporary Culture.* Cambridge, MA: Harvard University Press, p. 79.

24 Donna Gaines (1999), "How Schools Teach Our Kids to Hate," *Newsday,* April 25, 1999: B5.

Critical Pedagogy and the Politics of Youth

CHAPTER 5

No Bailouts for Youth

Education and Pedagogy in an Era of Disposability

By almost any political, economic, and ethical measure, Barack Obama's election victory in 2008 inherits a set of problems produced by one of the darkest periods in American history.[1] In the eight years prior to Obama's presidency, not only did the spaces where genuine politics could occur largely disappear as a result of an ongoing assault by the market-driven forces of privatization, deregulation, and unrestrained corporate power, but there was also a radical hardening of the culture that increasingly disparaged democratic values, the public good, human dignity, and with these the safety nets provided by a once robust but now exiled social state. George W. Bush, the privileged and profligate son of a wealthy Texas oilman, became the embodiment of a political era in which willful immaturity and stubborn civic illiteracy found their match in an emerging culture of excess and irresponsibility.[2] As the age of finance capital reigned supreme over American society, the ongoing work of democratization along with the public spheres needed to sustain it became an increasingly fragile, perhaps even dysfunctional, project. Market principles now reached far beyond the realm of the economic and played a formative role in influencing and organizing every domain of human activity and interaction, while simultaneously launching a frontal attack on notions of a common good, public purpose, non-commodified values, and democratic modes of governing.

Yet — even in the aftermath of the October 2008 global financial crisis and the historic election of Barack Obama as the first African American president of the United States — the vocabulary and influence of corporate power and hapless governance can still be heard as the expansion of market fundamentalism continues, albeit more slowly, along the trajectory of privileging corporate interests over the needs of the public good and ignoring the rising demands of millions of people struggling for economic, racial, and political justice. Tragically, the Obama administration seems complicit with what has become an element of common sense for a large and noisy segment of the populace — that the market, rather than politics, gives people what they want. This state of affairs suggests not only a perilous future for the social state and a government willing to intervene on behalf of its citizens, but also a view of governance in which economic priorities dominate and suppress important social needs, rather than being carefully adjusted toward the goal of fostering a more just, more democratic society.

Under the reign of a largely deregulated and privatized society, social problems become utterly individualized and removed from the index of public considerations. As public concerns collapse into private issues, it becomes more difficult to connect individual problems with broader social considerations. Or, as C. Wright Mills once put it, the sociological imagination withers as troubles become privatized and the lives and concerns of individuals are disconnected from matters of history and larger public issues.[3] With the bonds of sociality now severed, stunned and isolated individuals negotiate life's problems as best they can — like so many amputees willfully forgetting or fitfully haunted by a phantom limb.[4] Pressing social issues, such as the unprecedented ecological crisis, skyrocketing levels of unemployment, home foreclosures, wage stagnation, persistent racism, homelessness, poverty, and an unprecedented war debt, lose their political capacity to compel citizens to organize and act. The privatized utopias of consumerist society offer the public a market-based language that produces narrow modes of subjectivity, defining what people should know and how they should act within the constricted interests and values of what Zygmunt Bauman has called "an order of egoism."[5] The consequences involve not only the undoing of social bonds but also the endless reproduction of much-narrowed registers of character and individual responsibility as a substitute for any analysis of wider social problems. Such reductive logics make it more socially acceptable to blame the destitute, homeless, uninsured, jobless, poor minority youth, and other disadvantaged individuals and groups for their plight, while reinforcing the merging of the market state with the punishing state.

It appears ever more unlikely that the current change of government will undo the havoc wrought by the Bush administration (itself the culmination of a decades-long trend toward market deregulation) or reverse the effects of a rampant free-market fundamentalism now unleashed across the globe. As the financial crisis looms large in the lives of the majority of Americans, government funds are used to bail out Wall Street bankers rather than being used to address either the growing impoverishment of the many people who have lost homes, jobs, and hope of a better future or the structural conditions that created such problems. In this scenario, a privileged minority retains the freedom to purchase time, goods, services, and security, while the vast majority of people are relegated to a life without protections, benefits, and safety supports. For those populations considered expendable, redundant, and invisible by virtue of their race, class, and age, life becomes increasingly precarious.

Youth, in particular, are assaulted by market forces that commodify almost every aspect of their lives, though different groups of young people bear unequally the burden of this market-driven assault. Newspapers and other popular media treat their audiences to an endless stream of alarming images and dehumanizing stories about rampaging young people who allegedly occupy a domestic war zone. Youth are no longer categorized as Generation X, Y, and Z. On the contrary, they are now defined rhetorically in mainstream media as "Generation Kill," "Killer Children," or as one CNN television special labeled them, "Killers in Our Midst."[6] Capitalizing on shocking and sensational imagery not only swells the media's bottom line. It also adds fuel to a youth panic that insidiously portrays young people as pint-size nihilists and an ever-present threat to public order. Such negative and demeaning views have had disastrous consequences for young people as their lives are increasingly subjected to policies and modes of governance defined through the logic of punishment, surveillance, and carceral control. Moreover, under the reign of an expanding, punishing state coupled with the persistent structural racism of the criminal justice system, the situation for a growing number of impoverished young people and youth of color is getting much worse. These are young people whose labor is unneeded, who are locked out of the commodity market, and who often inhabit the impoverished and soul-crushing margins of society. Too often they fall prey to the dictates of a youth-governing complex that increasingly subjects them to harsh disciplinary controls while criminalizing more and more aspects of their behavior.

THE POLITICS OF DISPOSABILITY

Today, what we see spread out across this neoliberal landscape are desolate communities, gutted public services, weakened labor unions, 40 million impoverished people (many living in their cars or the ever-growing tent cities), and 46 million Americans without health insurance — one result of which, according to a Harvard University study, is the needless deaths of 45,000 people every year.[7] It gets worse. According to a study released by the Johns Hopkins Children's Center, the "lack of adequate health care may have contributed to the deaths of some 17,000 US children over the past two decades."[8] Couple this landscape of human suffering with the 30 million who constitute the number of unemployed, and we end up wondering, along with *New York Times* columnist Bob Herbert, how "this nation could be so dysfunctional at the end of the first decade of the 21st century."[9]

This harsh, dehumanizing reality and its culture of disposability and cruelty are captured in a story told by Chip Ward, a thoughtful administrator at the Salt Lake City Public Library, who writes poignantly about his observations of a homeless woman named Ophelia. Ophelia spends time at the library because, like many of the homeless, she has nowhere else to go to use the bathroom, experience some temporary relief from bad weather, or simply be able to rest. Excluded from the American dream and treated as both expendable and a threat, Ophelia, in spite of her mental illness, defines her own existence using a chilling metaphor. Ward describes Ophelia's presence and actions in the following way:

Ophelia sits by the fireplace and mumbles softly, smiling and gesturing at no one in particular. She gazes out the large window through the two pairs of glasses she wears, one windshield-sized pair over a smaller set perched precariously on her small nose. Perhaps four lenses help her see the invisible other she is addressing. When her "nobody there" conversation disturbs the reader seated beside her, Ophelia turns, chuckles at the woman's discomfort, and explains, *"Don't mind me, I'm dead. It's okay. I've been dead for some time now."* *She pauses, then adds reassuringly, "It's not so bad. You get used to it."* Not at all reassured, the woman gathers her belongings and moves quickly away. Ophelia shrugs. Verbal communication is tricky. She prefers telepathy, but that's hard to do since the rest of us, she informs me, "don't know the rules."[10]

Ophelia is just one of the 200,000 chronically homeless who now use public libraries and other accessible but shrinking public spaces to find shelter.[11] Many are sick, addicted to drugs and alcohol, or mentally disabled, and others are close to a nervous breakdown because of the stress, insecurity, and danger they face daily. In this country, as many as 3.5 million human beings experience homelessness each year,[12] and they are often treated like criminals — as if punishment is the appropriate civic response to poverty, mental illness, and human suffering. Ophelia's comments should not be dismissed as the ramblings of a mentally disturbed woman because they point to something much deeper about the current state of American society and its abandonment of entire populations who are now considered the unrecyclable human waste of a neoliberal social order.

Under the ruthless dynamics of predatory capitalism, there has been a shift away from the possibility of getting ahead economically and living a life of dignity toward the much more deadly task of struggling to stay alive. Many now argue that this new form of economic Darwinism is conditioned by a permanent state of class and racial exception in which, as Achille Mbembe asserts, "vast populations are subject to conditions of life conferring upon them the status of living dead."[13] These disposable populations are increasingly relegated to the frontier zones and removed from public view. Such populations are often warehoused in schools that resemble boot camps,[14] dispersed to dank and dangerous workplaces far from the enclaves of the tourist industries, incarcerated in prisons that privilege punishment over rehabilitation, and consigned to the ranks of the permanently unemployed. What Orlando Patterson in his discussion of slavery called "social death" has now become the fate of more and more people as the socially strangulating neoliberal values of hyper-individualism, self-interest, and consumerism become the organizing principles of everyday life.[15]

THE PLIGHT OF TODAY'S YOUTH

The devastation wreaked by neoliberal economic policies has been largely financed in the hard currency of human suffering that such policies have imposed on children, readily evident in some astounding statistics that suggest a profound moral and political contradiction at the heart of one of the richest democracies in the world. The notion that children should be treated as a crucial social resource and represent for any healthy society important ethical and political considerations about the quality of public life, the allocation of social provisions, and the role of the state as a guardian of public interests, appears to be lost. Children, for example, make up a disproportionate share of the poor in the United States in that "they are 26 per cent of the total population, but constitute 39 per cent of the poor."[16] Just as alarming, over 8 million children lack health insurance,[17] and millions lack affordable childcare and decent early childhood education. One of the most damaging statistics revealing how low a priority children are in America can be seen in the fact that among the industrialized nations in the world the United States ranks first in billionaires and in defense expenditures and yet ranks an appalling 29th in infant mortality.[18] As we might expect, behind these dire statistics lies a series of decisions to favor those already advantaged economically at the expense of the poor and socially vulnerable.

The toll in human suffering that results from these policies of punishment and neglect becomes clear in shocking stories about those marginalized by race and class who literally die because they lack health insurance, often have to fend for themselves in the face of life's tragedies, and increasingly are excommunicated from the sphere of human concern. Too many youth are now rendered invisible and disposable in a world in which short-term investments yield quick profits while long-term social investments in young people are viewed as a drag on the economy. It gets worse. In what amounts to a national disgrace, one out of every five children currently lives in poverty, which amounts to over 13 million young people.[19] With home foreclosures still on the rise, school districts across the nation have identified and enrolled almost 800,000 homeless children.[20] Their numbers are growing at an exponential rate, as one in 50 children are now living in crowded rooms in seedy welfare hotels, in emergency shelters, or with relatives, or they simply live on the streets.[21] What is unique about these kids is not just the severity of deprivations they experience daily, but how they have been forced to view the world and redefine the nature of their own childhood between the borders of hopelessness and despair. There is little sense of a bright future lying just beyond the shadows of highly policed and increasingly abandoned urban spaces. An entire generation of youth will not have access to the jobs, material comforts, or social securities available to previous generations. These children are a new generation of youth forced to grow up fast — they think, act, and talk like adults. They worry about their families, which may be headed by a single parent or two out of work and searching for a job; they wonder how their parents are going to get the money to buy food and what it will take to pay for a doctor. And these children are no longer confined to so-called ghettoes. As the burgeoning landscape of poverty and despair spreads across our cities, suburbs, and rural areas, these children make their presence felt everywhere

— there are just too many to ignore or hide away in the usually contained and invisible spaces of disposability. These kids constitute a new and more unsettling scene of suffering, one that reveals not only vast inequalities in our economic landscape but also portends a future that has no purchase on the hope that should characterize an aspiring democracy.

In one episode of the CBS television series *Children of the Recession*, a 12-year-old, Michael Rotundo, living in a motel room with his parents, complains that he can't think straight in school and is failing. His mind is filled not with the demands of homework, sports, girls, or hanging out with his friends, but with grave concerns about his parents not having enough money to pay rent or put down a payment on a house. His voice is eerily precocious as he tells the interviewer that he dreams about having a normal kid's life, but he is not hopeful. Another child, when asked what he does when he is hungry, states — with a sadness no child should experience — "I just cry." In another exchange, a young boy says the unthinkable for any child. He says that his life is ruined and that all he now thinks about is death because he doesn't see any way out of the circumstances he and his family find themselves in. And a 13-year-old named Lewis Roman tells an interviewer he wants to get a job to help his mother; when asked how he copes with being hungry, he says he hides it from people because he doesn't want them to know. His only recourse from gnawing hunger is to try to fall asleep.

These narratives just scratch the surface of a new social and economic reality, as millions of children now find themselves suffering physical, psychological, and developmental problems that thus far go unacknowledged by the Obama administration, as it bails out the automotive industries, banks, and other financial institutions. What kind of country have we become that we cannot protect our children or offer them even the most basic requirements to survive? What does it mean to witness this type of suffering among so many children and not do anything about it — our attentions quickly diverted to view the spectacles and moral indifference that characterize so much of the cut-throat world of reality TV, zombie politics, and a consumer culture that shapes the sensibilities and inner lives of adults and children alike.

While all young people have to bear the consequences of a diminishing public concern about their care, dignity, and future, adult indifference and disrespect bear down on some youth much harder than on others. There is a long history in the United States of youth, particularly those of color, being associated in the media and by politicians with a rising crime wave. What is really at stake in this discourse is the emergence of a *punishment wave*, one that reveals a society that does not know how to address those social problems that undercut any viable sense of agency, possibility, and future for many young people. Dystopian fears about youth in the United States have intensified since the events of 9/11, as has the public's understanding of youth as an unruly and unpredictable threat to law and order. This tragedy is made obvious by the many "get tough" policies that have rendered young people as criminals, while depriving them of basic healthcare, education, and social services. Punishment and fear have replaced compassion and social responsibility as the most important modalities mediating the relationship of youth to the larger social order. Youth within the last two decades have come to be seen as a source of trouble rather than as a resource for investing in the future, and, in the case of poor white, black, and Hispanic youth, are increasingly treated as disposable populations. These youth are largely recruited as cannon fodder for unwinnable wars abroad or subject to a coming-of-age crisis marked by an ever-expanding police order with its paranoid machinery of security and criminalization.

THE YOUTH CRIME-CONTROL COMPLEX

If the commodification of youth culture in American society represents a soft war on children, then the hard war takes a different and more extreme form, as poor youth and youth of color are subject to the harshest elements, values, and dictates of a growing youth "crime complex"[22] that governs them through a logic of punishment, surveillance, and control. In this instance, even as the corporate state is in turmoil, it is transformed into a punishing state, and certain segments of the youth population become the object of a new mode of governance based on the crudest forms of disciplinary control. As this recession unfolds, too many young people, especially poor minorities, are not completing high school but are instead bearing the brunt of a system that leaves them uneducated and jobless, and ultimately offers them one of the few bailouts available for populations who no longer have available roles to play as producers or consumers — either poverty or prison. A 2009 study counted nearly 6.2 million high school dropouts in the United States.[23] Nearly one in ten male high school dropouts is either in jail or in juvenile detention.[24] These figures become even more alarming when analyzed through the harsh realities of economic deprivation and persistent racial disadvantage. The jobless rate for African American dropouts aged 16–24 is a staggering 69 percent, while for whites it is 54 percent.[25] For African American male youth, the incarceration rate jumps to one in four high school dropouts ending up in prison.[26] What becomes clear is that level of education and unemployment are increasingly driving staggering incarceration rates for young people. What does it say about a society that can put trillions of dollars into two politically and ethically dubious and likely unwinnable wars, offer generous tax cuts for the rich, and bail out corrupt banks and insurance industries, but cannot provide a decent education and job training opportunities for its most disadvantaged youth?

As youth incarceration rates soar, the model of the prison increasingly appears to influence almost every major institution that impacts directly on youth — both expanding the culture of cruelty and worsening its impact on young people. For Jonathan Simon, an obsession with crime and punishment has become an axis for how Americans come to "know and act on ourselves, our families, and our communities."[27] Simon argues that the aggressive rhetoric and policies emerging from a crime-and-punishment mentality constitute not only a crisis of politics but the emergence of a new politics of "governing through crime." One consequence of governing through crime has been the development of what Angela Davis calls "the imprisonment binge" of the last 30 years.[28] Even as violent crime fell by 25 percent in the past 20 years, states have increased their spending on corrections, with 13 states now spending more than one billion dollars a year in general funds on their corrections systems.[29] Five states spend as much or more on corrections than on higher education, while they jettison a range of important social programs that provide for people's welfare.[30] As a disciplinary model, the prison reinforces modes of violence and control that are now central to the efforts of the punishing state to align its values and practices with a number of other important commanding economic, political, and social institutions. Its deeply structured politics of disposability, racist principles, and modes of authoritarian governance become part of the fabric of common sense, an unquestioned element of effective governance.

As the war against poverty is transformed into a rabid war against crime, young people are often subjected to intolerable conditions that inflict irreparable harm on their minds and bodies. Many youth now have to endure drug tests, surveillance cameras, invasive monitoring, random searches, security forces in schools, and a host of other militarizing and monitoring practices typically used against suspected criminals, terrorists, and other groups represented as a threat to the state. Under such circumstances, education has given way to modes of confinement whose purpose is to ensure "custody and control."[31] Hence, it is not surprising that "school officials and the criminal justice system are criminalizing children and teenagers all over the country, arresting them and throwing them in jail for behavior that in years past would never have led to the intervention of law enforcement."[32] As Bob Herbert points out, young people being ushered "into the bowels of police precincts and jail cells" for minor offenses "is a problem that has gotten out of control."[33] Egregious examples of children being treated like criminals abound. According to Barbara Ehrenreich:

[A] growing number of cities have taken to ticketing and sometimes handcuffing teenagers found on the streets during school hours [while in] New York City, a teenager caught in public housing without an ID — say, while visiting a friend or relative — can be charged with criminal trespassing and wind up in juvenile detention.[34]

According to a 2007 report put out by the Children's Defense Fund, a "Black boy born in 2001 has a 1 in 3 chance of going to prison in his lifetime [while] a Latino boy born in 2001 has a 1 in 6 chance of going to prison in his lifetime . . . Minority youth make up 39 percent of the juvenile population but are 60 percent of committed juveniles."[35] Shockingly, in the land of the free and the home of the brave, a "jail or detention cell . . . is the only universally guaranteed child policy in America."[36]

One consequence of the punishment focus of these policies is the elimination of intervention programs, which has the effect of increasing the number of youth in prisons and keeping them there for longer periods of time. And when these young people are placed in adult prisons, the outcome is even more disturbing. Youth in adult prisons are "five times as likely to be raped, twice as likely to be beaten, and eight times as likely to commit suicide than adults in the adult prison system."[37] Juvenile detention centers are not much better. According to Professor Barry Feld, "The daily reality of juveniles confined in many 'treatment' facilities is one of violence, predatory behavior, and punitive incarceration."[38] In some juvenile facilities, young people are abused and tortured in a manner associated with the treatment detainees have received at Abu Ghraib, Guantanamo, and various detention centers in Afghanistan and Iraq. For example, the United States Department of Justice reported in 2009 that children at four juvenile detention centers in New York were often severely abused and beaten, leading to concussions, broken teeth, and bone fractures.[39] The use of excessive force by the staff was indiscriminate and ruthlessly applied. According to one report, "anything from sneaking an extra cookie to initiating a fistfight may result in full prone restraint with handcuffs."[40] In one instance, a boy simply glared at a staff member and for that infraction was put into a sitting restraint. His arms were pulled behind his back with such force that his collarbone, which had been previously injured, was broken.[41] It should also be noted that the United States is one of the few countries in the world that sentences children under the age of 18 who commit violent crimes to life without parole.[42] As of 2009, there were more than 2000 of these children in our prisons.[43]

The alarming physical and psychological violence directed at youth is also increasingly visible in many public schools. Traditionally viewed as nurturing, child-friendly spaces dedicated to protecting and educating children, schools have become one of the most punitive institutions young people are compelled to face — on a daily basis. Educating for citizenship, work, and the public good has been replaced with models of schooling in which students are viewed either as threats and perpetrators of violence, on the one hand, or as infantilized potential victims of crime who must endure modes of surveillance that are demeaning and repressive, on the other. As the logic of the market and "the crime complex" frame a number of school policies, students are now subjected to zero-tolerance laws that are used primarily to humiliate, punish, repress, and exclude them.[44] School has become a model for a punishing society in which children who violate a rule as minor as a dress-code infraction or slightly act out in class can be handcuffed, booked, and put in a jail cell. The Chicago public school system in 2003 had over 8,000 students arrested, often for trivial infractions such as pushing, tardiness, and using spitballs. The grim consequence of zero-tolerance policies in Chicago schools is also evident in the number of expulsions having "mushroomed from 32 in 1995 to 3,000 in the school year 2003–2004,"[45] mostly affecting poor black youth. All across America, poor black and brown youth in urban school systems are being suspended or expelled at rates much higher than their white counterparts who commit similar behavioral infractions. Howard Witt, writing in the *Chicago Tribune* points out:

> In the average New Jersey public school, African-American students are almost 60 times as likely as white students to be expelled for serious disciplinary infractions . . . And on average across the nation, black students are suspended and expelled at nearly three times the rate of white students.[46]

Unfortunately, many youth of color in urban school systems are not just being suspended or expelled from school but also have to bear the terrible burden of being ushered into the dark precincts of juvenile detention centers and subjected to the harsh dictates of the juvenile justice system — a trajectory that has been described as the school-to-prison pipeline and one that mirrors the race-based discrimination characteristic of the carceral state. Between 2000 and 2004, the Denver public school system experienced a 71 percent increase in the number of student referrals to law enforcement, many for non-violent behaviors.

Equally disturbing is the reality that students are more and more the victims of harmful and degrading treatment, defended by school authorities and politicians under the rubric of school safety. For instance, according to the 2005 report *Education on Lockdown*, in Chicago, "in February 2003, a 7-year-old boy was cuffed, shackled, and forced to lie face down for more than an hour while being restrained by a security officer at Parker Community Academy on the Southwest Side. Neither the principal nor the assistant principal came to the aid of the first grader, who was so traumatized by the event he was not able to return to school."[47] In another widely distributed news story accompanied by a disturbing video, a school-based police officer brutally beat a 15-year-old special-needs student because his shirt was not tucked into his pants. A few months later, the same cop was charged with raping a young woman.[48]

As the culture of fear, crime, and repression embrace American public schools, especially inner-city schools, the culture of schooling is reconfigured through the allocation of resources used primarily to hire more police and security staff, and purchase more technologies of control and surveillance. In some cases, schools such as those in the Palm Beach County system have established their own police departments. Under such circumstances, schools begin to take on the obscene and violent contours one associates with the "all [too] familiar procedures of efficient prison management":[49] including unannounced locker searches, armed police patrolling the corridors, mandatory drug testing, and the ever-present phalanx of lock-down security devices such as metal detectors, X-ray machines, surveillance cameras, and other technologies of fear and control. The sociologist Randall Beger is right in suggesting that the new "security culture in public schools [has] turned them into 'learning prisons' where the students unwittingly become 'guinea pigs' to test the latest security devices."[50] Saturating schools with police and security personnel has created a host of problems for schools, teachers, and students — not to mention that such practices tap into financial resources otherwise used for actually enhancing learning. Trust and respect now give way to fear, disdain, and suspicion, creating an environment in which critical pedagogical practices wither, while pedagogies of punishment, surveillance, and testing flourish. Moreover, the combination of school punishments and criminal penalties has proven a lethal mix for many poor and minority youth and has transformed too many schools from spaces of youth advocacy, protection, hope, and equity to military fortresses, increasingly well-positioned to mete out injustice and humiliation. Unfortunately, such policies and practices make it easier for young people to look upon their society and their futures with suspicion and despair, rather than anticipation and hope.

At this moment in history, it is more necessary than ever to register youth as a central theoretical, moral, and political concern. Doing so reminds adults of their ethical and political responsibility to future generations and will further legitimate what it means to invest in youth as a symbol for nurturing civic imagination and collective resistance in response to the suffering of others. Youth provide a powerful referent for a critical discussion about the long-term consequences of neoliberal policies, while also gesturing towards the need for putting into place those conditions that make a democratic future possible.

The crisis of youth is symptomatic of the crisis of democracy, and as such it hails us as much for the threat that it poses as for the challenges and possibilities it invokes. One way of addressing our collapsing intellectual and moral visions regarding young people is to imagine those educational policies, values, opportunities, and pedagogies that both invoke adult responsibility and reinforce the ethical imperative to provide young people, especially those marginalized by race and class, with the economic, social, and educational conditions that make life livable and the future sustainable. Clearly, the issue at stake here is not a one-off bailout or temporary fix but real structural reforms. At the very least, as Dorothy Roberts has argued, this suggests fighting for a child welfare system that would reduce "family poverty by increasing the minimum wage," and mobilizing for legislation that would institute "a guaranteed income, provide high-quality subsidized child care, preschool education, and paid parental leaves for all families."[51] Young people need a federally funded jobs-creation program and wage subsidy that would provide year-round employment for out-of-school youth and summer jobs that target in-school low-income youth. Public and higher education, increasingly shaped by corporate and instrumental values, must be reclaimed as democratic public spheres committed to teaching young people about how to govern rather than merely be governed. Incarceration should be the last resort, not the first resort, for dealing with our children.

Any viable notion of educational reform must include equitable funding schemes for schools, reinforced by the recognition that the problems facing public schools cannot be solved with corporate solutions or with law enforcement strategies. We need to get the police out of public schools, greatly reduce spending for prisons and military expenditures, and hire more teachers, support staff, and community people in order to eliminate the school-to-prison pipeline. In order to make life livable for young people and others, basic supports must be put in place, such as a system of national health insurance that covers everybody, along with provisions for affordable housing. At the very least, we need guaranteed heathcare for young people and we need to lower the age of eligibility for Medicare to 55 years in order to keep poor families from going bankrupt. And, of course, none of this will take place unless the institutions, social relations, and values that legitimate and reproduce current levels of inequality, power, and human suffering are dismantled. The widening gap between the rich and the poor has to be addressed if young people are to have a viable future. And that requires pervasive structural reforms that constitute a real shift in both power and politics away from a market-driven system that views too many children as disposable. We need to reimagine what liberty, equality, and freedom might mean as truly democratic values and practices. Higher education is one crucial public sphere where politics and pedagogy can come together to address the many crises facing young people today.

DEFENDING YOUTH IN THE TWENTY-FIRST CENTURY: A CHALLENGE FOR HIGHER EDUCATION

In order for higher education to become a meaningful site for educating youth for a democratic future, educators and others need to reclaim higher education as an ethical and political response to the demise of democratic public life. At stake here is the role of higher education as a public sphere committed to increasing the possibilities of democratic identities, values, and relations. This approach suggests new models of leadership, organization, power, and vision dedicated to opening higher education up to all groups, creating a critical citizenry, providing specialized work skills for jobs that really require them, democratizing relations of governance among administrators, faculty, and students, and taking seriously the imperative to disseminate an intellectual and artistic culture. Higher education may be one of the few sites left in which students learn the knowledge and skills that enable them not only to mediate critically between democratic values and the demands of corporate power and the national security state, but also to distinguish between identities founded on democratic principles and identities steeped in forms of competitive, unbridled individualism that celebrate self-interest, profit-making, militarism, and greed.

Addressing education as a democratic endeavor begins with the recognition that higher education is more than an investment opportunity;

citizenship is more than conspicuous consumption; learning is more than preparing students for the workplace, however important that task might be; and democracy is more than making choices at the local mall. Reclaiming higher education as a public sphere begins with the crucial project of challenging, among other things, those market fundamentalists, religious extremists, and rigid ideologues who harbor a deep disdain for critical thought and healthy scepticism, and who look with displeasure upon any form of education that teaches students to read the world critically and to hold power and authority accountable. Education is not only about issues of work and economics, but also about questions of justice, social freedom, and the capacity for democratic agency, action, and change, as well as the related issues of power, exclusion, and citizenship. These are educational and political issues, and they should be addressed as part of a broader effort to re-energize the global struggle for social justice and democracy.

If higher education is to reclaim itself a site of critical thinking, collective work, and public service, educators and students will have to redefine the knowledge, skills, research, and intellectual practices currently favored in the university. Central to such a challenge is the need to position intellectual practice as part of a complex web of rigor, morality, and responsibility that enables academics to speak with conviction, use the public sphere to address important social problems, and demonstrate alternative models for bridging the gap between higher education and the broader society. Lacking a self-consciously democratic political focus, teachers are often reduced to the role of a technician or functionary engaged in formalistic rituals, unconcerned with the disturbing and urgent problems that confront the larger society or the consequences of one's pedagogical practices and research undertakings. In opposition to this model, with its claims to and conceit of political neutrality, I argue that academics should combine the mutually interdependent roles of critical educator and active citizen. This requires finding ways to connect the practice of classroom teaching with the operation of power in the larger society and to provide the conditions for students to view themselves as critical agents capable of making those who exercise authority and power accountable. Academics who assume the role of public intellectuals must function within institutions, in part, as an exile, as someone who raises uncomfortable questions, makes authority responsible, encourages thoughtful exchanges, connects knowledge to the wider society, and addresses important social issues. In this instance, the educator as public intellectual becomes responsible for linking the diverse experiences that produce knowledge, identities, and social values in the university to the quality of moral and political life in wider society. Such an intellectual does not train students solely for jobs, but also educates them to question critically the institutions, policies, and values that shape their lives, relationships to others, and their connection to the larger world.

In addition to their responsibility to prepare students to engage critically with the world, academics must also recognize the impact their students will have on a generation of young people twice removed from the university. Education cannot be decoupled from democracy; and as such must be understood as a deliberately informed and purposeful political and moral practice, as opposed to one that is either doctrinaire, instrumentalized, or both. Moreover, a critical pedagogy should be engaged at all levels of schooling. It must gain part of its momentum in higher education among students who will go back to the schools, churches, synagogues, and workplaces in order to produce new ideas, concepts, and critical ways of understanding the world in which young people and adults live. This is a notion of intellectual practice and responsibility that refuses the insular, overly pragmatic, and privileged isolation of the academy while affirming a broader vision of learning that links knowledge to the power of self-definition and to the capacities of students to expand the scope of democratic freedoms, particularly those that address the crisis of education, politics, and the social as part and parcel of the crisis of democracy itself. This is the kind of intellectual practice that Zygmunt Bauman calls "taking responsibility for our responsibility,"[52] one that is attentive to the suffering of others and "will not allow conscience to look away or fall asleep."[53]

In order for pedagogy that encourages critical thought to have a real effect, it must include the message that all citizens, old and young, are equally entitled, if not equally empowered, to shape the society in which they live. If educators are to function as public intellectuals, they need to provide the opportunities for students to learn that the relationship between knowledge and power can be emancipatory, that their histories and experiences matter, and that what they say and do counts in their struggle to unlearn dominating privileges, productively reconstruct their relations with others, and transform, when necessary, the world around them. Put simply, educators need to argue for forms of pedagogy that close the gap between the university and everyday life. Their curricula need to be organized around knowledges of communities, cultures, and traditions that give students a sense of history, identity, and place. The late Edward Said illuminated the process when he urged academics and students to accept the demands of "worldliness," which include "lifting complex ideas into the public space," recognizing human injury inside and outside of the academy, and using theory as a critical resource to change things.[54] Worldliness suggests we not be afraid of controversy, that we make connections that are otherwise hidden, deflate the claims of triumphalism, and bridge intellectual work and the operation of politics. It means combining rigor and clarity on the one hand, and civic courage and political commitment on the other.

A critically engaged pedagogy also necessitates that we incorporate in our classrooms those electronically mediated knowledge forms that constitute the terrain of mass and popular culture. I am referring here to the world of media texts and screen culture — videos, films, internet, podcasts, and other elements of the new electronic technologies that operate through a combination of visual, aural, and print culture. Such an approach not only challenges the traditional definition of schooling as the only site of pedagogy by widening the application and sites of education to a variety of cultural locations but also alerts students to the educational force of the culture at large, what I have called elsewhere the field of public pedagogy. This mode of education has become central to shaping the desires, values, and identities of young people, often in ways that that not only depoliticize but also enhance tactics and reach of a larger corporate culture and its need to commodify everything. Such a pedagogy must be open to critique as both an ideological and a political force and also as a site and technology that can be rewritten and understood in the interests of more democratic goals, shared values, and modes of engaged civic intervention.

Any viable notion of critical pedagogy should affirm and enrich the meaning, language, and knowledge forms that students actually use to negotiate and inform their lives. Academics can, in part, exercise their role as public intellectuals via such approaches by giving students the opportunity to understand how power is organized through an enormous number of "popular" cultural spheres including libraries, movie theaters, schools, and high-tech media conglomerates that circulate signs and meanings through newspapers, magazines, advertisements, new information technologies, computers, films, and television programs. Needless to say, this position challenges Roger Kimball's neoconservative claim that "Popular culture is a tradition essential to uneducated Americans."[55] By laying claim to popular media, public pedagogy not only asks important questions about how knowledge is produced and taken up, but also provides the conditions for students to become competent and critically versed in a variety of literacies (not just the literacy of print), while at the same time expanding the conditions and options for the roles they might play as cultural producers (as opposed to simply teaching them to be critical readers). At stake here is an understanding of literacy as both a set of competencies to be learned and a crucial condition for developing ways of intervening in the world.

I have suggested that central to intellectual life is the pedagogical and political imperative that academics engage in rigorous social criticism while becoming a stubborn force for challenging false prophets, fighting against the imposed silence of normalized power, "refusing to allow conscience to look away or fall asleep," and critically engaging all those social relations that promote material and symbolic violence.[56] There is a lot of talk among social theorists about the death of politics brought on by a negative globalization characterized by markets without frontiers, deregulation, militarism, and armed violence, which not only feed each other but produce global lawlessness and reduce politics to merely an extension of war.[57] I would hope that of all groups, educators would vocally and tirelessly challenge this myth by making it clear that expanding the public good and promoting democratic social change are at the very heart of critical education and the precondition for global justice.

The potential for a better future further increases when critical education is directed toward young people. As a result, public and higher education may be among the few spheres left in which the promise of youth can be linked to the promise of democracy. Education in this instance becomes both an ethical and a political referent; it furnishes an opportunity for adults to provide the conditions for young people to become critically engaged social agents. Similarly, it points to a future in which a critical education, in part, creates the conditions for each generation of youth to struggle anew to sustain the promise of a democracy that has no endpoint, but which must be continuously expanded into a world of new possibilities and opportunities for keeping justice and hope alive.

Finally, I want to suggest that struggles over how we view, represent, and treat young people should be part of a larger public dialogue about how to imagine a democratic future. The war against youth and critical education demands a new politics, a new analytic of struggle, and a new understanding of the connection between critical and public pedagogy. But most importantly, it demands a renewed sense of imagination, vision, and hope. Making human beings superfluous is the essence of totalitarianism, and the promise of a radical democracy is the antidote in urgent need of being recovered. To do so, we need to address what it means to make the political more pedagogical; that is, we need a discourse that will allow us to re-envision civic engagement and social transformation while forming a new understanding of the pedagogical conditions that enable and nurture thoughtfulness, critical agency, compassion, and democracy itself. We have entered a period in which the war against youth, especially poor youth of color, offers no apologies because it is too arrogant and ruthless to imagine any resistance. But the collective need and potential struggle for justice should never be underestimated, even in the darkest of times.

NOTES

1 I have taken up this issue in more detail in Henry A. Giroux (2008), *Against the Terror of Neoliberalism*. Boulder: Paradigm Publishers. See also Chris Hedges (2006), *American Fascists: The Christian Right and the War on America*. New York: Free Press; and Sheldon S. Wolin (2008), *Democracy Incorporated: Managed Democracy and the Specter of Inverted Totalitarianism*. Princeton, NJ: Princeton University Press.

2 For an excellent analysis of this issue, see Chris Hedges (2009), *Empire of Illusion: The End of Literacy and the Triumph of Spectacle*. New York: Knopf Canada. See also George Monbiot (2008), "The Triumph of Ignorance," *AlterNet*, October 31, 2008. Available online at: www.alternet.org/story/105447/the_triumph_of_ignorance:_how_morons_succeed_in_u.s._politics/. Accessed October 31, 2008. For an extensive study of anti-intellectualism in America, see Richard Hofstadter (1963), *Anti-Intellectualism in American Life*. New York: Vantage House; and Susan Jacoby (2008), *The Age of American Unreason*. New York: Pantheon.

3 C. Wright Mills (2000), *The Sociological Imagination*. New York: Oxford University Press, especially pp. 3–24.

4 The collapse of the social into the realm of the private has been the subject of

a number of books. In addition to *The Sociological Imagination*, see Zygmunt Bauman (1999), *In Search of Politics*. Stanford: Stanford University Press; and Henry A. Giroux (2003), *Public Spaces/Private Lives*. Lanham: Rowman and Littlefield.

5 This term is used by Zygmunt Bauman, who acknowledges that it was first used by John Dunn. See Zygmunt Bauman (2007), *Consuming Life*. London: Polity, p. 140.

6 "Generation Kill" is the name of a seven-part HBO television mini-series about what the *New York Times* calls "a group of shamelessly and engagingly profane, coarse and irreverent marines . . . that spearhead the invasion" in the second Iraq war. See Alessandra Stanley (2008), "Comrades in Chaos, Invading Iraq," *New York Times*, July 11, 2008: B1. The term "Killer Children" appears as the title of a *New York Times* book review. See Kathryn Harrison (2008), "Killer Children," *New York Times Book Review*, July 20, 2008: 1, 8.

7 US Census Bureau Press Release (2009), *Income, Poverty and Health Insurance Coverage in the United States: 2008*, US Department of Commerce, Washington, DC, September 10, 2009. Available online at: www.census.gov/prod/2009pubs/p60-236.pdf. Paul Kleyman (2009), "Harvard Study: 45,000 People Die Every Year," *Facing South*, September 18, 2009. Available online at: www.southernstudies.org/2009/09/uninsured-die-every-year.html. Accessed September 18, 2009.

8 Editorial (2009), "Lack of Health Care Led to 17,000 US Child Deaths," *Agence France-Presse*, October 29, 2009. Available online at: www.truth-out.org/1030099. Accessed October 29, 2009.

9 Bob Herbert (2009), "Our Crumbling Foundation," *New York Times*, May 26, 2009: A19.

10 Chip Ward (2007), "America Gone Wrong: A Slashed Safety Net Turns Libraries into Homeless Shelters," *TomDispatch.com*, April 2, 2007. Available online at: www.alternet.org/story/50023. Accessed April 7, 2007.

11 National Alliance to End Homelessness (2007), *Fact Checker: Chronic Homelessness*, March, 2007. Available online at: www.endhomelessness.org/files/1623_file_10483_FactChecker_Chronic_2_.pdf. Accessed September 1, 2008.

12 National Alliance to End Homelessness (2009), *Homelessness Looms as Potential Outcome of Recession*, January 23, 2009. Available online at: www.azceh.org/PDF/Projected%20Homelessness%20Increases.pdf. Accessed December 5, 2010.

13 Achille Mbembe (2003), "Necropolitics," trans. Libby Meintjes, *Public Culture*, 15, (1): 40.

14 Kenneth Saltman and David Gabard (eds) (2003), *Education as Enforcement: The Militarization and Corporatization of Schools*. New York: Routledge.

15 Orlando Patterson (1982), *Slavery and Social Death: A Comparative Study*. Cambridge, MA: Harvard University Press.

16 César Chelala (2006), "Rich Man, Poor Man: Hungry Children in America," *Seattle Times*, January 4, 2006. Available online at: www.commondreams.org/views06/0104-24.htm. Accessed January 5, 2006.

17 The Henry J. Kaiser Family Foundation (2009), *The Uninsured: A Primer*, October. Available online at: www.kff.org/uninsured/upload/7451-06.pdf. Accessed April 01, 2011.

18 Marian F. MacDorman and T. J. Mathews (2008), *Recent Trends in Infant Mortality in the United States*. National Center for Health Statistics, October 2008. Available online at: www.cdc.gov/nchs/data/databriefs/db09.htm. Accessed September 4, 2010.

19 Kenneth C. Land (2009), *The 2009 Foundation for Child Development Child and Youth Well-Being Index (CWI) Report*, May. Available online at: www.fcd-us.org/Final-2009CWIReport.pdf. See also Sarah Fass and Nancy K. Cauthen (2008), "Who Are America's Poor Children? The Official Story," National Center for Children in Poverty, October, 2008. Available online at: www.nccp.org/publications/pdf/text_843.pdf. Accessed November 20, 2010.

20 Kenneth C. Land (2009), *Education for Homeless Children and Youths Program*. Foundation for Child Development, April. Available online at: www.fcd-us.org/ usr_doc/Final-2009CWIReport.pdf. Accessed January 15, 2009.

21 National Center on Family Homelessness (2009), *America's Youngest Outcasts: State Report Card on Child Homelessness*, March 2009. Available online at: www. homelesschildrenamerica.org/report.php. Accessed January 18, 2009.

22 Central to such a bleak future is what Victor Rios calls a "youth control complex . . . an ecology of interlinked institutional arrangements that manages and controls the everyday lives of inner-city youth of color"; this complex has "a devastating grip on the lives of many impoverished male youth of colour" and continues to promote the hypercriminalization of black and Latino youth in the United States. See Victor M. Rios (2007), "The Hypercriminalization of Black and Latino Male Youth in the Era of Mass Incarceration," in Ian Steinberg, Manning Marable, and Keesha Middlemass (eds), *Racializing Justice, Disenfranchising Lives*. New York: Palgrave, p. 17.

23 Center for Labor Market Studies at Northeastern University (2009), *Left Behind in America: The Nation's Dropout Crisis*, May 5, 2009. Available online at: www. clms.neu.edu/publication/documents/CLMS_2009_Dropout_Report.pdf. Accessed January 5, 2010.

24 Andrew Sum, Ishwar Khatiwada, Joseph McLaughlin, and Sheila Palma (2009), *The Consequences of Dropping Out of High School: Joblessness and Jailing for High School Dropouts and the High Cost for Taxpayers*. Boston: Center for Labor Market Studies, Northeastern University, October, 2009. Available online at: www.clms. neu.edu/publication/documents/The_Consequences_of_Dropping_Out_of_High_ School.pdf. Accessed February 10, 2010.

25 Ibid.

26 Ibid.

27 Jonathan Simon (2007), *Governing Through Crime: How the War on Crime Transformed American Democracy and Created a Culture of Fear*. New York: Oxford University Press, p. 5.

28 Angela Y. Davis (2005), *Abolition Democracy: Beyond Empire, Prisons, and Torture*. New York: Seven Stories Press, p. 41.

29 Pew Center on the States (2008), *One in 100: Behind Bars in America 2008*, February 2008, p. 11. Available online at: www.pewcenteronthestates.org/uploaded Files/8015PCTS_Prison08_FINAL_2-1-1_FORWEB.pdf. Accessed February 10, 2009.

30 Ibid., p. 16.

31 Zygmunt Bauman (2004), *Wasted Lives*. London: Polity Press, p. 82.

32 Bob Herbert (2007), "School to Prison Pipeline," *New York Times*, June 9, 2007: A29.

33 Ibid.

34 Barbara Ehrenreich (2009), "Is It Now a Crime to Be Poor?" *New York Times*, August 8 ,2009: WK9. Available online at: www.nytimes.com/2009/08/09/ opinion/09ehrenreich.html . Accessed September 15, 2010.

35 These figures are taken from Children's Defense Fund (2007), *Summary Report: America's Cradle to Prison Pipeline*, pp. 4, 38. Available online at: www.childrens defense.org/site/DocServer/CPP_report_2007_summary.pdf?docID=6001. Accessed September 10, 2010.

36 Children's Defense Fund (2007), *America's Cradle to Prison Pipeline*, October, 2007, p. 77. Available online at: www.childrensdefense.org/child-research-data- publications/data/cradle-prison-pipeline-report-2007-full-lowres.pdf. Accessed November 10, 2008.

37 Quoted in Evelyn Nieves (2000), "California Proposal Toughens Penalties for Young Criminals," *New York Times*, March 6, 2000: A1, A15.

38 Barry Feld (1993), "Criminalizing the American Juvenile Court," *Crime and Justice*, 17: 251.

39 US Department of Justice (2009), *Report: Investigation of the Lansing Residential Center, Louis Gossett, Jr. Residential Center, Tryon Residential Center, and Tryon Girls Center*. Washington, DC: US Government. Available online at: www.usdoj. gov/crt/split/documents/NY_juvenile_facilities_findlet_08-14-2009.pdf. Accessed January 8, 2010.

40 Ibid. See also Nicholas Confessore (2009), "4 Youth Prisons in New York Used Excessive Force," *New York Times*, August 25, 2009: A1.

41 US Department of Justice, *Report: Investigation of the Lansing Residential Center*.

42 Facts on File News Services (2009), "Sentencing Juvenilles to Life Without Parole." *Issues & Controversies*, 21 August, 2009. Available online at: http://www.2facts.com/ PrintPage.aspx?PIN=i1400440. Accessed April 1, 2011.

43 Altman & Altman (2009), "More than 2,000 US Inmates Sentenced to Life in Prison without Parole Committed their Crimes when they were Minors," *Boston Criminal Lawyer Blog*, April 9, 2009. Available online at: www.bostoncriminallawyerblog. com/2009/04/more_than_2000_us_inmates_sent.html. Accessed April 1, 2011.

44 For an extensive treatment of zero-tolerance laws and the militarization of schools, see Christopher Robbins (2008), *Expelling Hope: The Assault on Youth and the Militarization of Schooling*. Albany: SUNY Press; and Kenneth Saltman and David Gabbard (eds) (2003), *Education as Enforcement: The Militarization and Corporatization of Schools*. New York: Routledge.

45 Advancement Project in partnership with Padres and Jovenes Unidos, Southwest Youth Collaborative (2005), *Education on Lockdown: The Schoolhouse to Jailhouse Track*. Chicago: Children & Family Justice Center of Northwestern University School of Law, March 24, 2005, p. 31.

46 Howard Witt (2007), "School Discipline Tougher on African Americans," *Chicago Tribune*, September 25, 2007. Available online at: www.chicagotribune.com/news/ nationworld/chi-070924discipline,0,22104.story?coll=chi_tab01_layout. Accessed October 25, 2007.

47 Advancement Project, *Education on Lockdown*, p. 33.

48 Henry A. Giroux (2009), "Brutalizing Kids: Painful Lessons in the Pedagogy of School Violence," *Truthout*, October 8, 2009. Available online at: www.truthout. org/10080912 . Accessed September 18, 2010.

49 Zygmunt Bauman (2004), *Wasted Lives*. London: Polity Press, p. 82.

50 Beger, "Expansion of Police Power," p. 120.

51 Dorothy Roberts (2008), *Shattered Bonds: The Color of Child Welfare*. New York: Basic Civitas Books, p. 268.

52 Cited in Madeline Bunting (2003), "Passion and Pessimism," *The Guardian*, April 5, 2009. Available online at: http://books.guardian.co.uk/print/0,3858,4640858,00.html. Accessed February 10, 2008.

53 Edward Said, *Humanism and Democratic Criticism*, p. 143.

54 Edward Said (2000), "Scholarship and Commitment: An Introduction," in *Profession 2000*, p. 7.

55 Kimball, cited in Lawrence W. Levine (1996), *The Opening of the American Mind*. Boston: Beacon Press, p. 19.

56 All of these ideas and the quote itself are taken from Edward Said (2004), *Humanism and Democratic Criticism*. New York: Columbia, p. 142.

57 Zygmunt Bauman (2007), *Liquid Times: Living in an Age of Uncertainty*. London: Polity, p. 8.

CHAPTER 6

Higher Education and the Politics and Pedagogy of Educated Hope

Children are the future of any society. If you want to know the future of a society, look at the eyes of the children. If you want to maim the future of any society, you simply maim the children. The struggle for the survival of our children is the struggle for the survival of our future. The quantity and quality of that survival is the measurement of the development of our society.[1]

Ngugi Wa Thiong'O

Education has as its object the formation of character.

Herbert Spencer

YOUTH AND THE CRISIS OF THE FUTURE

Any discourse about the future has to begin with the issue of youth, because more than any other group youth embody the projected dreams, desires, and commitment of a society's obligations to the future. This echoes a classical principle of modernity in which youth both symbolize society's responsibility to the future and offer a measure of its progress. For most of this century, Americans have embraced as a defining feature of politics the idea that all levels of government would assume a large measure of responsibility for providing the resources, social provisions, security, and modes of education that simultaneously offered young people a future as it expanded the meaning and depth of a substantive democracy. In many respects, youth not only registered symbolically the importance of modernity's claim to progress; they also affirmed the importance of the liberal, democratic tradition of the social contract in which adult responsibility was mediated through a willingness to fight for the rights of children, enact reforms that invested in their future, and provide the educational conditions necessary for them to make use of the freedoms they have while learning how to be critical citizens. Within such a modernist project, democracy was linked to the well-being of youth, while the status of how a society imagined democracy and its future was contingent on how it viewed its responsibility towards future generations.

But the category of youth did more than affirm modernity's social contract rooted in a conception of the future in which adult commitment was articulated as a vital public service; it also affirmed those vocabularies, values and social relations central to a politics capable of both defending vital institutions as a public good and contributing to the quality of public life. Such a vocabulary was particularly important for higher education, which often defined and addressed its highest ideals through the recognition that how it educated youth was connected to both the democratic future it hoped for and its claim as an important public sphere.

Yet, at the dawn of the new millennium, it is not at all clear that we believe any longer in youth, the future, or the social contract, even in its minimalist version. Since the Reagan/Thatcher revolution of the 1980s, we have been told that there is no such thing as society and, indeed, following that nefarious pronouncement, institutions committed to public welfare have been disappearing ever since. Those of us who, against the prevailing common sense, insist on the relationship between higher education and the future of democracy have to face a disturbing reversal in priorities with regard to youth and education, a reversal which now defines the United States and other regions under the reign of neoliberalism. Rather than being cherished as a symbol of the future, youth are now seen as a threat to be feared and a problem to be contained. If youth once symbolized the moral necessity to address a range of social and economic ills, they are now largely portrayed as being the source of most of society's problems. Hence, youth now constitute a crisis that has less to do with improving the future than with denying it.

No longer "viewed as a privileged sign and embodiment of the future,"[2] youth are now demonized by the popular media and derided by politicians looking for quick-fix solutions to crime, joblessness, and poverty. In a society deeply troubled by their presence, youth prompt a public rhetoric of fear, control, and surveillance, which translates into social policies that signal the shrinking of democratic public spheres, the hijacking of civic culture, and the increasing militarization of public space. Nurturance, trust, and respect now give way to fear, disdain, and suspicion. In many suburban malls, young people, especially urban youth of color, cannot shop or walk around without having appropriate identification cards or being in the company of a parent. Children have fewer rights than almost any other group and fewer institutions protecting these rights. Consequently, their voices and needs are almost completely absent from the debates, policies, and legislative practices that are constructed in terms of their needs. One consequence of such a betrayal can be seen in youthful protests now extending from the Middle East and Western Europe to various cities in the United States.

Instead of providing a decent education to poor young people, American society offers them the growing potential of being incarcerated, buttressed by the fact that the US is one of the few countries in the world that sentences minors to death and spends "three times more on each incarcerated citizen than on each public school pupil."[3] Instead of guaranteeing them food, decent health care, and shelter, we serve them more standardized tests; instead of providing them with vibrant public spheres, we offer them a commercialized culture in which consumerism is the only obligation of citizenship. In the hard currency of human suffering, children pay a heavy price in one the richest democracies in the world: 20 percent of children are poor during the first three years of life and over 15.5 million live in poverty; 9.2 million children lack health insurance; millions lack affordable childcare and decent early childhood education; in many states more money is being spent on prison construction than on education; and the infant mortality rate in the United States is the highest of any other industrialized nation. When broken down along racial categories, the figures become even more despairing. For example, "In 1998, 36 percent of black and 34 percent of Hispanic children lived in poverty, compared with 14 percent of white children."[4] In some cities, such as the District of Columbia, the child poverty rate is as high as 45 percent.[5] While the United States ranks first in military technology, military exports, defense expenditures, and the number of millionaires and billionaires, it is ranked 18th among the industrialized nations in the gap between rich and poor children, 12th in the percent of children in poverty, 17th in the efforts to lift children out of poverty, and 29th in infant mortality.[6] One of the most shameful figures on youth as reported in 2002 by Jennifer Egan, a writer for the *New York Times*, indicates that "1.4 million children are homeless in America for a time in any given year . . . and these children make up 40 percent of the nation's homeless population."[7] In short, economically, politically, and culturally, the situation of youth in the United States is intolerable and obscene. It is all the more unforgivable since President Bush insisted during the 2000 campaign that "the biggest percentage of our budget should go to children's education." He then passed a 2002 budget in which 40 times more money went for tax cuts for the wealthiest 1 percent of the population rather than for education.[8] Under the Obama administration, children make up one third of all people living under the poverty line. While social protections for the poor and unemployed are being dismantled, **the 400 richest families in the United States have a combined wealth of $1.57 trillion more than the combined wealth of 50 percent of the US population.**[9]

Youth have become the central site onto which the anxieties of living in an age where "there is no such thing as society" are projected. Their very presence represents *both* the broken promises of democracy in an age of corporate deregulation and downsizing and a collective fear of the consequences wrought by systemic class inequalities, racism, and a culture of "infectious greed" that has created a generation of displaced and unskilled youth who have been expelled from the "universe of moral obligations."[10] Youth within the economic, political, and cultural geography of neoliberal capitalism occupy a degraded borderland in which the spectacle of commodification exists side by side with the imposing threat of the prison-industrial complex and the elimination of basic civil liberties. As neoliberalism disassociates economics from its social costs, "the political state has become the corporate state."[11] Under such circumstances, the state does not disappear, but, as Pierre Bourdieu has brilliantly reminded us,[12] is refigured as its role in providing social provisions, intervening on behalf of public welfare, and regulating corporate plunder is weakened. The neoliberal state no longer invests in solving social problems; it now punishes those who are caught in the downward spiral of its economic policies. Under such circumstances, the social state is transformed into a corporate and punishing state.[13] Punishment, incarceration, and surveillance represent the face of the new state. One consequence is that the implied contract between the state and citizens is broken, and social guarantees for youth as well as civic obligations to the future vanish from the agenda of public concern. Similarly, as market values supplant civic values, it becomes increasingly difficult "to translate private worries into public issues and, conversely, to discern public issues in private troubles."[14] Alcoholism, homelessness, poverty, and illiteracy, among other issues, are not seen as social but as individual problems — matters of character, individual fortitude, and personal responsibility.

The war against youth, in part, can be understood within those fundamental values and practices that characterize a rapacious, neoliberal capitalism. For many young people and adults today, the private sphere has become the only space in which to imagine any sense of hope, pleasure, or possibility. Culture as an activity in which people actually produce the conditions of their own agency through dialogue, community participation, resistance, and political struggle is being replaced by a "climate of cultural and linguistic privatization,"[15] in which culture becomes something you consume and the only kind of speech that is acceptable is that of the savvy shopper. Neoliberalism, with its emphasis on market forces and profit margins, narrows the legitimacy of the public sphere by redefining it around the related issues of privatization, deregulation, consumption, and safety. Big government, recalled from exile after 9/11, is now popularly presented as a guardian of security — security not in terms of providing adequate social provisions or a social safety net but associated with increasing the state's role as a policing force. The desire to protect market freedoms and wage a war against terrorism, ironically, has not only ushered in a culture of fear but also dealt a lethal blow to civil freedoms. Resting in the balance of this contradiction is both the fate of democracy and the civic health and future of a generation of children and young people.

What is happening to children in America and what are its implications for addressing the future of higher education? Lawrence Grossberg argues that "the current rejection of childhood as the core of our social identity is, at the same time, a rejection of the future as an affective investment."[16] But the crisis of youth not only signals a dangerous state of affairs for the future; it also portends a crisis in the very idea of the political and ethical constitution of the social and the possibility of articulating the relevance of democracy itself. It is in reference to the crisis of youth, the social, and democracy that I want to address the relationship between higher education and the future.

HIGHER EDUCATION AND THE CRISIS OF THE SOCIAL

There is a prominent educational tradition in the United States, extending from W. E. B. Du Bois and John Dewey to C. Wright Mills, in which the future of the university is premised on the recognition that in order for freedom to flourish in the worldly space of the public realm, citizens have to be educated for the task of self-government. Education in this context is linked to public life through democratic values such as equality, justice, and freedom, rather than viewed as an adjunct of the corporation whose knowledge and values are defined largely through the prism of commercial interests. For Dewey, Mills, and Du Bois, education was crucial to a notion of individual agency and public citizenship. It was integral to defending the relationship between an autonomous society — rooted in an ever-expanding process of self-examination, critique, and reform — and autonomous individuals, for whom critical inquiry is propelled by the need to engage in an ongoing pursuit of ethics and justice as a matter of public good. In many ways, higher education has been faithful, at least in theory, to a project of modern politics whose purpose is to create citizens capable of defining and implementing universal goals such as freedom, equality, and justice as part of a broader attempt to deepen the relationship between an expanded notion of the social and the enabling ground of a vibrant democracy.

Within the last two decades a widespread pessimism about public life and politics has developed in the United States. Under neoliberalism, hope becomes dystopian as the public sphere disappears and, as Peter Beilharz argues, "politics becomes banal, for there is not only an absence of citizenship but a striking absence of agency."[17] As power is increasingly separated from the specificity of traditional politics and public obligations, corporations are less subject to the control of the state and "there is a strong impulse to displace political sovereignty with the sovereignty of the market, as if the latter has a mind and morality of its own."[18] Under the auspices of neoliberalism, the language of the social is either devalued or ignored altogether as the idea of the public sphere is equated with a predatory space rife with danger and disease — as in reference to public restrooms, public transportation, and urban public schools. Dreams of the future are now modeled around the narcissistic, privatized, and self-indulgent needs of consumer culture and the dictates of the alleged free market. This may be one reason that young people are not protesting the assault on public and higher education in the United States in ways similar to the protests waged by their counterparts in France, Greece, Italy, and England.

Within this impoverished sense of politics and public life, the university is gradually being transformed into a training ground for the corporate workforce. As universities become increasingly strapped for money, corporations provide the needed resources for research and funds for endowed chairs, exerting a powerful influence on both the hiring of faculty and how research is conducted and for what purposes. In addition, universities now offer up buildings and stadiums as billboards for brand-name corporations in order to procure additional sources of revenue while also adopting the values, management styles, cost-cutting procedures, and the language of excellence that has been the hallmark of corporate culture. Under the reign of neoliberalism and corporate culture, the boundaries between commercial culture and public culture become blurred as universities rush to embrace the logic of industrial management while simultaneously forfeiting those broader values both central to a democracy and capable of limiting the excesses of corporate power. Although the university has always had ties to industry, there is a new intimacy between higher education and corporate culture, characterized by what Larry Hanley calls a "new, quickened symbiosis."[19] As Masao Miyoshi points out, the result is "not a fundamental or abrupt change perhaps, but still an unmistakable radical reduction of its public and critical role."[20] What was once the hidden curriculum of many universities — the subordination of higher education to capital — has now become an open and much-celebrated policy of both public and private higher education.[21]

How do we understand the university in light of both the crisis of youth and the related crisis of the social that have emerged under the controlling hand of neoliberalism? How can the future be grasped given the erosion of the social and public life over the last 20 years? What are the implications for the corporatization of higher education in light of these dramatic changes? Any concern about the future of the university has to both engage and challenge this transformation while simultaneously reclaiming the role of the university as a democratic public sphere. In what follows, I want to analyze the university as a corporate entity within the context of a crisis of the social. In particular, I will focus on how this crisis is played out not only through the erosion of public space, but through the less explained issues of public versus corporate time, on the one hand, and the related issues of agency, pedagogy, and public mission on the other.

PUBLIC TIME VERSUS CORPORATE TIME

Questions of time are crucial to how a university structures its public mission, the role of faculty, the use of space, student access, and the legitimation of particular forms of knowledge, research, and pedagogy. Time is not simply a question of how to invoke the future. It is also used to legitimate particular social relations and make claims on human behavior, representing one of the most important battlefields for determining how the future of higher education is played out in political and ethical terms. Time refers not only to the way in which it is mediated differently by institutions, administrators, faculty, and students but also to how it shapes and allocates power, identities, and space through a particular set of codes and interests. More importantly, time is a central feature of politics and orders not merely the pace of the economic, but the time available for consideration, contemplation, and critical thinking. When reduced to a commodity, time often becomes the enemy of deliberation and thoughtfulness and undermines the ability of political culture to function critically.

For the past 20 years, time as a value and the value of time have been redefined through the dictates of neoliberal economics, which has largely undermined any notion of public time guided by non-commodified values central to a political and social democracy. As Peter Beilharz observes:

> [T]ime has become our enemy. The active society demands of us that we keep moving, keep consuming, experience everything, travel, work as good tourists more than act as good citizens, work, shop and die. To keep moving is the only way left in our cultural repertoire to push away . . . meaning . . . [and consequently] the prospects and forms of social solidarity available to us shrink before our eyes.[22]

Without question, the future of the university will largely rest on the outcome of the current struggle between the university as a public space with the capacity to slow down time in order to question what Jacques Derrida calls the powers that limit "a democracy to come"[23] and a corporate university culture wedded to a notion of accelerated time in which the principle of self-interest replaces politics and consumerism becomes a tawdry substitute for a broader notion of social agency. A meaningful and inclusive democracy is indebted to a notion of public time, while neoliberalism celebrates what I call corporate time. Public time as a condition and critical referent makes visible how politics is played out through the unequal access different groups have to "institutions, goods, services, resources, and power and knowledge."[24] That is, it offers a critical category for interrogating how the ideological and institutional mechanisms of higher education work to grant time to some faculty and students and to withhold it from others, how time is mediated differently within different disciplines and among diverse faculty and students, and how time can work across the canvas of power and space to create new identities and social formations capable of "intervening in public debate for the purpose of affecting positive change in the overall position and location in society."[25] When linked to issues of power, identity, ideology, and politics, public time can be an important social construct for orientating the university towards a vision of the future in which critical learning becomes central to increasing the scope of human rights, individual freedom, and the operations of a substantive democracy.

Public time rejects the fever-pitch appeals of "just in time" or "speed time," demands often made within the context of "ever faster technological transformation and exchange"[26] and buttressed by corporate capital's golden rule: "time is money." Public time slows down time, not as a simple refusal of technological change or a rejection of all calls for efficiency but as an attempt to create the institutional and ideological conditions that promote long-term analyses, historical reflection, and deliberations over what our collective actions might mean for shaping the future. Rejecting an instrumentality that evacuates questions of history, ethics, and justice, public time fosters dialogue, thoughtfulness, and critical exchange. Public time offers room for knowledge that contributes to society's self-understanding, enables it to question itself, and seeks to legitimate intellectual practices that are collective and non-instrumental, deepening democratic values while encouraging pedagogical relations that question the future in terms that are political, ethical, and social. As Cornelius Castoriadis observes, public time puts into question established institutions and dominant authority, rejecting any notion of the social that either eliminates the question of judgment or "conceals . . . the question of responsibility."[27] Rather than maintaining a passive attitude towards power, public time demands and encourages forms of political agency based on a passion for self-governing, actions informed by critical judgment, and a commitment to linking social responsibility and social transformation. Public time legitimates those pedagogical practices that provide the basis for a culture of questioning, one that enables the knowledge, skills, and social practices necessary for resistance, a space of translation, and a proliferation of discourses. Public time unsettles common sense and disturbs authority while encouraging critical and responsible leadership. As Roger Simon observes, public time

> presents the question of the social — not as a space for the articulation of pre-formed visions through which to mobilize action, but as the movement in which the very question of the possibility of democracy becomes the frame within which a necessary radical learning (and questioning) is enabled.[28]

Put differently, public time affirms a politics without guarantees and a notion of the social that is open and contingent. Public time also provides a conception of democracy that is never complete and determinate but constantly open to different understandings of the contingency of its decisions, mechanisms of exclusions, and operations of power.[29] Public time challenges neoliberalism's willingness to separate the economic from the social as well as its failure to address human needs and social costs.

At its best, public time renders governmental power explicit, and in doing so it rejects the language of religious rituals and the abrogation of the conditions necessary for the assumption of basic freedoms and rights. Moreover, public time considers civic education the basis, if not essential dimension, of justice because it provides individuals with the skills, knowledge, and passions to talk back to power while simultaneously emphasizing both the necessity to question that accompanies viable forms of political agency and the assumption of public responsibility through active participation in the very process of governing. Expressions of public time in higher education can be found in shared notions of governance between faculty and administration, in modes of academic labor that encourage forms of collegiality tied to vibrant communities of exchange and democratic values, and in pedagogical relations in which students do not just learn about democracy but experience it through a sense of active participation, critical engagement, and social responsibility. The notion of public time has a long history in higher education and has played a formative role in shaping some of the most important principles of academic life. Public time, in this instance, registers the importance of pedagogical practices that provide the conditions for a culture of questioning in which teachers and students engage in critical dialogue and unrestricted discussion in order to affirm their role as social agents, inspect their own past, and engage the consequences of their own actions in shaping the future.

As higher education becomes increasingly corporatized, public time is replaced by corporate time. In corporate time, the "market is viewed as a master design for all affairs";[30] profit-making becomes the defining measure of responsibility; and consumption is the privileged site for determining value between the self and the larger social order. Corporate time fosters a narrow sense of leadership, agency, and public values and is largely indifferent to those concerns that are critical to a just society, but are not commercial in nature. The values of hierarchy, materialism, competition, and excessive individualism are enshrined under corporate time and play a defining role in how it allocates space, manages the production of particular forms of knowledge, and regulates pedagogical relations. Hence, it is not surprising that corporate time accentuates privatized and competitive modes of intellectual activity, largely removed from public obligations and social responsibilities. Divested of any viable democratic notion of the social, corporate time measures relationships, productivity, space, and knowledge according to the dictates of cost-efficiency, profit, and a market-based rationality. Within this framework, time is accelerated rather than slowed down and reconfigures academic labor, increasingly through, though not limited to, new computer generated technologies, which are making greater demands on faculty time, creating larger teaching loads, and producing bigger classes. And as Peter Euben observes, under such circumstances a particular form of rationality emerges as common sense in which speed rules and "calculation and logic are in [while] moral imagination and reasoned emotions are out. With speed at a premium, shorthand, quantification and measurements become dominant modes of thought."[31]

Corporate time maps faculty relationships through self-promoting market agendas and narrow definitions of self-interest. Caught on the treadmill of getting more grants, teaching larger classes, and producing more revenue for the university, faculty become another casualty of a business ideology that attempts to "extract labor from campus workers at the lowest possible cost, one willing to sacrifice research independence and integrity for profit."[32] Under the reign of corporatization, time is accelerated and fragmented. Overworked and largely isolated, faculty are now rewarded for intellectual activities privileged as entrepreneurial, "measured largely in the capacity to transact and consume."[33] Faculty are asked to spend more time in larger classrooms while they are simultaneously expected to learn and use new instructional technologies such as power point, the web, and various multi-media pedagogical activities. Grounded in the culture of competitiveness and self-interest, corporate time reworks faculty loyalties. Faculty interaction is structured less around collective solidarities built upon practices which offer a particular relationship to public life than through corporate-imposed rituals of competition and production that conform to the "narrowly focused ideas of the university as a support to the economy."[34]

Under such conditions, faculty solidarities are weakened even more as corporate time evokes cost-efficient measures by outsourcing instruction to part-time faculty who lack health benefits and are underpaid, overworked, and deprived of any power to shape the conditions under which they work. Powerlessness breeds resentment and anger among part-time faculty, and fear and insecurity among full-time faculty, who no longer believe that their tenure is secure. Hence, the divide between part-time and full-time faculty is reproduced by the heavy hand of universities as they downsize and outsource under the rubric of fiscal responsibility and accountability, especially in a post-9/11 era.[35] But more is reproduced than structural dislocations among faculty; there is also a large pool of crippling fear, insecurity, and resentment that makes it difficult for faculty to take risks, forge bonds of solidarity, engage in social criticism, and perform as public intellectuals rather than as technicians in the service of corporate largesse.

Leadership under the reign of corporate culture and corporate time has been rewritten as a form of homage to business models of governance. As Stanley Aronowitz points out, "Today . . . leaders of higher education wear the badge of corporate servants proudly."[36] Gone are the days when university presidents were hired for intellectual status and public roles. College presidents are now labeled as Chief Executive Officers, and are employed primarily because of their fundraising abilities. Deans of various colleges are often pulled from the ranks of the business world and pride themselves on the managerial logic and cost-cutting plans they adopt from the corporate culture of Microsoft, Disney, and IBM. Bill Gates and Michael Eisner replace John Dewey and Robert Hutchins as models of educational leadership. Rather than defend the public role of the university, academic freedom, and worthy social causes, the new corporate heroes of higher education now focus their time selling off university services to private contractors, forming partnerships with local corporations, searching for new patent and licensing agreements, and urging faculty to engage in research and grants that generate external funds. Under this model of leadership the university is being transformed from a place to think to a place to imagine stock options and profit windfalls.

Corporate time provides a new framing mechanism for faculty relations and modes of production and suggests a basic shift in the role of the intellectual. Academics now become less important as a resource to provide students with the knowledge and skills they need to engage the future as a condition of democratic possibilities. In the "new economy," they are entrepreneurs who view the future as an investment opportunity and research as a private career opportunity rather than a civic and collective effort to improve public life. Increasingly, academics find themselves being deskilled as they are pressured to teach more service-oriented and market-based courses and devote less time to their roles either as well-informed, public intellectuals or as cosmopolitan intellectuals who perform a valuable public service.[37]

Corporate time not only transforms the university as a democratic public sphere into a space for training while defining faculty as market-oriented producers; it also views students as both customers and potential workers, as well as a source of revenue. As customers, students "are conceptualized in terms of their ability to pay . . . and the more valued customers are those who can afford to pay more."[38] One consequence is that student access to higher education is "now shaped less by considerations of social justice than [by] revenue potential."[39] Consequently, those students who are poor and under-serviced are increasingly denied access to the benefits of higher education. Of course, the real problem is one of not merely potential decline, but "long-term and continuing failure to offer all citizens, especially minorities of class and color, equal educational opportunities,"[40] a failure that has been intensified under the authority of the corporate university. As a source of revenue, students are now subjected to higher fees and tuition costs and are bombarded by brand-name corporations who either lease space on the university commons to advertise their goods or run any one of a number of students services from the dining halls to the university book store. Almost every aspect of public space in higher education is now designed to attract students as consumers and shoppers, constantly subjecting them to forms of advertisements mediated by the rhythms of corporate time that keep students moving through a marketplace of brand-name products rather than ideas. Such hyper-commercialized spaces increasingly resemble malls, transforming all available university space into advertising billboards and bringing home the message that the most important identity available to students is that of a consuming subject. As the line between public and commercial space disappears, the gravitational pull of Taco Bell, McDonald's, Starbucks, Barnes & Noble, American Express, and Nike, among others, creates a "geography of nowhere,"[41] a consumer placelessness in which all barriers between a culture of critical ideas and branded products simply disappear.[42]

Corporate time not only translates faculty into multinational operatives and students into sources of revenue and captive consumers; it also makes a claim on how knowledge is valued, how the classroom is to be organized, and how pedagogy is defined. Knowledge under corporate time is valued as a form of capital. As Michael Peters observes, entire disciplines and bodies of knowledge are now either valued or devalued on the basis of their "ability to attract global capital and . . . potential for serving transnational corporations. Knowledge is valued for its strict utility rather than as an end in itself or for its emancipatory effects."[43] Good value for students means taking courses labeled as "relevant" in market terms, which are often counterposed to courses in the social sciences, humanities, and the fine arts that are concerned with forms of learning that do not readily translate into either private gain or commercial value. Under the rule of corporate time, the classroom is no longer a public space concerned with issues of justice, critical learning, or the knowledge and skills necessary for civic engagement. As training replaces education, the classroom, along with pedagogy itself, is transformed as a result of the corporate restructuring of the university.

What is crucial to recognize in the rise of corporate time is that while it acknowledges that higher education should play a crucial role in offering the narratives that frame society, it presupposes that faculty, in particular, will play a different role and assume a "different relation to the framing of cultural reality."[44] Many critics have pointed to the changing nature of governance and management structures in the university as a central force in redefining the relationship of the university to the larger society, but little has been said about how the changing direction of the university impacts on the nature of academic activity and intellectual relations. While at one level, the changing nature of the institution suggests greater control of academic life by administrators and an emerging class of managerial professionals, it also points to the privileging of those intellectuals in the techno-sciences whose services are indispensable to corporate power, while recognizing information as the reigning commodity of the new economy. Academic labor is now prized for how it fuses with capital, rather than how it contributes to what Geoff Sharp calls "society's self-understanding."[45] The changing institutional and social forms of the university reject the elitist and reclusive models of intellectual practice that traditionally have refused to bridge the gap between higher education and the larger social order, theory and practice, the academic and the public. Within the corporate university, transformation rather than contemplation is now a fundamental principle for judging and rewarding intellectual practice. Removed from matters of either social justice or democratic possibilities, transformation is defined through a notion of the social that is increasingly rooted in privileging the material interests of the market. Higher education's need for new sources of funding neatly dovetails with the inexhaustible need on the part of corporations for new products. Within this symbiotic relationship, knowledge is directly linked to its application in the market, mediated by a collapse of the distinction between knowledge and the commodity. Knowledge has become capital to invest in the market but has little to do with the power of self-definition, civic commitments, or ethical responsibilities that "require an engagement with the claims of others"[46] and with questions of justice. At the same time, the conditions for scholarly work are being transformed through technologies that eliminate face-to-face contact, speed up the labor process, and define social exchange in terms that are more competitive, instrumental, and removed from direction interaction.

Electronic, digital, and image-based technologies shape notions of the social in ways that were unimaginable a decade ago. Social exchanges can now proceed without the presence of "real" bodies. Contacts among faculty and between teachers and students are increasingly virtual, yet these practices profoundly delineate the nature of the social in instrumental, abstract, and commodified terms. As John Hinkson and Geoff Sharp have pointed out, these new intellectual practices and technological forms are redefining the nature of the social in higher education in ways that radically delimit the free sharing of ideas and cooperativeness, as collegiality seems to be disappearing among faculty.[47] This is an especially important issue since such social values serve as a "condition for the development of intellectual practices devoted to public service."[48] Within these new forms of instrumental framing and intellectual practice, the ethic of public service that once received some support in higher education is being eliminated and with it those intellectual relations, scholarly practices, and forms of collegiality that leave some room for addressing a less commodified and democratic notion of the social.

In opposition to this notion of corporate time, instrumentalized intellectual practices, and a deracinated view of the social, I want to reassert the importance of academic social formations that view the university as a site of struggle and resistance. Central to such a challenge is the necessity to define intellectual practice "as part of an intricate web of morality, rigor and responsibility"[49] that enables academics to speak with conviction, enter the public sphere in order to address important social problems, and demonstrate alternative models for what it means to bridge the gap between higher education and the broader society. This is a notion of intellectual practice that refuses both the instrumentality and the privileged isolation of the academy, while affirming a broader vision of learning that links knowledge to the power of self-definition and the capacities of administrators, academics, and students to expand the scope of democratic freedoms, particularly as they address the crisis of the social as part and parcel of the crisis of both youth and democracy itself. Implicit in this notion of social and intellectual practice is a view of academics as public intellectuals. Following Edward Said, I am referring to those academics engaged in rigorous intellectual practices who interpret and question power rather than merely consolidate it, enter into the public sphere in order to alleviate human suffering, make the connections of power visible, and work individually and collectively to create the pedagogical and social conditions necessary for what the late Pierre Bourdieu has called "realist utopias."[50] I want to conclude this chapter by taking up how the role of both the university as a democratic public sphere and the function of academics as public intellectuals can be further enabled through what I call a politics of educated hope.

TOWARDS A POLITICS OF EDUCATED HOPE

Higher education should be defended as a crucial democratic public sphere where teachers and students have the chance to resist and rewrite those modes of pedagogy, time, and rationality that refuse to include questions of judgment and issues of responsibility. Understood as such, higher education is viewed neither as a consumer driven product nor as a form of training and career preparation but as a mode of critical education that renders all individuals fit "to participate in power . . . to the greatest extent possible, to participate in a common government,"[51] to be capable as Aristotle reminds us of both governing and being governed. If higher education is to bring democratic public culture and critical pedagogy back to life, educators need to provide students with the knowledge and skills that enable them not only to judge and choose between different institutions but also to create those institutions they deem necessary for living lives of decency and dignity. As Castoriadis insists, "People should have not just the typical right to participate; they should also be educated in every aspect (of leadership and politics) in order to be able to participate"[52] in governing society. Higher education may be one of the few sites left in which students can learn how to address critically the tension between the democratic imperatives and possibilities of public institutions and their everyday realization within a social order dominated by market principles. It is also one of the few spheres in which students are provided with the tools not only for citizen participation in public life, but also for exercising forms of critical leadership. Toni Morrison is right in arguing:

> If the university does not take seriously and rigorously its role as a guardian of wider civic freedoms, as interrogator of more and more complex ethical problems, as servant and preserver of deeper democratic practices, then some other regime or menage of regimes will do it for us, in spite of us, and without us.[53]

Only if this struggle is taken seriously by educators and others can the university be reclaimed as a space of debate, discussion, and at times dissidence.

Education is not only about issues of work and economics, but also about questions of justice, social freedom, and the capacity for democratic agency, action, and change as well as the related issues of power, exclusion, and citizenship. These are educational and political issues and should be addressed as part of a broader concern for renewing the struggle for social justice and democracy. Such a struggle demands, as the writer Arunhdhati Roy points out, that as intellectuals we ask ourselves some very "uncomfortable questions about our values and traditions, our vision for the future, our responsibilities as citizens, the legitimacy of our 'democratic institutions,' the role of the state, the police, the army, the judiciary, and the intellectual community."[54]

Against the increasing corporatization of the university, educators need to resurrect a language of resistance and possibility, a language that embraces an oppositional utopianism while constantly being attentive to those forces that seek to turn such hope into a new slogan or punish and dismiss those who dare look beyond the horizon of the given. Hope as a form of oppositional utopianism is one of the preconditions for individual and social struggle and the ongoing practice of critical education in a wide variety of sites — the attempt to make a difference by being able to imagine otherwise in order to act in other ways. Educated hope is utopian, as Ruth Levitas observes, in that it is understood "more broadly as the desire for a better way of living expressed in the description of a different kind of society that makes possible that alternative way of life."[55] Educated hope also demands a certain amount of courage on the part of intellectuals, requiring from them the willingness to articulate social possibilities, mediate the experience of injustice as part of a broader attempt to contest the workings of oppressive power, undermine various forms of domination, and fight for alternative ways to imagine the future. This is no small challenge at a time in American history when jingoistic patriotism is the only obligation of citizenship and dissent is viewed increasingly as the refuge of those who support terrorists.

Educated hope as a utopian longing becomes all the more urgent given the bleakness of the times, but also because it opens horizons of comparison by evoking not just different histories but different futures; at the same time, it substantiates the importance of ambivalence while problematizing certainty, or as Paul Ricoeur has suggested, it is "a major resource as the weapon against closure."[56] As a form of utopian thinking, educated hope provides a theoretical service in that it pluralizes politics by generating dissent against the claims of a false harmony, and it provides an activating presence in promoting social transformation. Jacques Derrida has observed in another context that if higher education is going to have a future that makes a difference in promoting democracy, it is crucial for educators to take up the "necessity to rethink the concepts of the possible and the impossible."[57] What Derrida is suggesting is that educated hope provides a vocabulary for challenging the presupposition that there are no alternatives to the existing social order, while simultaneously stressing the dynamic, still unfinished elements of a democracy to be realized.[58]

Utopian thinking in this view is neither a blueprint for the future nor a form of social engineering, but a belief that different futures are possible. Utopian thinking rejects a politics of certainty and holds open matters of contingency, context, and indeterminancy as central to any notion of agency and the future. This suggests a view of hope based on the recognition that it is only through education that human beings can learn the limits of the present and the conditions necessary for them to "combine a gritty sense of limits with a lofty vision of possibility."[59] Educated hope poses the important challenge of how to reclaim social agency within a broader discourse of ethical advocacy while addressing those essential pedagogical and political elements necessary for envisioning alternatives to global neoliberalism and its attendant assault on public time and space.

Educated hope takes as a political and ethical necessity the need to address what modes of education are required for a democratic future and further requires that we ask such questions as: What pedagogical projects, resources, and practices can be put into place that would convey to students the vital importance of public time and its attendant culture of questioning as an essential step towards self-representation, agency, and a substantive democracy? How might public time with its imperative to "take more time" compel respect rather than reverence, critique rather than silence, while challenging the narrow and commercial nature of corporate time? What kinds of social relations necessarily provide students with time for deliberation as well as spaces of translation in which they can critically engage those forms of power and authority that speak directly to them both within and outside of the academy? How might public time, with its unsettling refusal to be fixed or to collapse in the face of corporate time, be used to create pedagogical conditions that foster forms of self and social critique as part of a broader project of constructing alternative desires and critical modes of thinking, on the one hand, and democratic agents of change on the other? How to deal with these issues is a major question for intellectuals in the academic world today, and their importance resides in not just how they might provide teachers and students with the tools to fight corporatization in higher education, but also how they address the need for fundamental institutional change in the ongoing struggles for freedom and justice in a revitalized democracy.

Educated hope accentuates the ways in which the political can become more pedagogical and the pedagogical more political. Pedagogy merges politics and ethics with revitalized forms of civic education that provide the knowledge, skills, and experiences enabling individual freedom and social agency. Making the pedagogical more political demands that educators become more attentive to the ways in which institutional forces and cultural power are tangled up with everyday experience. It means understanding how higher education in the information age now interfaces with the larger culture, how it has become the most important site for framing public pedagogies and authorizing specific relations among the self, the other, and the larger society that often shut down democratic visions. Any viable politics of educated hope must tap into individual experiences while at the same time linking individual responsibility with a progressive sense of social agency. Politics and pedagogy alike spring "from real situations and from what we can say and do in these situations."[60] As an empowering practice, educated hope makes concrete the possibility for transforming higher education into an ethical practice and public event that confront the flow of everyday experience and the weight of social suffering with the force of individual and collective resistance and the promise of an ongoing project of democratic social transformation.

There is a long-standing tradition among critical theorists that pedagogy as a moral and political practice plays a crucial role in constituting the social. Far from innocent, pedagogical practices operate within institutional contexts that carry great power in determining what knowledge is of most worth, what it means for students to know something, and how such knowledge relates to a particular understanding of the self and its relationship to both others and the future. Connecting teaching as knowledge production to teaching as a form of self-production, pedagogy not only presupposes an ethical and political project that offers up a variety of human capacities; it also propagates diverse meanings of the social. Moreover, as an articulation of and intervention in the social, pedagogical practices always sanction particular versions of what knowledge is of most worth, what it means to know something, how to be attentive to the operations of power, and how we might construct representations of ourselves, others, and our physical environment. In the broadest sense, pedagogy is a principal feature of politics because it provides the capacities, knowledge, skills, and social relations through which individuals recognize themselves as social and political agents. As Roger Simon points out, "talk about pedagogy is simultaneously talk about the details of what students and others might do together and the cultural politics such practices support."[61]

The primary emphasis in many approaches to critical pedagogy suggests that its foremost responsibility is to provide a space where the complexity of knowledge, culture, values, and social issues can be explored in open and critical dialogue. This position is echoed by Judith Butler, who argues: "For me there is more hope in the world when we can question what is taken for granted, especially about what it is to be human."[62] Zygmunt Bauman goes further, positing that the resurrection of any viable notion of political and social agency is dependent upon a culture of questioning, whose purpose, as he puts it, is to

> keep the forever unexhausted and unfulfilled human potential open, fighting back all attempts to foreclose and pre-empt the further unraveling of human possibilities, prodding human society to go on questioning itself and preventing that questioning from ever stalling or being declared finished.[63]

Central to any viable notion of critical pedagogy is its willingness to take seriously those academic projects, intellectual practices, and social relations in which students have the basic right to raise, if not define, questions, both within and outside of disciplinary boundaries. Such a pedagogy also must bear the responsibility of being self-conscious about those forces that sometimes prevent people from speaking openly and critically, whether they are part of a hidden curriculum of either racism, class oppression, or gender discrimination or part of those institutional and ideological mechanisms that silence students under the pretext of a claim to professionalism, objectivity, or unaccountable authority. Crucial here is the recognition that a pedagogical culture of questioning is not merely about the dynamics of communication but also about the effects of power and the mechanisms through which it either constrains, denies, or excludes particular forms of agency — preventing some individuals from speaking in specific ways, in particular spaces, under specific circumstances. Clearly, such a pedagogy might include a questioning of the corporatization of the educational context itself, the role of foreign policy, the purpose and meaning of the burgeoning prison-industrial complex, and the declining nature of the welfare state. Pedagogy makes visible the operations of power and authority as part of its processes of disruption and unsettlement — an attempt, as Larry Grossberg points out, "to win an already positioned, already invested individual or group to a different set of places, a different organization of the space of possibilities."[64]

At its best, such a pedagogy is self-reflective, and views its own practices and effects not as pre-given but as the outcome of previous struggles. Rather than defined as either a technique, method, or "a kind of physics which leaves its own history behind and never looks back,"[65] critical pedagogy is grounded in a sense of history, politics, and ethics that uses theory as a resource to respond to particular contexts, problems, and issues. I want to suggest that as educators we need to extend this approach to critical pedagogy beyond the project of simply providing students with the critical knowledge and analytic tools that can be used in any way they wish. While this pedagogical approach rightly focuses on the primacy of dialogue, understanding, and critique, it does not adequately affirm the experience of the social and the obligations it evokes regarding questions of responsibility and social transformation. Such a pedagogy attempts to open up for students important questions about power, knowledge, and what it might mean for students to critically engage the conditions under which life is presented to them, but it does not directly address what it would mean for them to work to overcome those social relations of oppression that make living unbearable for those youths and adults who are poor, hungry, unemployed, refused adequate social services, and under the aegis of neoliberalism, viewed largely as disposable.

But to acknowledge that critical pedagogy is directed and interventionist is not the same as turning it into a religious ritual. Critical approaches to pedagogy do not guarantee certainty or impose particular ideologies, nor should they. But they should make a distinction between a rigorous ethical and scholarly approach to learning implicated in diverse relations of power and those forms of pedagogy that belie questions of responsibility and allow conversation and dialogue to degenerate into opinion and academic methods to be reduced to an unreflective and damaging ideological approach to teaching. Rather than deny the relationship between education and politics, it seems far more crucial to engage it openly and critically so as to prevent pedagogical relations from degenerating into forms of abuse, terrorism, or contempt immune from any viable form of self-reflection and analysis.

A pedagogy that simply promotes a culture of questioning says nothing about what kind of future is or should be implied by how and what educators teach; nor does it address the necessity of recognizing the value of a future in which matters of liberty, freedom, and justice play a constitutive role. While it is crucial for education to be attentive to those practices in which forms of social and political agency are denied, it is also imperative to create the conditions in which forms of agency are available for students to learn how not only to think critically but to act differently. Any notion of critical pedagogy has to foreground issues not only of understanding but also of social responsibility and address the implications the latter has for a democratic society. As Vaclav Havel has noted:

Democracy requires a certain type of citizen who feels responsible for something other than his own well-feathered little corner; citizens who want to participate in society's affairs, who insist on it; citizens with backbones; citizens who hold their ideas about democracy at the deepest level, at the level that religion is held, where beliefs and identity are the same.[66]

Responsibility breathes politics into educational practices and suggests both a different future and the possibility of politics itself. Responsibility makes politics and agency possible, because it does not end with matters of understanding since it recognizes the importance of students becoming accountable for others through their ideas, language, and actions. Being aware of the conditions that cause human suffering and the deep inequalities that generate dreadfully undemocratic and unethical contradictions for many people is not the same as resolving them. If pedagogy is to be linked to critical citizenship and public life, it needs to provide the conditions for students to learn in diverse ways how to take responsibility for moving society in the direction of a more realizable democracy. In this case, the burden of pedagogy is linked to the possibilities of understanding and acting, engaging knowledge and theory as a resource to enhance the capacity for civic action and democratic change.

The future of higher education is inextricably connected to the future that we make available to the next generation of young people. Finding our way to a more humane future means educating a new generation of scholars who not only defend higher education as a democratic public sphere, but who also frame their own agency as both scholars and citizen activists willing to connect their research, teaching, and service with broader democratic concerns over equality and justice, and with an alternative vision of what the university might be and what society might become.

NOTES

1 Ngugi Wa Thiong'O (1993), *Moving the Centre: The Struggle for Cultural Freedoms.* Portsmouth, NH: Heinemann, p. 76.

2 Lawrence Grossberg (2001), "Why Does Neo-Liberalism Hate Kids? The War on Youth and the Culture of Politics," *The Review of Education/Pedagogy/Cultural Studies,* 23, (2): 133.

3 Heather Wokusch (2002), "Leaving Our Children Behind," *Common Dreams News Center,* July 8, 2002. Available online at: www.commondreams.org/views02/0708-08.htm

4 These figures are taken from Child Research Briefs, "Poverty, Welfare, and Children: A Summary of the Data." Available online at: www.childtrends.org. Accessed January 3, 2010.

5 These figures are taken from Childhood Poverty Research Brief 2, "Child Poverty in the States: Levels and Trends From 1979 to 1998." Available online at: www.nccp. org. Accessed January 3, 2010.

6 These figures largely come from Children's Defense Fund (2002), *The State of Children in America's Union: A 2002 Action Guide to Leave No Child Behind.* Washington, DC: Children's Defense Fund Publication, pp. iv–v, 13.

7 Jennifer Egan (2002), "To Be Young and Homeless," *The New York Times Magazine*, March 24, 2002: p. 35.

8 Wokusch, "Leaving Our Children Behind," p. 1.

9 David DeGraw (2010), "The Richest 1% Have Captured America's Wealth — What's It Going to Take to Get It Back?" *AlterNet*. Available online at: www.alternet.org/module/printversion/145705. Accessed March 3, 2010.

10 Zygmunt Bauman (1999), *Work, Consumerism, and the New Poor*. Philadelphia, Open University Press, p. 77.

11 Noreena Hertz (2001), *The Silent Takeover: Global Capitalism and the Death of Democracy*. New York: The Free Press, p. 11.

12 Pierre Bourdieu (1998), *Acts of Resistance; Against the Tyranny of the Market*. New York: The New Press; Pierre Bourdieu, et al. (1999), *The Weight of the World: Social Suffering in Contemporary Society*. Stanford: Stanford University Press.

13 Loic Wacquant (2009). *Punishing the Poor: The Neoliberal Government of Social Insecurity*. Durham, NC: Duke University Press.

14 Zygmunt Bauman (1999), *In Search of Politics*. Stanford, CA: Stanford University Press, p. 2.

15 Naomi Klein (1999), *No Logo*. New York: Picador, p. 177.

16 Lawrence Grossberg (2001), "Why Does Neo-Liberalism Hate Kids? The War on Youth and the Culture of Politics," *The Review of Education/Pedagogy/Cultural Studies*, 23, (2): 133.

17 Peter Beilharz (2000), *Zygmunt Bauman: Dialectic of Modernity*. London: Sage, p. 160.

18 Jean Comaroff and John L. Comaroff, (2000) "Millennial Capitalism: First Thoughts on a Second Coming." *Public Culture*, 12, (2): 332.

19 Larry Hanley (2001), "Conference Roundtable," *Found Object*, 10: 103.

20 Masao Miyoshi (1998), "'Globalization,' Culture, and the University," in Fredric Jameson and Masao Miyoshi (eds), *The Cultures of Globalization*. Durham, NC: Duke University Press, p. 263.

21 Stanley Aronowitz (1998), "The New Corporate University," *Dollars and Sense*, p. 32.

22 Peter Beilharz (2000), *Zygmunt Bauman: Dialectic of Modernity*. London: Sage, p. 161.

23 Jacques Derrida (2000), "Intellectual Courage: An Interview," *Culture Machine*, 2: 9.

24 Michael Hanchard (1999), "Afro-Modernity: Temporality, Politics, and the African Diaspora," *Public Culture*, 11, (1): 253.

25 Ibid., p. 256.

26 Jerome Bind (2000), "Toward an Ethic of the Future," *Public Culture*, 12, (1): 52.

27 Cornelius Castoriadis (1991), "The Greek Polis and the Creation of Democracy," *Philosophy, Politics, Autonomy: Essays in Political Philosophy*. New York: Oxford University Press, pp. 113–14.

28 Roger I. Simon (2002), "On Public Time." Unpublished paper. Ontario Institute for Studies in Education, April 1, 2002, p. 4.

29 Simon Critchley (2002), "Ethics, Politics, and Radical Democracy — The History of a Disagreement," *Culture Machine*, 4 Available online at: www.culturemachine.net/index.php/cm/article/viewArticle/267/252 . Accessed November 15, 2010.

30 James Rule (1998), "Markets In their Place," *Dissent*, Winter: 30.

31 Peter Euben (2000), "Reforming the Liberal Arts," *The Civic Arts Review*, 2: 8.

32 Cary Nelson (2002), "Between Anonymity and Celebrity: The Zero Degrees of Professional Identity," *College English*, 64, (6): 717.

33 Comaroff and Comaroff, "Millennial Capitalism: First Thoughts on a Second Coming," p. 306.

34 Geoff Sharp (2002), "The Idea of the Intellectual and After," in Simon Cooper, John Hinkson, and Geoff Sharp (eds), *Scholars and Entrepreneurs*. Melbourne, VIC: Arena Publications, p. 280.

35 Gary Rhoades (2001), "Corporate, Techno Challenges, and Academic Space," *Found Object*, 10: 143.

36 Aronowitz, "The New Corporate University," p. 32.

37 I have taken up this issue in great detail in Henry A. Giroux (2005), *Border Crossings: Cultural Workers and the Politics of Education*, 2nd edn. New York: Routledge.

38 Gary Rhoades, "Corporate, Techno Challenges, and Academic Space," p. 122.

39 Ibid.

40 Cary Nelson (2002), "Between Anonymity and Celebrity: The Zero Degrees of Professional Identity," *College English*, 64, (6): 713.

41 Taken from James Howard Kunstler (1993), *The Geography of Nowhere*. New York: Touchstone.

42 The most extensive analysis of the branding of culture by corporations can be found in Naomi Klein (1999), *No Logo*. New York: Picador.

43 Michael Peters (2002), "The University in the Knowledge Economy," in Simon Cooper, John Hinkson, and Geoff Sharp (eds), *Scholars and Entrepreneurs: The University in Crisis*. Melbourne, VIC: Arena Publications, p. 148.

44 Geoff Sharp (2002), "The Idea of the Intellectual and After," in Cooper, Hinkson, and Sharp (eds), *Scholars and Entrepreneurs*, p. 275.

45 Ibid., pp. 284–5.

46 Nick Couldry (2001), "Dialogue in an Age of Enclosure: Exploring the Values of Cultural Studies," *The Review of Education/Pedagogy/Cultural Studies*, 23, (1): 17.

47 John Hinkson (2002), "Perspectives on the Crisis of the University," in Cooper, Hinkson, and Sharp (eds), *Scholars and Entrepreneurs*, pp. 233–67; Sharp, "The Idea of the Intellectual and After," in Cooper, Hinkson, and Sharp (eds), *Scholars and Entrepreneurs*.

48 Hinkson, "Perspectives on the Crisis of the University," p. 259.

49 Arundhati Roy (2001), *Power Politics*. Cambridge, MA: South End Press, p. 6.

50 The ideas on public intellectuals are taken directly from Edward Said (2001), *Reflections on Exile and Other Essays*. Cambridge, MA: Harvard University Press, pp. 502–3. For the reference to realist utopias, see Pierre Bourdieu (2000), "For a Scholarship with Commitment," *Profession*, 2000: 42.

51 Cornelius Castoriadis (1991), "The Nature and Value of Equity," in *Philosophy, Politics, Autonomy: Essays in Political Philosophy*. New York: Oxford University Press, p. 140.

52 Cornelius Castoriadis (1996), "The Problem of Democracy Today," *Democracy and Nature*, 8: 24.

53 Toni Morrison (2001), "How Can Values Be Taught in the University?" *Michigan Quarterly Review*, Spring: 278.

54 Roy, *Power Politics*, p. 3.

55 Ruth Levitas (1993), "The Future of Thinking About the Future," in Jon Bird, Barry Curtis, Tim Putman, Lisa Tickner (eds), *Mapping the Futures: Local Cultures, Global Change*. New York: Routledge, p. 257.

56 Cited in Zygmunt Bauman (1998), *Work, Consumerism and the New Poor*. Philadelphia: Open University Press, p. 98.

57 Jacques Derrida (2001), "The Future of the Profession or the Unconditional University," in Laurence Simmons and Heather Worth (eds), *Derrida Downunder*. Auckland: Dunmore Press, p. 7.

58 Samir Amin has captured this sentiment in his comment: "Neither modernity

nor democracy has reached the end of its potential development. That is why I prefer the term 'democratization,' which stresses the dynamic aspect of a still-unfinished process, to the term 'democracy,' which reinforces the illusion that we can give a definitive formula for it." See Samir Amin (2001), "Imperialization and Globalization," *Monthly Review*, June: 12.

59 Ron Aronson (1999), "Hope After Hope?" *Social Research*, 66, (2): 489.

60 Alain Badiou (2001), *Ethics: An Essay on the Understanding of Evil*. London: Verso, p. 96.

61 Roger Simon (1987), "Empowerment as a Pedagogy of Possibility," *Language Arts*, 64, (4): 371.

62 Cited in Gary A. Olson and Lynn Worsham (2000), "Changing the Subject: Judith Butler's Politics of Radical Resignification," *JAC*, 20, (4): 765.

63 Zygmunt Bauman and Keith Tester (2001), *Conversations with Zygmunt Bauman*. Malden, MA: Polity Press, p. 4.

64 Lawrence Grossberg (1994), "Introduction: Bringing It All Back Home — Pedagogy and Cultural Studies," in Henry A. Giroux and Peter McLaren (eds), *Between Borders: Pedagogy and the Politics of Cultural Studies*. New York: Routledge, p. 14.

65 Bauman and Tester, *Conversations with Zygmunt Bauman*, p. 20.

66 Cited in Paul Berman (1997), "The Philosopher-King is Mortal," *New York Times Magazine*, May 11, 1997: 36.

Neoliberalism, Public Pedagogy, and the Legacy of Paulo Freire

CHAPTER 7

Neoliberalism and the Politics of Public Pedagogy

Our age is the time of "individual utopias," of utopias privatized, and so it comes naturally (as well as being a fashionable thing to do) to deride and ridicule such projects which imply a revision of the options which are collectively put at the disposal of individuals.[1]

Zygmunt Bauman

NEOLIBERALISM AS PUBLIC PEDAGOGY

The ascendancy of neoliberal corporate culture into every aspect of American life both consolidates economic power in the hands of the few and aggressively attempts to break the power of unions, decouple income from productivity, subordinate the needs of society to the market, and deem public services and goods an unconscionable luxury. But it does more. It thrives on a culture of cynicism, insecurity, and despair. Conscripts in a relentless campaign for personal responsibility, Americans are now convinced that they have little to hope for — and gain from — the government, non-profit public spheres, democratic associations, public and higher education, or other non-governmental social forces. With few exceptions, the project of democratizing public goods has fallen into disrepute in the popular imagination as the logic of the market undermines the most basic social solidarities. The consequences include not only a weakened state but a growing sense of insecurity, cynicism, and political retreat on the part of the general public. The incessant calls for self-reliance that now dominate public discourse betray a hollowed-out and refigured state that neither provides adequate safety nets for its populace, especially those who are young, poor, or marginalized, nor gives any indication that it will serve the interests of its citizens in spite of constitutional guarantees. As Stanley Aronowitz and Peter Bratis argue: "The nation-state lives chiefly as a repressive power [though it] also has some purchase on maintaining a degree of ideological hegemony over . . . 'the multitude.'"[2] In short, private interests trump social needs, and economic growth becomes more important than social justice. The capitulation of labor unions and traditional working-class parties to neoliberal policies is matched by the ongoing dismantling of the welfare state. Within neoliberalism's market-driven discourse, corporate power marks the space of a new kind of public pedagogy, one in which the production, dissemination, and circulation of ideas emerge from the educational force of the larger culture. Public pedagogy in this sense refers to a powerful ensemble of ideological and institutional forces whose aim is to produce competitive, self-interested individuals vying for their own material and ideological gain. Corporate public pedagogy culture largely cancels out or devalues gender, class-specific, and racial injustices of the existing social order by absorbing the democratic impulses and practices of civil society within narrow economic relations. Corporate public pedagogy has become an all-encompassing cultural horizon for producing market identities, values, and practices.

Under neoliberalism, dominant public pedagogy, with its narrow and imposed schemes of classification and limited modes of identification, uses the educational force of the culture to negate the basic conditions for critical agency. As Pierre Bourdieu has pointed out, political action is only "possible because agents, who are part of the social world, have knowledge of this world and because one can act on the social world by acting on their knowledge of this world."[3] Politics often begins when it becomes possible to make power visible, to challenge the ideological circuitry of hegemonic knowledge, and to recognize that "political subversion presupposes cognitive subversion, a conversion of the vision of the world."[4] But another element of politics focuses on where politics happens, how proliferating sites of pedagogy bring into being new forms of resistance, raise new questions, and necessitate alternative visions regarding autonomy and the possibility of democracy itself.

What is crucial to recognize in the work of theorists such as Raymond Williams, Stuart Hall, Pierre Bourdieu, Noam Chomsky, Robert McChesney, and others is that neoliberalism is more than an economic theory; it also constitutes the conditions for a radically reconfigured cultural politics. That is, it provides, to use Raymond Williams' term, a new mode of "permanent education" in which dominant sites of pedagogy engage in diverse forms of pedagogical address to put into play a limited range of identities, ideologies, and subject positions that both reinforce neoliberal social relations and undermine the possibility for democratic politics.[5] The economist William Greider goes so far as to argue that the diverse advocates of neoliberalism currently in control of the American government want to "roll back the twentieth century literally"[6] by establishing the priority of private institutions and market identities, values, and relationships as the organizing principles of public life. This is a discourse that wants to squeeze out ambiguity from public space, dismantle the social provisions and guarantees provided by the welfare state, and eliminate democratic politics by making the notion of the social impossible to imagine beyond the isolated consumer and the logic of the market.[7] The ideological essence of this new public pedagogy is well expressed by Grover Norquist, the president of Americans for Tax Reform and arguably Washington's leading right-wing strategist, who says: "My goal is to cut government in half in twenty-five years, to get it down to the size where we can drown it in the bathtub."[8]

These new sites of public pedagogy, which have become the organizing force of neoliberal ideology, are not restricted to schools, blackboards, and test-taking. Nor do they incorporate the limited forms of address found in schools. Such sites operate within a wide variety of social institutions and formats, including sports and entertainment media, cable television networks, churches, and channels of elite and popular culture such as advertising. Profound transformations have taken place in the public space, producing new sites of pedagogy marked by a distinctive confluence of new digital and media technologies, growing concentrations of corporate power, and unparalleled meaning-producing capacities. Unlike traditional forms of pedagogy, knowledge and desire are inextricably connected to modes of pedagogical address mediated through unprecedented electronic technologies that include high-speed computers, new types of digitized film, and social media on the Internet. The result is a public pedagogy that plays a decisive role in producing a diverse cultural sphere that gives new meaning to education as a political force. What is surprising about the cultural politics of neoliberalism is that cultural studies theorists have either ignored or largely underestimated the symbolic and pedagogical dimensions of the struggle that neoliberal corporate power has put into place for the last 30 years, particularly under the ruthless administration of George W. Bush.

MAKING THE PEDAGOGICAL MORE POLITICAL

At this point in American history, neoliberal capitalism is not simply too overpowering; on the contrary, "democracy is too weak."[9] Hence, the increasing influence of money over politics; corporate interests overriding public concerns; and the growing tyranny of unchecked corporate power and avarice. There is also the educational force of the wider culture which now functions as a mode of permanent education and expands the reach of the pedagogical far beyond the confines of the school. As Raymond Williams insisted,

> The need for permanent education, in our changing society, will be met in one way or another. It is now on the whole being met, though with many valuable exceptions and efforts against the tide, by an integration of this teaching with the priorities and interests of a capitalist society, and of a capitalist society, moreover, which necessarily retains as its central principle the idea of a few governing, communicating with and teaching the many.[10]

Culture combines with politics to turn struggles over power into entertainment, as is the case in the California recall of Governor Davis and the emergence of Arnold Schwarzenegger as the new occupant in the Governor's office. But, more important, under neoliberalism, pedagogy has become thoroughly politicized in reactionary terms as it constructs knowledge, values, and identities through dominant media that have become a handmaiden of corporate power. For instance, soon after the invasion of Iraq, the *New York Times* released a survey indicating that 42 percent of the American public believed that Saddam Hussein was directly responsible for the 9/11 attacks on the World Trade Center and the Pentagon. CBS also released a news poll indicating that 55 percent of the public believed that Saddam Hussein directly supported the terrorist organization Al Qaeda. A majority of Americans also believed that Saddam Hussein had weapons of mass destruction, was about to build a nuclear bomb, and that he would unleash it eventually on an unsuspecting American public. None of these claims had any basis in fact, since no evidence existed to even remotely confirm that any of these assertions were true. Of course, these opinions, held by a substantial number of Americans, did not simply fall from the sky; they were ardently legitimated by President Bush, Vice President Cheney, Colin Powell, and Condoleezza Rice, while reproduced daily and uncritically in all of the dominant media. These misrepresentations and strategic distortions circulated in the dominant press either with uncritical, jingoistic enthusiasm, as in the case of the Fox News Channel, or through the dominant media's refusal to challenge such claims — both positions, of course, in opposition to foreign news sources such as the BBC, which repeatedly challenged such assertions. Such deceptions are never innocent and in this case appear to have been shamelessly used by the Bush administration to muster support for both the Iraqi invasion and an ideologically driven agenda "that overwhelmingly favors the president's wealthy supporters and is driving the federal government toward a long-term fiscal catastrophe."[11]

While not downplaying the seriousness of government deception, I believe there is another serious issue that underlies these events in which the most important casualty is not simply the integrity of the Bush administration, but democracy itself. One of the central legacies of modern democracy, with its roots in the Enlightenment classical liberal tradition, and most evident in the twentieth century in work by scholars as diverse as W. E. B. Du Bois, Raymond Williams, Cornelius Castoriadis, John Dewey, and Paulo Freire, among others, is the important recognition that a substantive democracy cannot exist without educated citizens. For some, the fear of democracy itself was translated into an attack on a truly public and accessible education for all citizens. For others, such as the progressive Walter Lippman, who wrote extensively on democracy in the 1920s, it meant creating two modes of education: one mode for the elite who would rule the country and be the true participants in the democratic process; and the other for the masses, whose education would train them to be spectators rather than participants in shaping democratic public life. Du Bois recognized that such a bifurcation of educational opportunity was increasingly becoming a matter of common sense, but rejected it outright.[12] Similarly, in opposition to the enemies of democracy and the elitists, radical social critics such as Cornelius Castoriadis, Paulo Freire, Stuart Hall, and others believed that education for a democratic citizenry was an essential condition of equality and social justice and had to be provided through public, higher, popular, and adult education.

While Castoriadis and others were right about linking education and democracy, they had no way in their time of recognizing that the larger culture would extend, if not supersede, institutionalized education as the most important educational force in the developed societies. In fact, education and pedagogy have been synonymous with schooling in the public mind. Challenging such a recognition does not invalidate the importance of formal education to democracy, but it does require a critical understanding of how the work of education takes place in a range of other spheres such as advertising, television, film, the internet, video games, and the popular press. Rather than invalidate the importance of schooling, it extends the sites of pedagogy, and in doing so broadens and deepens the meaning of cultural pedagogy. The concept of public pedagogy also underscores the central importance of formal spheres of learning that unlike their popular counterparts — driven largely by commercial interests that more often mis-educate the public — must provide citizens with those critical capacities, modes of literacies, knowledge, and skills that enable them to both read the world critically and participate in shaping and governing it. Pedagogy at the popular level must now be a central concern of formal schooling itself. I am not claiming that public or higher education are free from corporate influence and dominant ideologies, but that such models of education, at best, provide the spaces and conditions for prioritizing civic values over commercial interests (i.e., they self-consciously educate future citizens capable of participating in and reproducing a democratic society). In spite of its present embattled status and contradictory roles, institutional schooling remains uniquely placed to prepare students to both understand and influence the larger educational forces that shape their lives. Such institutions, along with their cultural studies advocates by virtue of their privileged position and dedication to freedom and democracy, also have an obligation to draw upon those traditions and resources capable of providing a critical and humanistic education to all students in order to prepare them for a world in which information and power have taken on new and powerful dimensions. One entry into this challenge is to address the contributions that cultural studies and critical pedagogy have made in the last few decades to such issues, particularly with respect to how the relationship between culture and power constitute a new site of both politics and pedagogy.

CULTURAL STUDIES AND THE QUESTION OF PEDAGOGY

My own interest in cultural studies emerges out of an ongoing project to theorize the regulatory and emancipatory relationships among culture, power, and politics as expressed through the dynamics of what can be called "public pedagogy." This project concerns, in part, the diverse ways in which culture functions as a contested sphere over the production, distribution, and regulation of power, and how and where it operates both symbolically and institutionally as an educational, political, and economic force. For instance, as Cornelius Castoriadis points out, the symbolic reach if not pedagogical intrusion of culture has now become ubiquitous. He writes: "City walls, books, spectacles, events educate — yet now they mostly *miseducate* their residents. Compare the lessons, taken by the citizens of Athens (women and slaves included), during the performances of Greek tragedies with the kind of knowledge which is today consumed by the spectator of *Dynasty* or *Perdue de vue*."[13] Drawing upon a long tradition in cultural studies work, culture is viewed as constitutive and political, not only reflecting larger forces but also constructing them. In this instance, culture not only mediates history; it shapes it. In this formulation, power is a central element of culture just as culture is a crucial element of power.[14] As Bauman observes:

> Culture is a permanent revolution of sorts. To say "culture" is to make another attempt to account for the fact that the human world (the world moulded by the humans and the world which moulds humans) is perpetually, unavoidably — and unremediably — *noch nicht geworden* (not-yet-accomplished), as Ernst Bloch beautifully put it.[15]

I am suggesting that culture is a crucial terrain for theorizing and realizing the political as an articulation and intervention into the social, a space in which politics is pluralized, recognized as contingent, and open to many formations.[16] But culture is also a crucial sphere for articulating the dialectical and mutually constitutive dynamics between the global political circuits that now frame material relations of power and a cultural politics in which matters of representation and meaning shape and offer concrete examples of how politics is expressed, lived, and experienced through the modalities of daily existence. Culture, in this instance, is the ground of both contestation and accommodation, and it is increasingly characterized by the rise of mega-corporations and new technologies that are transforming radically the traditional spheres of the economy, industry, society, and everyday life. I am referring not only to the development of new information technologies but also to the enormous concentration of ownership and power among a limited number of corporations that now control a diverse number of media technologies and markets.[17] Culture now plays a central role in producing narratives, metaphors, images, and desiring maps that exercise a powerful pedagogical force over how people think about themselves and their relationship to others. From this perspective, culture is the primary sphere in which individuals, groups, and institutions engage in the art of translating the diverse and multiple relations that mediate between private life and public concerns. It is also the sphere in which the translating and pedagogical possibilities of culture are under assault, particularly as the forces of neoliberalism dissolve public issues into utterly privatized and individualistic concerns.[18]

Against the neoliberal attack on all things social, culture must be defended as the site where exchange and dialogue become crucial as an affirmation of a democratically configured space of the social in which the political is actually taken up and lived out through a variety of intimate relations and social formations. Far from being exclusively about matters of representation and texts, culture becomes a site, event, and performance in which identities and modes of agency are configured through the mutually determined forces of thought and action, body and mind, and time and space. Culture is the public space where common matters, shared solidarities, and public engagements provide the fundamental elements of democracy. Culture is also the pedagogical and political ground in which shared solidarities and a global public sphere can be imagined as a condition of democratic possibilities. Culture offers a common space in which to address the radical demand of a pedagogy that allows critical discourse to confront the inequities of power and promote the possibilities of shared dialogue and democratic transformation. Culture affirms the social as a fundamentally political space just as it attempts within the current historical moment to deny its relevance and its centrality as a political necessity. And culture's urgency, as Nick Couldry observes, resides in its possibilities for linking politics to matters of individual and social agency as they are lived out in particular democratic spheres, institutional forms, and communities in process. He writes:

> For what is urgent now is not defending the full range of cultural production and consumption from elitist judgement but defending the possibility of any shared site for an emergent democratic politics. The contemporary mission of cultural studies, if it has one, lies not with the study of "culture" (already a cliche of management and marketing manuals), but with the fate of a "*common culture*," and its contemporary deformations.[19]

Central to any viable notion of cultural studies is the primacy of culture and power, organized through an understanding of how the political becomes pedagogical, particularly in terms of how private issues are connected to larger social conditions and collective forces; that is, how the very processes of learning constitute the political mechanisms through which identities are shaped, desires mobilized, and experiences take on form and meaning within those collective conditions and larger forces that constitute the realm of the social. In this context, pedagogy is no longer restricted to what goes on in schools, but becomes a defining principle of a wide-ranging set of cultural apparatuses engaged in what Raymond Williams has called "permanent education." Williams rightfully believed that education in the broadest sense plays a central role in any viable form of cultural politics:

> What [permanent education] valuably stresses is the educational force of our whole social and cultural experience. It is therefore concerned, not only with continuing education, of a formal or informal kind, but with what the whole environment, its institutions and relationships, actively and profoundly

teaches . . . [Permanent education also refers to] the field in which our ideas of the world, of ourselves and of our possibilities, are most widely and often most powerfully formed and disseminated. To work for the recovery of control in this field is then, under any pressures, a priority.[20]

Williams argued that any viable notion of cultural politics would have to pay closer "attention to the complex ways in which individuals are formed by the institutions to which they belong, and in which, by reaction, the institutions took on the color of individuals thus formed."[21] Williams also foregrounded the crucial political question of how agency unfolds within a variety of cultural spaces structured within unequal relations of power.[22] He was particularly concerned about the connections between pedagogy and political agency, especially in light of the emergence of a range of new technologies that greatly proliferated the amount of information available to people, while at the same time constricting the substance and ways in which such meanings entered the public domain. The realm of culture for Williams took on a new role in the latter part of the twentieth century because the actuality of economic power and its attendant networks of pedagogical control now exercised more influence than ever before in shaping how identities are produced and everyday social experiences acquire the force of common sense.[23] Williams clearly understood that making the political more pedagogical meant recognizing that where and how the psyche locates itself in public discourse, visions, and passions provide the groundwork for agents to enunciate, act, and reflect on themselves and their relations to others and the wider social order.

Unfortunately, Williams' emphasis on making the pedagogical more political has not occupied a central place in the work of most cultural studies theorists. Pedagogy in most cultural studies accounts is either limited to the realm of schooling, dismissed as a discipline with very little academic cultural capital, or rendered reactionary through the claim that it simply accommodates the paralyzing grip of governmental institutions that normalize all pedagogical practices. Within this discourse, pedagogy largely functions to both normalize relations of power and overemphasize agency at the expense of institutional pressures, embracing what Tony Bennett calls "all agency and no structure."[24] This criticism, however, does little to explore or highlight the complicated, contradictory, and determining ways in which the institutional pressures of schools and other pedagogical sites and the social capacities of educators are mediated within unequal relations of power. Instead, Bennett simply reverses the formula and buttresses his own notion of governmentality as a theory of structures without agents. Of course, this position also ignores the role of various sites of pedagogy and the operational work they perform in producing knowledge, values, identities, and subject positions. But more importantly it reflects the general refusal on the part of many cultural studies theorists to take up the relationship between pedagogy and agency, on the one hand, and the relationship among the crises of culture, education, and democracy on the other. Given such a myopic vision, left-leaning intellectuals who are dismissive of formal education sites have no doubt made it easier for the more corporate and entrepreneurial interests to dominate colleges and universities.

Unfortunately, many cultural studies theorists have failed to take seriously Antonio Gramsci's insight that "[e]very relationship of 'hegemony' is necessarily an educational relationship" — with its implication that education as a cultural pedagogical practice takes place across multiple sites as it signals how, within diverse contexts, education makes us both subjects of and subject to relations of power.[25] I want to build on Gramsci's insight by exploring in greater detail the connection among democracy, political agency, and pedagogy by analyzing some of the work of the late French philosopher, Cornelius Castoriadis. Castoriadis has made seminal, and often overlooked, contributions to the role of pedagogy and its centrality to political democracy. I focus on this radical tradition in order to reclaim a legacy of critical thinking that refuses to decouple education from democracy, politics from pedagogy, and understanding from public intervention. This tradition of critical thought signals for educators and cultural studies advocates the importance of investing in the political as part of a broader effort to revitalize notions of democratic citizenship, social justice, and the public good. But it also signals the importance of cultural politics as a pedagogical force for understanding how people buy into neoliberal ideology, how certain forms of agency are both suppressed and produced, how neoliberals work pedagogically to convince the public that consumer rights are more important than the rights people have as citizens and workers, and how pedagogy as a force for democratic change enables understanding, action, and resistance.

EDUCATION AND RADICAL DEMOCRACY

Castoriadis was deeply concerned about what it meant to think about politics and agency in light of the new conditions of capitalism that threatened to undermine the promise of democracy at the end of the twentieth century. Moreover, he argues, like Raymond Williams, that education in the broadest sense is a principal feature of politics because it provides the capacities, knowledge, skills, and social relations through which individuals recognize themselves as social and political agents. Linking such a broad-based definition of education to issues of power and agency also raises fundamental questions that go to the heart of any substantive notion of democracy: How do issues of history, language, culture, and identity work to articulate and legitimate particular exclusions? If culture in this sense becomes the constituting terrain for producing identities and constituting social subjects, education becomes the strategic and positional mechanism through which such subjects are addressed, positioned within social spaces, located within particular histories and experiences, and always arbitrarily displaced and decentered as part of a pedagogical process that is increasingly multiple, fractured, and never homogeneous.

Cornelius Castoriadis has over the last 30 years provided an enormous theoretical service in analyzing the space of education as a constitutive site for
democratic struggle. Castoriadis pursues the primacy of education as a political force by focusing on democracy both as the realized power of the people
and as a mode of autonomy. In the first instance, he insists that "democracy
means power of the people . . . a regime aspiring to social and personal"
freedom.[26] Democracy in this view suggests more than a simply negative
notion of freedom in which the individual is defended against power. On the
contrary, Castoriadis argues that any viable notion of democracy must reject
this passive attitude towards freedom with its view of power as a necessary
evil. In its place, he calls for a productive notion of power, one that is central
to embracing a notion of political agency and freedom that affirms the equal
opportunity of all to exercise political power in order to participate in shaping
the most important decisions affecting their lives.[27] He ardently rejected the
increasing "abandonment of the public sphere to specialists, to professional
politicians."[28] He also rejected any conception of democracy that did not create the means for "unlimited interrogation in all domains" or that closed off
in "advance not only every political question as well as every philosophical
one, but equally every ethical or aesthetic question."[29] Castoriadis refused a
notion of democracy restricted to the formalistic processes of voting while
at the same time arguing that the notion of participatory democracy cannot
remain narrowly confined to the political sphere.

Democracy, for Castoriadis, must also concern itself with the issue of
cultural politics. He rightly argues that progressives are required to address
the ways in which every society creates what he calls its "social imaginary
significations," which provide the structures of representations that offer
individuals selected modes of identification and set the standards for both the
ends of action and the criteria for what is considered acceptable or unaccept-
able behavior, while establishing the affective measures for mobilizing desire
and human action.[30] The fate of democracy for Castoriadis was inextricably
linked to the profound crisis of contemporary knowledge, characterized by
its increasing commodification, fragmentation, privatization, and the turn
toward racial and patriotic conceits. As knowledge becomes abstracted from
the demands of civic culture and is reduced to questions of style, ritual, and
image, it undermines the political, ethical, and governing conditions for
individuals and social groups to either participate in politics or construct
those viable public spheres necessary for debate, collective action, and solving urgent social problems. As Castoriadis suggests, the crisis of contemporary
knowledge provides one of the central challenges to any viable notion of
politics:

> Also in question is the relation of . . . knowledge to the society that produces
> it, nourishes it, is nourished by it, and risks dying of it, as well as the issues
> concerning for whom and for what this knowledge exists. Already at present
> these problems demand a radical transformation of society, and of the human

being, at the same time that they contain its premises. If this monstrous tree of knowledge that modern humanity is cultivating more and more feverishly every day is not to collapse under its own weight and crush its gardener as it falls, the necessary transformations of man and society must go infinitely further than the wildest utopias have ever dared to imagine.[31]

Castoriadis was particularly concerned about how progressives might address the crisis of democracy in light of how social and political agents were being produced through dominant public pedagogies in a society driven by the glut of specialized knowledge, consumerism, and a privatized notion of citizenship that no longer supported non-commercial values and increasingly dismissed as a constraint any view of society that emphasized public goods and social responsibility. What is crucial to acknowledge in Castoriadis' view of democracy is that the crisis of democracy cannot be separated from the dual crisis of representation and political agency. In a social order in which the production of knowledge, meaning, and debate are highly restricted not only are the conditions for producing critical social agents limited, but also lost is the democratic imperative of affirming the primacy of ethics as a way of recognizing a social order's obligation to future generations. Ethics in this sense recognizes that the extension of power assumes a comparable extension in the field of ethical responsibility, a willingness to acknowledge that ethics means being able to answer in the present for actions that will be borne by generations in the future.[32]

Central to Castoriadis' work is the crucial acknowledgment that society creates itself through a multiplicity of organized pedagogical forms that provide the "instituting social imaginary" or field of cultural and ideological representations through which social practices and institutional forms are endowed with meaning, generating certain ways of seeing the self and its possibilities in the world. Not only is the social individual constituted, in part, by internalizing such meanings, but he or she acts upon such meanings in order to also participate and, where possible, to change society. According to Castoriadis, politics within this framework becomes "the collective activity whose object" is to put into question the explicit institutions of society while simultaneously creating the conditions for individual and social autonomy.[33] Castoriadis' unique contribution to democratic political theory lies in his keen understanding that autonomy is inextricably linked to forms of civic education that provide the conditions for bringing to light how explicit and implicit power can be used to open up or close down those public spaces that are essential for individuals to meet, address public interests, engage pressing social issues, and participate collectively in shaping public policy. In this view, civic education brings to light "society's instituting power by rendering it explicit . . . it reabsorbs the political into politics as the lucid and deliberate activity whose object is the explicit [production] of society."[34] According to Castoriadis, political agency involves learning how to deliberate, make judgments, and exercise choices, particularly as the latter are brought to bear on critical activities that offer the possibility of change. Civic education as it is experienced and produced throughout a vast array of institutions provides individuals with the opportunity to see themselves as more than simply players within the existing configurations of power of any given society. Every society has an obligation to provide citizens with the capacities, knowledge, and skills necessary for them to be, as Aristotle claimed, "capable of governing and being governed."[35] A democracy cannot work if citizens are not autonomous, self-judging, and independent, qualities that are indispensable for them to make vital judgments and choices about participating in and shaping decisions that affect everyday life, institutional reform, and governmental policy. Hence, civic education becomes the cornerstone of democracy in that the very foundation of self-government is based on people not just having the "typical right to participate; they should also be educated [in the fullest possible way] in order to be *able* to participate."[36]

FROM A PEDAGOGY OF UNDERSTANDING TO A PEDAGOGY OF INTERVENTION

Williams and Castoriadis were clear that pedagogy and the active process of learning were central to any viable notion of citizenship and inclusive democracy. Pedagogy looms large for both of these theorists not as a technique or a priori set of methods but as a political and moral practice. As a political practice, pedagogy illuminates the relationship among power, knowledge, and ideology, while self-consciously, if not self-critically, recognizing the role it plays as a deliberate attempt to influence how and what knowledge and identities are produced within particular sets of social relations. As a moral practice, pedagogy recognizes that what cultural workers, artists, activists, media workers, and others teach cannot be abstracted from what it means to invest in public life, presuppose some notion of the future, or locate oneself in a public discourse.

The moral implications of pedagogy also suggest that our responsibility as public intellectuals cannot be separated from the consequences of the knowledge we produce, the social relations we legitimate, and the ideologies and identities we offer up to students. Refusing to decouple politics from pedagogy means, in part, that teaching in classrooms or in any other public sphere should not only simply honor the experiences students bring to such sites, including the classroom, but should also connect their experiences to specific problems that emanate from the material contexts of their everyday life. Pedagogy in this sense becomes performative in that it is not merely about deconstructing texts but about situating politics itself within a broader set of relations that addresses what it might mean to create modes of individual and social agency that enable rather than shut down democratic values, practices, and social relations. Such a project not only recognizes the political nature of pedagogy, but also situates it within a call for intellectuals to assume responsibility for their actions, to link their teaching to those moral principles that allow us to do something about human suffering, as Susan Sontag has suggested.[37] Part of this task necessitates that cultural studies theorists and educators anchor their own work, however diverse, in a radical project that seriously engages the promise of an unrealized democracy against its really existing and radically incomplete forms. Of crucial importance to such a project is rejecting the assumption that theory can understand social problems without contesting their appearance in public life. Yet, any viable cultural politics needs a socially committed notion of injustice if we are to take seriously what it means to fight for the idea of the good society. I think Zygmunt Bauman is right in arguing that "If there is no room for the idea of *wrong* society, there is hardly much chance for the idea of good society to be born, let alone make waves."[38]

Cultural studies theorists need to be more forceful, if not committed, to linking their overall politics to modes of critique and collective action that address the presupposition that democratic societies are never too just or just enough, and such a recognition means that a society must constantly nurture the possibilities for self-critique, collective agency, and forms of citizenship in which people play a fundamental role in critically discussing, administrating and shaping the material relations of power and ideological forces that bear down on their everyday lives. At stake here is the task, as Jacques Derrida insists, of viewing the project of democracy as a promise, a possibility rooted in an ongoing struggle for economic, cultural, and social justice.[39] Democracy in this instance is not a sutured or formalistic regime; it is the site of struggle itself. The struggle over creating an inclusive and just democracy can take many forms, offers no political guarantees, and provides an important normative dimension to politics as an ongoing process of democratization that never ends. Such a project is based on the realization that a democracy that is open to exchange, question, and self-criticism never reaches the limits of justice. As Bauman observes:

> Democracy is not an institution, but essentially an anti-institutional force, a "rupture" in the otherwise relentless trend of the powers-that-be to arrest change, to silence and to eliminate from the political process all those who have not been "born" into power . . . Democracy expresses itself in a continuous and relentless critique of institutions; democracy is an anarchic, disruptive element inside the political system; essentially, a force for *dissent* and change. One can best recognize a democratic society by its constant complaints that it is *not* democratic enough.[40]

By linking education to the project of an unrealized democracy, cultural studies theorists who work in higher education can move beyond those approaches to pedagogy that reduce it to a methodology like "teaching of the conflicts" or relatedly opening up a culture of questioning. In the most immediate sense, these positions fail to make clear the larger political, normative, and ideological considerations that inform such views of education, teaching, and visions of the future, assuming that education is predicated upon a particular view of the future that students should inhabit. Furthermore, both positions collapse the purpose and meaning of higher education, the role of educators as engaged scholars, and the possibility of pedagogy itself into a rather short-sighted and sometimes insular notion of method, particularly one that emphasizes argumentation and dialogue. This is a disquieting refusal in such discourses to raise broader questions about the social, economic, and political forces shaping the very terrain of higher education — particularly unbridled market forces, or racist and sexist forces that unequally value diverse groups of students within relations of academic power, or what it might mean to engage pedagogy as a basis not merely for understanding but also for participating in the larger world. There is also a general misunderstanding of how teacher authority can be used to create the conditions for an education in democracy without necessarily falling into the trap of simply indoctrinating students.[41] For instance, liberal educator Gerald Graff believes that any notion of critical pedagogy that is self-conscious about its politics and engages students in ways that offer them the possibility for becoming critical — or what Lani Guinier calls the need to educate students "to participate in civic life, and to encourage graduates to give back to the community, which through taxes, made their education possible"[42] — either leaves students out of the conversation or presupposes too much and simply represents a form of pedagogical tyranny. While Graff advocates strongly that educators create the educational practices that open up the possibility of questioning among students, he refuses to connect pedagogical conditions that challenge how they think at the moment to the next step of prompting them to think about changing the world around them so as to expand and deepen its democratic possibilities.

George Lipsitz criticizes academics such as Graff who believe that connecting academic work to social change is at best a burden and, at worst, a collapse into a crude form of propagandizing. Lipsitz suggests that students are subconsciously educated to accept cynicism about the ability of ordinary people to change the conditions under which they live.[43] Teaching students how to argue, draw on their own experiences, or engage in rigorous dialogue says nothing about why they should engage in these actions in the first place. How the culture of argumentation and questioning relates to giving students the tools they need to fight oppressive forms of power, make the world a more meaningful and just place, and develop a sense of social responsibility is missing in work like Graff's because this is part of the discourse of political education, which Graff simply equates to indoctrination or speaking to the converted.[44] Here propaganda and critical pedagogy collapse into each other. Propaganda is generally used to misrepresent knowledge, promote biased knowledge, or produce a view of politics that appears beyond question and critical engagement. While no pedagogical intervention should fall to the level of propaganda, a pedagogy that attempts to empower critical citizens can't and shouldn't avoid politics. Pedagogy must address the relationship between politics, and agency, knowledge and power, subject positions and values, and learning and social change while always being open to debate, resistance, and a culture of questioning. Liberal educators committed to simply raising questions have no language for linking learning to forms of public scholarship that would enable students to consider the important relationship between democratic public life and education, politics and learning. Disabled by a depoliticizing, if not slavish allegiance to a teaching methodology, they have little idea of how to encourage students pedagogically to enter the sphere of the political, enabling them to think about how they might participate in a democracy by taking what they learn "into new locations — a third-grade classroom, a public library, a legislator's office, a park"[45] or for that matter taking on collaborative projects that address the myriad of problems citizens face in a diminishing democracy.

In spite of the professional pretense to neutrality, academics need to do more pedagogically than simply teach students how to be adept at forms of argumentation. Students need to argue and question, but they need much more from their educational experience. The pedagogy of argumentation in and of itself guarantees nothing but it is an essential step towards opening up the space of resistance towards authority, teaching students to think critically about the world around them, and recognizing interpretation and dialogue as a condition for social intervention and transformation in the service an unrealized democratic order. As Amy Gutmann brilliantly argues, education is always political because it is connected to the acquisition of agency and the ability to struggle with ongoing relations of power, and is a precondition for creating informed and critical citizens. For Gutmann, educators need to link education to democracy and recognize pedagogy as an ethical and political practice tied to modes of authority in which the "democratic state recognizes the value of political education in predisposing [students] to accept those ways of life that are consistent with sharing the rights and responsibilities of citizenship in a democratic society."[46] This is a notion of education tied not to the alleged neutrality of teaching methods but to a vision of pedagogy that is directive and interventionist on the side of reproducing a democratic society. Democratic societies need educated citizens who are steeped in more than the skills of argumentation. And it is precisely this democratic project that affirms the critical function of education and refuses to narrow its goals and aspirations to methodological considerations. This is what makes critical pedagogy different from training. And it is precisely the failure to connect learning to its democratic functions and goals that provides rationales for pedagogical approaches that strip the meaning of what it means to be educated from its critical and democratic possibilities.

Raymond Williams and Castoriadis recognized that the crisis of democracy was about not only the crisis of culture but also the crisis of pedagogy and education. Cultural studies theorists would do well to take account of the profound transformations taking place in the public sphere and reclaim pedagogy as a central category of cultural politics. The time has come for cultural studies theorists to distinguish professional caution from political cowardice and recognize that their obligations extend beyond deconstructing texts or promoting a culture of questioning. These are important pedagogical interventions, but they do not go far enough. We need to link knowing with action, learning with social engagement, and this requires addressing the responsibilities that come with teaching students and others to fight for an inclusive and radical democracy by recognizing that education in the broadest sense is not just about understanding, however critical, but also about providing the conditions for assuming the responsibilities we have as citizens to expose human misery and to eliminate the conditions that produce it. I think Bauman is quite right in suggesting that as engaged cultural workers, we need to take up our work as part of a broader democratic project in which the good society

> is a society which thinks it is not just enough, which questions the sufficiency of any achieved level of justice and considers justice always to be a step or more ahead. Above all, it is a society which reacts angrily to any case of injustice and promptly sets about correcting it.[47]

Matters of responsibility, social action, and political intervention do not simply develop out of social critique but also require forms of self-critique. The relationship between knowledge and power on the one hand, and scholarship and politics on the other, should always be self-reflexive about its effects, how it relates to the larger world, whether or not it is open to new understandings, and what it might mean pedagogically to take seriously matters of individual and social responsibility. In short, this project points to the need for educators to articulate cultural studies not only as a resource for theoretical competency and critical understanding, but also as a pedagogical practice that addresses the possibility of interpretation as intervention in the world.

Neoliberalism not only places capital and market relations in a no man's land beyond the reach of compassion, ethics, and decency; it also undermines those basic elements of the social contract and the political and pedagogical relations it presupposes in which self-reliance, confidence in others, and a trust in the longevity of democratic institutions provide the basis for modes of individual autonomy, social agency, and critical citizenship. One of the most serious challenges faced by cultural studies is the need to develop a new language and theoretical tools for contesting a variety of forms of domination associated with neoliberalism in the new millennium. Part of this challenge demands recognizing that the struggles over cultural politics cannot be divorced from the contestations and struggles put into play through the forces of dominant economic and cultural institutions and their respective modes of education. Cultural studies advocates must address the challenge of how to problematize and pluralize the political, engage new sites of pedagogy as crucial and strategic public spheres, and situate cultural studies within an ongoing project that recognizes that the crisis of democracy is about the interrelated crises of politics, culture, and education.

NOTES

1 Zygmunt Bauman (1998), *Work, Consumerism and the New Poor*. Philadelphia: Open University Press, pp. 97–8.

2 Stanley Aronowitz and Peter Bratsis (2002), "State Power, Global Power," in Stanley Aronowitz and Peter Bratsis (eds), *Paradigm Lost: State Theory Reconsidered*. Minneapolis: University of Minnesota Press, p. xvii.

3 Pierre Bourdieu (2001), *Language and Symbolic Power*. Cambridge, MA: Harvard University Press, p. 127.

4 Ibid., p. 128.

5 For some general theoretical principles for addressing the new sites of pedagogy, see Jeffrey R. DiLeo, Walter Jacobs, and Amy Lee (2003), "The Sites of Pedagogy," *Symploke*, 10, (1–2): 7–12.

6 William Greider (2003), "The Right's Grand Ambition: Rolling Back the 20th Century," *The Nation*, May 12, 2003: 11.

7 One interesting analysis on the contingent nature of democracy and public space can be found in Rosalyn Deutsche (1998), *Evictions: Art and Spatial Politics*. Cambridge, MA: The MIT Press.

8 Cited in Robert Dreyfuss (2001), "Grover Norquist: 'Field Marshal' of the Bush Plan," *The Nation*, May 14, 2001. Available online at: www.thenation.com/doc. mhtml?i=20010514&s=dreyfuss. Accessed May 15, 2001.

9 Benjamin R. Barber (2002), "A Failure of Democracy, Not Capitalism," *New York Times*, July 29, 2002: A23.

10 Raymond Williams (1966), *Communications*, rev. edn. New York: Barnes & Noble, p. 15.

11 Bob Herbert (2003), "The Art of False Impression," *New York Times*, August 11, 2003: A17.

12 W. E. B. Du Bois (1985), *Against Racism:Unpublished Essays, Papers, Addresses, 1887–1961*, ed. by Herbert Aptheker Amherst: University of Massachusetts Press.

13 Cornelius Castoriadis, cited in Zygmunt Bauman (2001), *The Individualized Society*. London: Polity Press, p. 127.

14 Michele Barrett (1999), *Imagination in Theory*. New York: New York University Press, p. 161.

15 Zygmunt Bauman and Keith Tester (2001), *Conversations with Zygmunt Bauman*. Malden, MA: Polity Press, p. 32.

16 On the importance of problematizing and pluralizing the political, see Jodi Dean (2000), "The Interface of Political Theory and Cultural Studies," in Jodi Dean (ed.), *Cultural Studies and Political Theory*. Ithaca: Cornell University Press, pp. 1–19.

17 Robert W. McChesney and John Nichols (2002), *Our Media Not Theirs: The Democratic Struggle against Corporate Media*. New York: Seven Stories Press.

18 Zygmunt Bauman (1999), *In Search of Politics*. Stanford, CA: Stanford University Press.

19 Nick Couldry (2004), "In the Place of a Common Culture, What?" *Review of Education, Pedagogy & Cultural Studies*, 26, (1): 6.

20 Raymond Williams (1967), "Preface to Second Edition," *Communications*. New York: Barnes & Noble, pp. 15, 16.

21 Ibid., p. 14.

22 See especially, Raymond Williams (1977), *Marxism and Literature*. New York:

Oxford University Press; Raymond Williams (1983), *The Year 2000*. New York: Pantheon.

23 Williams, *Marxism and Literature*.

24 See Tony Bennett (1998), *Culture: A Reformer's Science*. Thousand Oaks, CA: Sage, p. 223.

25 Antonio Gramsci (1971), *Selections from the Prison Notebooks*. New York, NY: International Press, p. 350.

26 Cornelius Castoriadis (1996), "The Problem of Democracy Today," *Democracy and Nature*, 8: 19.

27 Cornelius Castoriadis (1991), "The Nature and Value of Equity," in *Philosophy, Politics, Autonomy: Essays in Political Philosophy*. New York: Oxford University Press, pp. 124–42.

28 Cornelius Castoriadis (1997), *The World in Fragments*, ed. and trans. by David Ames Curtis. Stanford: Stanford University Press, p. 91.

29 Both quotes are taken from Cornelius Castoriadis (1997), "Culture in a Democratic Society," in David Ames Curtis (ed.), *The Castoriadis Reader*. Malden, MA: Blackwell, pp. 343, 341.

30 Cornelius Castoriadis (1997), "The Crisis of the Identification Process," *Thesis Eleven*, 49: 87–8.

31 Cornelius Castoriadis (1993), "The Anticipated Revolution," *Political and Social Writings*, vol. 3, ed. and trans. by David Ames Curtis. Minneapolis: University of Minnesota Press, pp. 153–4.

32 John Binde (2000), "Toward an Ethic of the Future," *Public Culture*, 12, (1): 65.

33 Cornelius Castoriadis (1991), "The Greek Polis and the Creation of Democracy," in *Philosophy, Politics, Autonomy: Essays in Political Philosophy*. New York: Oxford University Press, p. 102.

34 Cornelius Castoriadis (1991), "Power, Politics, and Autonomy," in *Philosophy, Politics Autonomy: Essays in Political Philosophy*, pp. 144–5.

35 Castoriadis, "Democracy as Procedure and Democracy as Regime," p. 15. It is crucial here to note that Castoriadis develops his notion of democracy and the primacy of education in political life directly from his study of ancient Greek democracy.

36 Castoriadis, "The Problem of Democracy Today," p. 24.

37 Susan Sontag (2003), "Courage and Resistance," *The Nation*, May 5, 2003: 11–14.

38 Zygmunt Bauman (2002), *Society under Siege*. Malden, MA: Blackwell, p. 170.

39 Jacques Derrida (2000), "Intellectual Courage: An Interview," trans. by Peter Krapp, *Culture Machine*, 2: 1–15.

40 Zygmunt Bauman (2001), *The Individualized Society*. London: Polity Press, pp. 54–5.

41 Gerald Graff appears to have made a career out of this issue by misrepresenting the work of Paulo Freire and others, citing theoretical work by critical educators that is outdated and could be corrected by reading anything they might have written in the last five years, creating caricatures of their work, or holding up as an example of what people in critical pedagogy do (or more generally anyone who links pedagogy and politics) the most extreme and ludicrous examples. For more recent representations of this position, see Gerald Graff (2000), "Teaching Politically without Political Correctness," *Radical Teacher*, 58: 26–30; Gerald Graff (2003), *Clueless in Academe*. New Haven: Yale University Press.

42 Lani Guinier (2003), "Democracy Tested," *The Nation*, May 5, 2003: 6. Guinier's position is in direct opposition to that of Graff and is acolytes. For instance, see a conversation between Lani Guinier and Anna Deavere Smith (2002), "Rethinking Power, Rethinking Theater," *Theater*, 31, (3): 31–45.

43 George Lipsitz (2000), "Academic Politics and Social Change," in Jodi Dean (ed.),

Cultural Studies and Political Theory. Ithaca: Cornell University Press, pp. 81–2.

44 For a more detailed response to this kind of watered-down pedagogical practice, see Stanley Aronowitz (2000), *The Knowledge Factory.* Boston: Beacon Press; Henry A. Giroux (2003), *The Abandoned Generation: Democracy Beyond the Culture of Fear.* New York: Palgrave.

45 An interview with Julie Ellison (2002), "New Public Scholarship in the Arts and Humanities," *Higher Education Exchange,* (2002) 20.

46 Amy Gutmann (1998), *Democratic Education.* Princeton, NJ: Princeton University Press, p. 42.

47 Bauman and Tester, *Conversations with Zygmunt Bauman,* p. 63.

CHAPTER 8

Rethinking Education as the Practice of Freedom

Paulo Freire and the Promise of Critical Pedagogy

PAULO FREIRE'S LEGACY

Paulo Freire occupies a hallowed position among the founders of critical pedagogy.[1] The legacy of his work stands as a testimonial to a pedagogical project to which he devoted both his passion and his principles to help students develop a consciousness of freedom, recognize authoritarian tendencies, connect knowledge to power and agency, and learn to read both the word and the world as part of a broader struggle for justice and democracy. Not only did he infuse critical pedagogy with his visionary contributions, but he also played a crucial role in developing a highly successful literacy campaign in Brazil before the onslaught of the *junta* in 1964. Once the military took over the government, Freire was imprisoned for a short time for his efforts to advance the educational movement. He was eventually released and went into exile for a number of years, first in Chile and later in Geneva, Switzerland. Once a semblance of democracy returned to Brazil, he went back to his country in 1980 and played a significant role in shaping its educational policies until his untimely death in 1997. His book *Pedagogy of the Oppressed* is considered one of the classic texts of critical pedagogy and has sold over a million copies, influencing generations of teachers and intellectuals in the United States and abroad. Since the 1980s there has been no intellectual on the North American educational scene who has matched either his theoretical rigor or his moral courage. Indeed, Freire's contribution to a progressive politics of education has become that much more conspicuous in recent years, when many colleges have become dominated by conservative ideologies, hooked on methods, slavishly wedded to instrumentalized accountability measures, and increasingly run by administrators who lack either a broader vision or a critical understanding of education as a force for strengthening the imagination and expanding democratic public life. Within this increasingly oppressive context, critical pedagogy continues to offer the best — perhaps the only — model enabling educators and young people to develop and assert a sense of their rights and responsibilities to participate in self-governance despite growing antidemocratic tendencies in educational theory and practice.

Freire's example is more important now than ever before. With institutions of public and higher education increasingly under siege by a host of neoliberal and conservative forces, it is imperative for educators to acknowledge Freire's understanding of the empowering and democratic potential of education. As the market-driven logic of neoliberal capitalism continues to devalue all aspects of the public interest, one consequence is that the educational concern with excellence has been removed from matters of equity, while higher education, once conceptualized as a public good, has been stripped of its collective meaning and reduced to a private good. Universities now largely conform to the corporate demand that they provide the skills, knowledge, and credentials to build a workforce that will enable the United States to compete against blockbuster growth in China and other Southeast Asian markets and maintain its role as the major global economic and military power. On the other hand, public education has increasingly fallen sway to the forces of privatization, commodification, high-stakes testing, and standardization. Public schools largely inhabited by minorities of class and color fare even worse as they are subject to disciplinary ideologies and measures modeled after prisons.[2] Consequently, there is little interest in understanding the pedagogical foundation of either public or higher education as a deeply civic, political, and moral practice — that is, pedagogy as a practice for freedom. As schooling is increasingly defined by a corporate order and a governing-through-crime paradigm, any vestige of critical education is replaced by training, containment, and the promise of economic security. Similarly, the empowering potential of pedagogy is now subordinated to the narrow regime of "teaching to the test" coupled with an often harsh system of disciplinary control exerted upon not only the students but teachers as well. Teachers are increasingly reduced to the status of technicians and denied any control over their classrooms or school governance structures. Teaching to the test and the corporatization of education provide mutual reinforcement as they become a way of "taming" students and invoking modes of corporate governance in which public school teachers become deskilled, while an increasing number of higher education faculty are reduced to part-time positions and now constitute a new subaltern class of academic labor.

But there is more at stake here than a crisis of authority, the exploitation of faculty labor, and economic considerations taking precedence over all else (to the ultimate detriment of the country's social and economic well-being). Too many classrooms at all levels of schooling now resemble a "dead zone" where any vestige of critical thinking, self-reflection, and imagination quickly migrates to sites outside of the school only to be mediated and corrupted by a corporate-driven media culture. The major issue now driving public schooling is not how to foster civic engagement but how to teach test-taking while finding ways to discipline poorly performing students, many of whom enter the educational system at a disadvantage by virtue of their class or race. Rather than support those students to offset the social factors impacting their educational performance, schools simply try to get rid of any students whose test results may undermine a school district's ranking in what is becoming an ethically sterile and bloodless world of high-stakes testing and empirical score cards.[3] Higher education mimics this logic by reducing its public vision to the interests of capital and redefining itself largely as a credentializing factory for students and as a petri dish for downsizing academic labor. Under such circumstances, rarely do educators ask questions about how schools can prepare students to be informed citizens, nurture their civic imagination, or teach them to be self-reflective about public issues and the world in which they live. As Stanley Aronowitz puts it:

> Few of even the so-called educators ask the question: What matters beyond the reading, writing, and numeracy that are presumably taught in the elementary and secondary grades? The old questioning of what a kid needs to become an informed "citizen" capable of participating in making the large and small public decisions that affect the larger world as well as everyday life receives honorable mention but not serious consideration. These unasked questions are symptoms of a new regime of educational expectations that privileges job readiness above any other educational values.[4]

There is little interest in understanding the pedagogical foundation of higher education as a deeply civic and political project that provides the conditions for individual autonomy and takes liberation and the practice of freedom as a collective goal.

EDUCATION AS THE PROJECT OF FREEDOM

Against this regime of "banking education," "scientific" schooling, and "bare pedagogy" stripped of all critical elements of teaching and learning, Freire believed that education was part of a project of freedom in its broadest sense and eminently political because it offered students the conditions for self-reflection, a self-managed life, and empowering forms of critical agency. Pedagogy in this sense connected learning to social change; it was a project and provocation that challenged students to critically engage with the world so they could act on it. As Aronowitz puts it in his analysis of Freire's work on literacy and critical pedagogy:

> Thus, for Freire literacy was not a means to prepare students for the world of subordinated labor or "careers," but a preparation for a self-managed life. And self-management could only occur when people have fulfilled three goals of education: self-reflection, that is, realizing the famous poetic phrase, "know thyself," which is an understanding of the world in which they live, in its economic, political and, equally important, its psychological dimensions.

Specifically, "critical" pedagogy helps the learner become aware of the forces that have hitherto ruled their lives and especially shaped their consciousness. The third goal is to help set the conditions for producing a new life, a new set of arrangements where power has been, at least in tendency, transferred to those who literally make the social world by transforming nature and themselves.[5]

What Freire made clear in *Pedagogy of the Oppressed*, his most influential work, is that pedagogy at its best is not about training in techniques or methods, nor does it involve coercion or political indoctrination. Indeed, far from being a mere method or an a priori technique to be imposed on all students, pedagogy is a political and moral practice that provides the knowledge, skills, and social relations that enable students to explore the possibilities of what it means to be critical citizens while expanding and deepening their participation in the promise of a substantive democracy. Critical thinking for Freire was not an object lesson in test-taking, but a tool for self-determination and civic engagement. Critical pedagogy could afford students the opportunity to read, write, and learn from a position of agency — to engage in a culture of question that demands far more than competency in rote learning. Critical pedagogy, for Freire, was imagining literacy as not simply the mastering of specific skills also a mode of intervention, a way of learning about and reading the word as a basis for intervening in the world. It was not about the task of memorizing so-called facts, decontextualized and unrelated to present conditions. To the contrary, it was about offering a way of thinking beyond the seeming naturalness or inevitability of the current state of things, challenging assumptions validated by "common sense," soaring beyond the immediate confines of one's experiences, entering into a critical dialogue with history, and imagining a future that would not merely reproduce the present.

By way of illustration, Freirean pedagogy might stage the dynamic interplay of audio, visual, and print texts as part of a broader examination of history itself as a site of struggle, one that might offer some insights into students' own experiences and lives in the contemporary moment. For example, a history class might involve reading and watching films about school desegregation in the 1950s and 1960s as part of a broader pedagogical engagement with the civil rights movement and the massive protests that developed over educational access and student rights to literacy. The classroom would also open up opportunities to talk about why these struggles are still part of the experience of many American youth today, particularly those marginalized by class and color who are denied equality of opportunity by virtue of market-based rather than legal segregation. Students could be asked to write short papers that speculate on the meaning and the power of literacy and why it was so central to the civil rights movement. These may be read by the entire class with each student elaborating his or her position and offering commentary as a way of entering into a critical discussion of the history of racial exclusion, reflecting on how its ideologies and formations still haunt American society in spite of the triumphal dawn of an allegedly post-racial Obama era. In this pedagogical context, students learn how to expand their own sense of agency, while recognizing that to be voiceless is to be powerless.

Central to such a pedagogy is shifting the emphasis from teachers to students and making visible the relationships among knowledge, authority, and power. Giving students the opportunity to be problem-posers and engage in a culture of questioning in the classroom foregrounds the crucial issue of who has control over the conditions of learning and how specific modes of knowledge, identities, and authority are constructed within particular sets of classroom relations. Under such circumstances, knowledge is not simply received by students, but actively transformed, open to be challenged, and related to the self as an essential step towards agency, self-representation, and learning how to govern rather than simply be governed. At the same time, students also learn how to engage others in critical dialogue and be held accountable for their views.

For Freire, critical thinking offered a way of not simply understanding the present but thinking beyond it. Theodor Adorno captures the spirit of Freire's notion of critical thinking by insisting:

> Thinking is not the intellectual reproduction of what already exists anyway. As long as it doesn't break off, thinking has a secure hold on possibility. Its insatiable aspect, its aversion to being quickly and easily satisfied, refuses the foolish wisdom of resignation . . . Open thinking points beyond itself.[6]

Like Adorno, Freire rejected those regimes of educational degradation organized around the demands of the market, instrumentalized knowledge, and the priority of training over the pursuit of the imagination, critical thinking, and the teaching of freedom and social responsibility. Rather than assume the mantle of a false impartiality, Freire believed that critical pedagogy involved the recognition of both the ways in which human life is conditioned, though not determined, and the crucial necessity of not only reading the world critically but also intervening in the larger social order as part of the responsibility of an informed citizenry.

Freire argued that the political and moral demands of pedagogy amount to more than the school and classroom being merely the instrument of official power or assuming the role of an apologist for the existing order, as the Obama administration seems to believe — given its willingness to give Bush's reactionary educational policies a new name and a new lease on life. Freire rejected those modes of pedagogy that supported economic models and modes of agency in which freedom is reduced to consumerism and economic activity is freed from any criteria except profitability and the reproduction of a rapidly expanding mass of wasted humans.

PEDAGOGY AS A PERFORMATIVE PRACTICE

Critical pedagogy attempts to understand how power works through the production, distribution, and consumption of knowledge within particular institutional contexts and seeks to constitute students as informed subjects and social agents. In this instance, the issue of how identities, values, and desires are shaped in the classroom becomes the ground of politics. Critical pedagogy is thus invested in both the practice of self-criticism about the values that inform teaching and a critical self-consciousness regarding what it means to equip students with analytical skills to be self-reflective about the knowledge and values they confront in classrooms. Moreover, such a pedagogy attempts not only to provide the conditions for students to understand texts and different modes of intelligibility, but also opens up new avenues for them to make better moral judgments that will enable them to assume some sense of responsibility to the other in light of those judgments. For Freire, pedagogy has to be meaningful in order to be critical and transformative. This means that personal experience becomes a valuable resource that gives students the opportunity to relate their own narratives, social relations, and histories to what is being taught. It also signifies a resource to help students locate themselves in the concrete conditions of their daily lives while furthering their understanding of the limits often imposed by such conditions. Under such circumstances, experience becomes a starting point, an object of inquiry that can be affirmed, critically interrogated, and used as a resource to engage broader modes of knowledge and understanding.

Freire was acutely aware that what makes critical pedagogy so dangerous to ideological fundamentalists, the ruling elites, religious extremists, and right-wing nationalists all over the world is that central to its very definition is the task of educating students to become critical agents who actively question and negotiate the relationships between theory and practice, critical analysis and common sense, and learning and social change. Critical pedagogy opens up a space where students should be able to come to terms with their own power as critically engaged citizens; it provides a sphere where the unconditional freedom to question and assert one's convictions is made central to the purpose of public schooling and higher education, if not democracy itself. And as political and moral practice, a way of knowing, and literate engagement, critical pedagogy attempts to "make evident the multiplicity and complexity of history."[7] History in this sense is engaged as a narrative open to critical dialogue rather than a predefined text to be memorized and accepted unquestioningly. Pedagogy in this instance provides the conditions to cultivate in students a healthy scepticism about power, a "willingness to temper any reverence for authority with a sense of critical awareness."[8] As a performative practice, pedagogy takes as one of its goals the opportunity for students to be able to reflectively frame their own relationship to the ongoing project of an unfinished democracy. It is precisely this relationship between democracy and pedagogy that is so threatening to so many of our educational leaders and spokespersons today, and it is also the reason why Freire's work on critical pedagogy and literacy is more relevant today than when it was first published.

According to Freire, all forms of pedagogy represent a particular way of understanding society and a specific commitment to the future. Critical pedagogy in particular presupposes a notion of a more equal and just future; and, as such, it always functions as a provocation that takes students beyond the world they know in order to expand the range of human possibilities and democratic values. Unlike dominant modes of teaching, critical pedagogy insists that one of the fundamental tasks of educators is to make sure that the future points the way to a more socially just world, a world in which critique and possibility — in conjunction with the values of reason, freedom, and equality — function to alter, as part of a broader democratic project, the ground upon which life is lived. Though it rejects a notion of literacy as the transmission of facts or skills tied to the latest market trends, critical pedagogy is hardly a prescription for political indoctrination, as the advocates of standardization and testing often insist. It offers students new ways to think and act creatively and independently while making clear that the educator's task, as Aronowitz points out, "is to encourage human agency, not mold it in the manner of Pygmalion."[9]

Critical pedagogy gives education its most valued purpose and meaning, and for this very reason it is a position that threatens right-wing private advocacy groups, neoconservative politicians, and conservative extremists. Such individuals and groups are keenly aware that critical pedagogy with its emphasis on the hard work of critical analysis, moral judgments, and social responsibility goes to the very heart of what it means to address real inequalities of power at the social level and to conceive of education as a project for freedom while at the same time foregrounding a series of important and often ignored questions such as: What is the role of teachers and academics as public intellectuals? Whose interests do public and higher education serve? How might it be possible to understand and engage the diverse contexts in which education takes place? What is the role of education as a public good? How do we make knowledge meaningful in order to make it critical and transformative? How do we democratize governance? Against the right-wing view that equates any suggestion of politics with indoctrination, critical pedagogy is concerned with offering students new ways to think critically and act with authority as independent political agents in the classroom and in larger society. In other words, it is concerned with providing students with the skills and knowledge necessary for them to expand their capacities, first to question the deep-seated assumptions and myths that legitimate the archaic and disempowering social practices structuring every aspect of society and then to take responsibility for intervening in the world they inhabit.

THE POLITICS OF ACADEMIC LABOR

What critical pedagogy does insist upon is that education cannot be neutral. It is inevitably a deliberate attempt to influence how and what knowledge, values, desires, and identities are produced within particular sets of class and social relations. Moreover, it is always directive in its attempt to teach students to inhabit a particular mode of agency; enable them to understand the larger world and one's role in it in a specific way; define their relationship, if not responsibility, to diverse others; and experience in the classroom some sort of understanding of a more just, imaginative, and democratic life. Pedagogy is by definition directive, but that does not mean it is merely a form of indoctrination. On the contrary, as Freire argued, education as a practice for freedom must expand the capacities necessary for human agency, and hence the possibilities for how academic labor should be configured to ensure such a project that is integral to democracy itself. Foundational to critical pedagogy is the recognition that the way we educate our youth is related to the future that we hope for and that such a future should offer students a life that leads to the deepening of freedom and social justice. Surely this suggests that even within the privileged precincts of higher education, educators should nourish those pedagogical practices that promote "a concern with keeping the forever unexhausted and unfulfilled human potential open, fighting back all attempts to foreclose and pre-empt the further unravelling of human possibilities, prodding human society to go on questioning itself and preventing that questioning from ever stalling or being declared finished."[10] In other words, critical pedagogy forges an expanded notion of politics and agency through a language of scepticism and possibility, and a culture of openness, debate, and engagement — all those elements now at risk because of the recent attacks being waged against public and higher education. This language of critique and educated hope was Paulo Freire's legacy, one that invokes dangerous memories and for this very reason is increasingly absent from any conservative discourse about current educational problems and appropriate avenues of reform. Unfortunately, it is also absent from much of the discussion on the current status of academic labor.

When I began my career teaching high school students, Freire became an essential influence in helping me to understand the broad contours of my ethical responsibilities as a teacher. Later, his work would help me come to terms with the complexities of my relationship to universities as powerful and privileged institutions that seemed far removed from the daily life of the working-class communities in which I had grown up. I first met Paulo in the early 1980s, just after I had been denied tenure by John Silber, then the notorious right-wing President of Boston University. Paulo was giving a talk at the University of Massachusetts and he came to my house in Boston for dinner. Given Paulo's reputation as a powerful intellectual, I recall initially being astounded by his profound humility. I remember being greeted with such warmth and sincerity that I felt completely at ease with him. We talked for a long time that night about his exile, how I had been attacked by a right-wing university administration, what it meant to be a working-class intellectual, and the risks one had to take to make a difference. I was in a very bad place after being denied tenure and had no idea what the future would hold. On that night, a friendship was forged that would span almost two decades until Paulo's death. I am convinced that had it not been for Paulo Freire and Donaldo Macedo[11] — a linguist, translator, and a friend of Paulo's and mine — I might not have stayed in the field of education. Their passion for education and their profound humanity convinced me that teaching was not a job like any other job, but a crucial site of struggle. With their examples in mind, I also arrived at the conclusion that ultimately whatever risks had to be taken to defend education as a source of empowerment for teachers and students were well worth it.

I have encountered many intellectuals throughout my career in academe, but Paulo was exceptionally generous, eager to help young intellectuals publish their work, willing to write letters of support, and always gave as much as possible of himself in the service of others. The early 1980s were exciting years in education studies in the United States, and Paulo was really at the center of it. Paulo and I together started a Critical Education and Culture series with Bergin & Garvey Publishers, which brought out the work of more than 60 young authors, many of whom went on to have a significant influence in universities. Jim Bergin became Paulo's patron as his American publisher; Donaldo became his translator and co-author; Ira Shor also played an important role in spreading Paulo's work and wrote a number of brilliant books integrating both theory and practice as part of Paulo's notion of critical pedagogy. Together we worked tirelessly to circulate Paulo's work, always with the hope of inviting him back to America so we could meet, talk, drink good wine, and deepen a commitment to critical education that had all marked us in different ways. Of course, it is difficult to write simply about Paulo as a person because who he was and how he entered one's space and the world could never be separated from his politics. Hence, I want to try to provide a broader context for my own understanding of him as well as those ideas that consistently shaped our relationship and his relationship with others.

BIOGRAPHY AS THE PEDAGOGY OF HOPE

Paulo, occupying the often difficult space between existing politics and the as yet possible, spent his life guided by the belief that the radical elements of democracy are worth struggling for, that critical education is a basic element of social change, and that how we think about politics is inseparable from how we come to understand the world, power, and the moral life we aspire to lead. In many ways, Paulo embodied the important but often complicated relationship between the personal and the political. His own life was a testimonial not only to his belief in democratic principles, but also to the notion that one's life had to come as close as possible to modeling the social relations and experiences that spoke to a more humane and democratic future. At the same time, Paulo never moralized about politics; he never employed the discourse of shame, or collapsed the political into the personal when talking about social issues. For him, private problems were always to be understood in relation to larger public issues. Everything about him suggested that the first order of politics was humility, compassion, and a willingness to fight against human injustices. For example, Paulo never reduced an understanding of homelessness, poverty, and unemployment to the failing of individual character, laziness, indifference, or a lack of personal responsibility, but instead viewed such issues as complex systemic problems generated by economic and political structures that produced massive amounts of inequality, suffering, and despair — and social problems far beyond the reach of limited individual capacities to cause or redress.

Freire's belief in democracy as well as his deep and abiding faith in the ability of people to resist the weight of oppressive institutions and ideologies were forged in a spirit of struggle tempered by the grim realities of his own imprisonment and exile and mediated by both a fierce sense of outrage and the belief that education and hope are the conditions of social action and political change. Acutely aware that many contemporary versions of hope occupied their own corner in Disneyland, Freire fought against such appropriations and was passionate about recovering and rearticulating hope through, in his words, an "understanding of history as opportunity and not determinism."[12] Hope for Freire was a practice of witnessing, an act of moral imagination that enabled progressive educators and others to think otherwise in order to act otherwise. Hope demanded an anchoring in transformative practices, and one of the tasks of the progressive educator was to "unveil opportunities for hope, no matter what the obstacles may be."[13] Underlying Freire's politics of hope was a view of radical pedagogy that located itself on the dividing lines where the relations between domination and oppression, power and powerlessness, continued to be produced and reproduced. For Freire, hope as a defining element of politics and pedagogy always meant listening to and working with the poor and other subordinate groups so that they might speak and act in order to alter dominant relations of power. Whenever we talked, Paulo never allowed himself to become cynical. He was always full of life, taking great delight in eating a good meal, listening to music, opening himself up to new experiences, and engaging in dialogue with a passion that both embodied his own politics and confirmed the lived presence of others.

Committed to the specific, the play of context, and the possibility inherent in what he called the unfinished nature of human beings, Freire offered no recipes for those in need of instant theoretical and political fixes. I was often amazed at how patient Paulo always was in dealing with people who wanted him to provide menu-like answers to the problems they raised about education, people who did not realize that their demands undermined his own insistence that critical pedagogy is defined by its context and must be approached as a project of individual and social transformation — that it could never be reduced to a mere method. Contexts mattered to Paulo. He was concerned with how contexts mapped in distinctive ways the relationships among knowledge, language, everyday life, and the machineries of power. For Freire, pedagogy was strategic and performative: considered as part of a broader political practice for democratic change, critical pedagogy was never viewed as an a priori discourse to be asserted or a methodology to be implemented, or for that matter a slavish attachment to forms of knowledge that are deemed to be quantifiable. On the contrary, Freirean pedagogy was a conscientious act arising from a deep awareness of one's situatedness and organized around the "instructive ambivalence of disrupted borders,"[14] a complex practice of bafflement, interruption, understanding, and intervention that emerged from ongoing historical, social, and economic struggles. Paulo's profound patience and wisdom in refusing to provide simple answers and instead articulating and rearticulating these complexities were always instructive for me, and I am convinced that it was only later in my life that I was able to begin to emulate his approach in my own interactions with audiences.

Paulo was a cosmopolitan intellectual who never overlooked the details in everyday life and the connections the latter had to a much broader, global world. He consistently reminded us that political struggles are won and lost in those specific yet hybridized spaces that anchored narratives of everyday experience within the social gravity and material force of institutional power. Any pedagogy that calls itself Freirean must acknowledge this key principle that our current knowledge is contingent on particular historical contexts and political forces. For example, each classroom will be affected by the different experiences students bring to the class, the resources made available for classroom use, the relations of governance bearing down on teacher–student relations, the authority exercised by administrations regarding the boundaries of teacher autonomy, and the theoretical and political discourses used by teachers to read and frame their responses to the diverse historical, economic, and cultural forces informing classroom dialogue. Any understanding of the project and practices that inform critical pedagogy has to begin with recognizing the forces at work in such contexts and which must be confronted by educators and schools everyday. Although Freire was a theoretician of radical contextualism, he also acknowledged the importance of understanding the particular and the local in relation to larger global and transnational forces. For Freire, literacy as a way of reading and changing the world had to be reconceived within a broader understanding of citizenship, democracy, and justice that was global and transnational. Making the pedagogical more political in this case meant moving beyond the celebration of specialized disciplines and developing a praxis that foregrounded "power, history, memory, relational analysis, justice (not just representation), and ethics as the issues central to transnational democratic struggles."[15] Culture and politics mutually informed each other in ways that spoke to histories whose presences and absences had to be narrated as part of a larger struggle over democratic values, relations, and modes of agency.

Freire recognized that it was through the complex production of experience within multilayered registers of power and culture that people recognized, narrated, and transformed their place in the world. Paulo challenged the separation of cultural experiences from politics, pedagogy, and power itself, but he did not make the mistake of many of his contemporaries by conflating cultural experience with a limited notion of identity politics. While he had a profound faith in the ability of ordinary people to shape history and their own destinies, he refused to romanticize individuals and cultures that experienced oppressive social conditions. Of course, he recognized that power privileged certain forms of cultural capital — certain modes of speaking, living, being, and acting in the world — but he did not believe that subordinate or oppressed cultures were free of the contaminating effects of oppressive ideological and institutional relations of power. Consequently, culture — as a crucial educational force influencing larger social structures as well as the most intimate spheres of identity formation — could be viewed as nothing less than an ongoing site of struggle and power in contemporary society.

Freire's insistence that education was about the making and changing of contexts did more than seize upon the political and pedagogic potentialities to be found across a spectrum of social sites and practices in society, which, of course, included but were not limited to the school. He also challenged the separation of culture from the political sphere by calling attention to how diverse technologies of power work pedagogically within governing institutions to produce, regulate, and legitimate particular forms of knowing, belonging, feeling, and desiring. For Freire, political engagement was also about creating the conditions for people to govern rather than just be governed and for individuals to become capable of mobilizing social movements against the oppressive economic, racial, and sexist practices put into place by colonization, global capitalism, and other oppressive structures of power.

Paulo Freire left behind a corpus of work that emerged out of a lifetime of struggle and commitment. Refusing the comfort of master narratives, Freire's work was always unsettled and unsettling, restless yet engaging. Unlike so much of the politically arid and morally vacuous academic and public prose that characterizes contemporary intellectual discourse, Freire's work was consistently fuelled by a healthy moral rage over the needless oppression and suffering he witnessed throughout his life as he travelled all over the globe. Similarly, his work exhibited a vibrant and dynamic quality that allowed it to grow, refuse easy formulas, and open itself to new political realities and projects. Freire's genius was to elaborate a theory of social change and engagement that was neither vanguardist nor populist. Combining theoretical rigor, social relevance, and moral compassion, Freire gave new meaning to the politics of daily life while affirming the importance of theory in opening up the space of critique, possibility, politics, and practice. For the critical educators influenced by Freire's insights, experience is a fundamental element of teaching and learning, but its distinctive configuration among different groups does not guarantee the legitimacy of particular versions of the truth; rather, experience must itself become an object for analysis. How students experience the world and speak to that experience is always a function of unconscious and conscious commitments, of politics, of access to multiple languages and literacies — thus experience always has to take a detour through theory as an object of self-reflection, critique, and possibility. For Freire, theory and language were sites of struggle and possibility that gave experience, meaning, and action a political direction, and any attempt to reproduce the binarism of theory versus politics was repeatedly condemned by Freire.[16] At the same time, while Paulo loved theory, he never reified it. When he talked about Freud, Marx, or Erich Fromm, one could feel his intense passion for ideas. Yet, he never treated theory as an end in itself; it was always a resource whose value lay in understanding, critically engaging, and transforming the world as part of a larger project of freedom and justice. Not only did history and experience become contested sites of struggle, but theory and language were also constantly subject to critical reflection. To say that Paulo's joy around such matters was infectious is to understate the formidable impact that his presence played in the intellectual and political lives of so many people he met throughout his life.

I had a close personal relationship with Paulo for over 15 years, and I was always moved by the way in which his political courage and intellectual reach were matched by a love of life and generosity of spirit. The political and the personal mutually informed Freire's life and work. He was always the curious student, even as he assumed the role of a critical teacher. As he moved between the private and the public, he revealed an astonishing gift for making everyone he met feel valued. His very presence embodied what it meant to combine political struggle and moral courage, to make hope meaningful and despair unpersuasive. Vigilant in bearing witness to the individual and collective suffering of others, Paulo shunned the role of the isolated intellectual as an existential hero who struggles alone. He believed that intellectuals must respond to the call for making the pedagogical more political with a continuing effort to build those coalitions, affiliations, and social movements capable of mobilizing real power and promoting substantive social change. Politics was more than a gesture of translation, representation, and dialogue: to be effective, it had to be about creating the conditions for people to become critical agents alive to the responsibilities of democratic public life. Paulo understood keenly that democracy was threatened by a powerful military-industrial complex, the rise of extremists groups, and the increased power of the warfare state. He also recognized the pedagogical force of a corporate and militarized culture that eroded the moral and civic capacities of citizens to think beyond the common sense of official power, its legitimating ideologies, and the hatemongering of a right-wing media apparatus. Paulo strongly believed that democracy could not last without providing critical counter-narratives against the dominant pedagogy and restoring the formative culture which made democratic public life possible.

Educational sites within both schools and the broader culture represented some of the most important venues through which to affirm public values, support a critical citizenry, and resist those who would deny the empowering functions of teaching and learning. He never lost sight of Robert Hass' claim that the job of education "is to refresh the idea of justice going dead in us all the time."[17] Against the growing forces of authoritarian pedagogy that are taking hold in the United States and other countries, Freire's work offers both a resource for critique and a language of possibility. His legacy and work stand as a reminder that even in the worst of times, pedagogy is crucial to the meaning of politics because it not only works to create the pedagogical practices that make self and social agency possible, but also recognizes the necessity of enabling students and others to struggle collectively in order to build the formative culture — "a complex of beliefs, values and practices that nurture equality, cooperation and freedom"[18] — necessary to affirm public values, inspire the social imagination, and sustain democratic institutions.

NOTES

1 One of the best sources on the life and work of Paulo Freire is Peter Mayo (2004), *Liberating Praxis: Freire's Legacy for Radical Education and Politics*. New York: Praeger. Two of the best translators of Freire's work to the American context are Donaldo Macedo (1994), *Literacies of Power*. Boulder: Westview; and Ira Shor (1987), *Freire for the Classroom*. Portsmouth, NH: Boynton/Cook.

2 I have take up this issue extensively in Henry A. Giroux (2010), *Youth in a Suspect Society: Democracy or Disposability?* New York: Palgrave. See also Kenneth Saltman and David Gabbard (eds), *Education as Enforcement: The Militarization and Corporatization of Schools*, 2nd edn. New York: Routledge.

3 On the issue of containment and the pedagogy of punishment, see Jenny Fisher, "'The Walking Wounded': The Crisis of Youth, School Violence, and Precarious Pedagogy," *Review of Education, Cultural Studies, and Pedagogy* (in press).

4 Stanley Aronowitz (2008), *Against Schooling: For an Education That Matters*. Boulder, CO: Paradigm Publishers, p. xii.

5 Stanley Aronowitz (2009), "Forward," in Sheila L. Macrine (ed.), *Critical Pedagogy in Uncertain Times: Hope and Possibilities*. New York: Palgrave MacMillan, p. ix.

6 Theodor Adorno (1998), "Education after Auschwitz," in *Critical Models: Interventions and Catchwords*. New York: Columbia University Press, pp. 291–2.

7 Edward Said (2001), *Reflections on Exile and Other Essays*. Cambridge, MA: Harvard University Press, p. 141.

8 Ibid., p. 501.

9 Stanley Aronowitz (1998), "Introduction," in Paulo Freire, *Pedagogy of Freedom*. Boulder: Rowman and Littlefield, pp. 10–11.

10 Zygmunt Bauman and Keith Tester (2001), *Conversations with Zygmunt Bauman*. Malden, MA: Polity Press, p. 4.

11 See Paulo Freire and Donaldo Macedo (1987), *Literacy: Reading the Word and the World*. Amherst, MA: Bergin and Garvey.

12 Paulo Freire (1994), *Pedagogy of Hope*. New York: Continuum, p. 91.

13 Ibid., p. 9.

14 Cited in Homi Bhabha (1994), "The Enchantment of Art," in Carol Becker and Ann Wiens (eds), *The Artist in Society*. Chicago: New Art Examiner, p. 28.

15 M. Jacqui Alexander and Chandra Talpade Mohanty (1997), "Introduction: Genealogies, Legacies, Movements," in *Feminist Genealogies, Colonial Legacies, Democratic Futures*. New York: Routledge, p. xix.

16 Surely, Freire would have agreed wholeheartedly with Stuart Hall's insight that "It is only through the way in which we represent and imagine ourselves that we come to know how we are constituted and who we are. There is no escape from the politics of representation." Stuart Hall (1992), "What is this 'Black' in Popular Culture?" in Gina Dent (ed.), *Black Popular Culture*. Seattle: Bay Press, p. 30.

17 Robert Hass, cited in Sarah Pollock (1992), "Robert Hass," *Mother Jones*, March/April: 22.

18 Sheldon S. Wolin (2008), *Democracy Incorporated: Managed Democracy and the Specter of Inverted Totalitarianism*. Princeton, NJ: Princeton University Press, pp. 260–1.

Does Critical Pedagogy Have a Future?

CHAPTER 9

Does Critical Pedagogy Have a Future?

Henry A. Giroux
Interviewed by Manuela Guilherme[1]

Manuela Guilherme: In your work, you show a deep and consistent concern for civic life in a globalized world. How do you define a more globalized form of citizenship?

Henry Giroux: Citizenship invokes a notion of the social in which individuals have duties and responsibilities to others. A globalized notion of citizenship extends the concept of the social contract beyond the boundaries of the nation-state, invoking a broader notion of democracy in which the global becomes the space for exercising civic courage, social responsibility, politics, and compassion for the plight of others. Clearly, for example, citizens' obligations to the environment cannot be seen as merely a national problem. At the same time, a globalized notion of citizenship accentuates matters of responsibility and interdependence, invoking citizenship not just as a political issue of rights and entitlements but also as an ethical challenge to narrow the gap between the promise and the reality of a global democracy. It is also important to recognize that the idea of citizenship cannot be separated from the spaces in which citizenship is developed and nurtured. This suggests that any struggle over a globalized and meaningful notion of citizenship that encourages debate and social responsibility must include fostering and developing democratic public spheres such as schools, media, and other institutions in which critical civic pedagogies can be developed. The notion of global citizenship suggests that politics must catch up with power, which today has removed itself from local and state control. New political structures, global institutions, and social movements that can reach and control the flows of uncontrolled power, particularly economic power, must develop. Real citizenship in the global sense means enabling people to have a say in the shaping of international laws governing trade, the environment, labor, criminal justice, social protections, and so on. Citizenship as

169

the essence of politics has to catch up with new social formations that the current political and social institutions of the nation-state cannot influence, contain, or control.

MG: What specific capacities does this new cosmopolitan citizen need to develop?

HG: Citizens for a global democracy need to be aware of the interrelated nature of all aspects of physical, spiritual, and cultural life. This means having a deep-rooted understanding of the relational nature of global dependencies, whether we are talking about the ecosphere or the circuits of capital. Second, citizens need to be multi-literate in ways that not only allow them access to new information and media-based technologies but also enable them to be border-crossers capable of engaging, learning from, understanding, and being tolerant of and responsible to matters of difference and otherness. This suggests reclaiming, as central to any viable notion of citizenship, the values of mutual worth, dignity, and ethical responsibility. At stake here is the recognition that there is a certain civic virtue and ethical value in extending our exposure to difference and otherness. Citizens need to cultivate loyalties that extend beyond the nation-state, beyond a theoretical distinction in which the division between friend and enemy is mediated exclusively by national boundaries. Clearly, citizenship as a form of empowerment means acquiring the skills that enable one to critically examine history and to resuscitate those dangerous memories in which knowledge expands the possibilities for self-knowledge and critical and social agency. Knowledge need not be only indigenous to be empowering. Individuals must also have some distance from the knowledge of their birth, origins, and specificity of place. This suggests appropriating that knowledge that emerges through dispersal, travel, border-crossings, diaspora, and through global communications. A cosmopolitan notion of citizenship must recognize the importance of a culture of questioning to any global concept of democracy. The global public sphere must be a place where authority can be questioned, power held accountable, and dissent seen as having a positive value. There is a growing authoritarianism in many parts of the world, particularly the United States. In facing this threat to democracy around the globe, it is crucial for educators, parents, young people, workers, and others to fight the collapse of citizenship into forms of jingoistic nationalism. This means educators and others will have to reinvigorate democracy by assuming the pedagogical project of prioritizing debate, deliberation, dissent, dialogue, and public spaces as central to any viable notion of global citizenship. In addition, if citizenship is to be global, it must develop a sense of radical humanism that comprehends social and environmental justice beyond national boundaries. Human suffering does not stop at the borders of nation-states.

MG: In my view, one of your most inspiring proposals is the claim for

a more dignified and committed role of the educator at all levels of the educational system. Do you agree with this being one of your main goals? How do you summarize the main goals of your writing?

HG: I have always argued that teachers must be treated as a critical public resource, essential not only to the importance of an empowering educational experience for students but also to the formation of a democratic society. At the institutional level, this means giving teachers an opportunity to exercise power over the conditions of their work. We cannot separate what teachers do from the economic and political conditions that shape their work, that is, their academic labor. This means they should have both the time and the power to institute structural conditions that allow them to produce curricula, collaborate with parents, conduct research, and work with communities. Moreover, school buildings must be limited in size to permit teachers and others to construct, maintain, and enhance a democratic community for themselves and their students. We are talking not only about the issue of class size but also about how space is institutionally constructed as part of a political project compatible with the formation of lived, democratic communities. Second, teachers should be given the freedom to shape the school curricula, engage in shared research with other teachers and with others outside of the school, and play a central role in the governance of the school and their labor. Educational empowerment for teachers cannot be separated from issues of power and governance. Educators should be valued as public intellectuals who connect critical ideas, traditions, disciplines, and values to the public realm of everyday life. But at the same time, educators must assume the responsibility for connecting their work to larger social issues, while raising questions about what it means to provide students with the skills they need to write policy papers, be resilient against defeat, analyze social problems, and learn the tools of democracy and how to make a difference in one's life as a social agent.

MG: You also propose a close link between theory and practice, which have been made separate in our academic systems and in our societies. Can you please expand on the advantages of linking them for the purposes of citizenship education?

HG: Citizenship education must take seriously the connections between theory and practice, reflection and action. All too often, theory in academia slides into a form of theoreticism in which it either becomes an end in itself, relegated to the heights of an arcane, excessive, and utterly ethereal existence, or degenerates into a form of careerism, offering the fastest track to academic prominence. But theory is hardly a luxury connected to the fantasy of intellectual power. On the contrary, theory is a resource that enables us to both define and respond to problems as they emerge in particular contexts. Its transformative power resides in the possibility of enabling forms of agency, not in its ability to solve problems. Its politics is linked to the ability to imagine the world differently and then to act differently, and this is its offering to any viable notion of citizenship education. At stake here is not the question of whether theory matters, which should be as obvious as asking whether critical thought matters, but the issue of what the political and public responsibilities of theory might be, particularly in theorizing a global politics for the twenty-first century. Theory is not just about contemplation or paving a way to academic stardom; it is foremost about intervention in the world, raising ideas to the worldly space of public life, social responsibility, and collective intervention. If learning is a fundamental part of social change, then theory is a crucial resource for studying the full range of everyday practices that circulate throughout diverse social formations and for finding better forms of knowledge and modes of intervention in the face of the challenge of either a growing authoritarianism or a manufactured cynicism.

MG: You have often been accused of equating education with instilling ideological propaganda in students, and you have rejected these accusations by pointing to critical pedagogy. How do you think critical pedagogy promotes a free mind?

HG: Far from instilling propaganda in students, I think critical pedagogy begins with the assumption that knowledge and power should always be subject to debate, held accountable, and critically engaged. Central to the very definition of critical pedagogy is a common concern for reforming schools and developing modes of pedagogical practice in which teachers and students become critical agents actively questioning and negotiating the relationships between theory and practice, critical analysis and common sense, and learning and social change. This is hardly a prescription for propaganda. I think critical pedagogy is often seen as dangerous because it is built around a project that goes to the very heart of what education is about and is framed around a series of important and often ignored questions such as: Why do we, as educators, do what we do the way we do it? Whose interest does schooling serve? How might it be possible to understand and engage the diverse contexts in which education takes place? But critical pedagogy is not simply concerned with offering students new ways to think critically and act with authority as agents in the classroom; it is also concerned with providing teachers and students with the skills and knowledge to expand their capacities both to question deep-seated assumptions and myths that legitimate the most archaic and disempowering social practices that structure every aspect of society and to take responsibility for intervening in the world. In other words, critical pedagogy forges critique and agency through a language of skepticism and possibility.

MG: The relevance of humanities departments in universities worldwide is being reconsidered by the university management, by the labor market

and the wider society more generally. In your opinion, how can those departments face the challenge not only of survival but also of countering the "crisis of culture," which you cite from Raymond Williams, and of reclaiming their relevance?

HG: In recent years, I have been working on a series of projects that address a number of interrelated concerns: the substantive role of culture, in particular popular culture, as the primary site where pedagogy and learning take place, especially for young people; the role that academics and cultural workers might assume as public intellectuals mindful of the constitutive force culture plays in shaping public memory, moral awareness, and political agency; the significance of the university, specifically the humanities, as a public sphere essential to sustaining a vibrant democracy yet under assault by the forces of corporatization; and the centrality of youth as an ethical register for measuring the changing nature of the social contract since the 1980s and its implications for a broader discourse on hope and the future. The humanities traditionally has offered both a refuge and a possibility for thinking about these issues, though under historical conditions which bear little resemblance to the present. This is particularly evident as the conditions for the production of knowledge, national identity, and citizenship have changed in a rapidly globalizing, post-9/11 world order marked by the expansion of new electronic technologies; the consolidation of global media; Western de-industrialization, deregulation, and downsizing; the privatization of public goods and services; and the marketization of all aspects of social life.

The "crisis" in the humanities reflects a crisis within the larger society about the meaning and viability of institutions that define themselves as serving a public rather than private good. The ongoing vocationalization of higher education, the commodification of the curriculum, the increasing role the university plays as part of the national security state, and the transformation of students into consumers have undermined the humanities in its efforts to offer students the knowledge and skills they need for learning how to govern as well as develop the capacities necessary for deliberation, reasoned arguments, and social action. The incursion of corporate and military culture into university life undermines the university's responsibility to provide students with an education that allows them to recognize the dream and promise of a substantive democracy. While it is true that the humanities must keep up with developments in the sciences, the new media, technology, and other fields, its first responsibility is treat these issues not merely pragmatically as ideas and skills to be learned but as sites of political and ethical intervention, deeply connected to the question of what it means to create students who can imagine a democratic future for all people.

In its best moments, this era of crisis, fear, and insecurity has reinvigorated the debate over the role that the humanities and the university more generally might play in creating a pluralized public culture essential for animating basic precepts of democratic public life. Matters of history, global relations, ethical concerns, creativity, and the development of new literacies and modes of communication should be central to any humanities education and the conversation it enables. But at the same time, such conversations have for the most part failed to consider more fundamental issues about the need to revitalize the language of civic education as part of a broader discourse of political agency and critical citizenship in a globalized society. More specifically, a better understanding of why the humanities has avoided the challenge of those critical discourses capable of interrogating how the society represents itself (for example, the gap suggested by the apogee of democracy at the precise moment of its hollowing out) and how and why individuals fail to critically engage such representations is crucial if educators are to intervene in the oppressive social relationships they often legitimate.

Given these contexts, educators in the humanities must ask new kinds of questions, beginning with: How do educators respond to value-based questions regarding the "usefulness" of the humanities and the range of purposes it should serve? What knowledges are of most worth? What does it mean to claim authority in a world where borders are constantly shifting? What role does the humanities have in a world in which the "immaterial production" of knowledge becomes the most important form of capital? How might pedagogy be understood as a political and moral practice rather than a technical strategy in the service of corporate culture? And what relation should the humanities have to young people as they develop a sense of agency, particularly in relation to the obligations of critical citizenship and public life in a radically transformed cultural and global landscape? As citizenship becomes increasingly privatized and youth are increasingly educated to become consuming subjects rather than critical social subjects, it becomes all the more imperative for educators working within the humanities to rethink the space of the social and to develop a critical language in which notions of the public good, public issues, and public life become central to overcoming the privatizing and depoliticizing language of the market. Central to this issue for me is the role that higher education might play as a democratic public sphere.

MG: You challenge the traditional understanding of the word "intellectual." How does this notion apply to the contemporary world?

HG: I have always believed that the notion of the intellectual carries with it a number of important political, cultural, and social registers. In contrast to the notion that intellectuals are a specialized group of experts, I have argued that everybody is an intellectual in that we all have the capacity to think, produce ideas, be self-critical, and connect knowledge (wherever it comes from) to forms of self- and social development. At the same time, those intellectuals who have the luxury of defining their social function through the production of intellectual ideas have a special responsibility to address how power works through institutions, individuals, social formations, and everyday life so as to enable or close down democratic values, identities,

174

and relations. More specifically, I believe that the most important obligation that intellectuals have to knowledge is only fulfilled through understanding their relationship to power not as a complementary relation but as one of opposition. I think intellectuals, whether in or outside of the academy, must connect ideas to the world and engage their skills and knowledge as part of a larger struggle over democracy and justice. Intellectuals have a responsibility not only to make truth prevail in the world and fight injustice wherever it appears but also to organize their collective passions to prevent human suffering, genocide, and diverse forms of unfreedom linked to domination and exploitation. Intellectuals have a responsibility to analyze how language, information, and meaning work to organize, legitimate, and circulate values, structure reality, and offer up particular notions of agency and identity. For public intellectuals, the latter challenge demands a new kind of literacy and critical understanding with respect to the emergence of the new media and electronic technologies, and the new and powerful role they play as instruments of public pedagogy. Critical reflection is an essential dimension of justice and is central to civic education, and it is precisely with respect to keeping justice and democracy alive in the public domain that intellectuals have a responsibility to the global world.

Today, the concept of the intellectual, as Pierre Bourdieu reminds us, has become synonymous with public relations experts, sycophantic apologists, and fast-talking media types. Educators as public intellectuals need a new vocabulary for linking hope, social citizenship, and education to the demands of substantive democracy. I am suggesting that educators need a new vocabulary for connecting not only how we read critically but also how we engage in movements for social change. I also believe that simply invoking the relationships between theory and practice, critique and social action, will not do. Any attempt to give new life to a substantive democratic politics must address both how people learn to be political agents and what kind of educational work is necessary within many kinds of public spaces. People need to use their full intellectual resources to provide a profound critique of existing institutions and to struggle towards fulfilling the promise of a radical global democracy. As public intellectuals, educators and other cultural workers need to understand more fully why the tools we used in the past feel awkward in the present, often failing to respond to problems now facing the United States and other parts of the globe. More specifically, we face the challenge posed by the failure of existing critical discourses to bridge the gap between how society represents itself and how and why individuals fail to understand and critically engage such representations in order to intervene in the oppressive social relationships they often legitimate. By combining the mutually interdependent roles of critic and active citizen, intellectual work at its best can exercise civic courage as a political practice, a practice that begins when one's life can no longer be taken for granted. Such a stance not only connects intellectual work to making dominant power accountable but also makes concrete the possibility for transforming hope and politics into an ethical space and public act that confront the flow of everyday experience and the weight of social suffering with the force of individual and collective resistance and the unending project of democratic social transformation. The road to authoritarianism begins when societies stop questioning themselves, and, when such questioning stops, it is often because intellectuals either have become complicit with such silence or actively produce it. Clearly, critical intellectuals have a responsibility to oppose this deafening quiet in the face of an emerging global barbarism, evidence of which can be seen in a number of growing religious, political, and economic fundamentalisms.

MG: One of your most radical statements is that every educational act is political and that every political act is pedagogical. In the same way that your work crosses into different disciplinary areas, you have also tried to link different institutional divisions in which pedagogy takes place: education, politics, and the media, just to name a few. What are your reasons for doing this and the risks of such an undertaking?

HG: In the last few decades, I have tried to resurrect the profound insights of theorists such as Antonio Gramsci, Raymond Williams, Edward Said, and others who have argued that the educational force of the broader culture has become one of the most important political sites in the struggle over ideas, values, and agency. Permanent education is a fundamental part of what it means to create those identities and values that constitute the narrative of the political. In the past, education was limited to schooling. But it has become clear that most of the education that takes place today, which is so vital to any democracy, occurs in a broader number of sites, including screen culture, popular culture, the internet, and in the all-encompassing old and new media. I have stressed that these new sites of education, which I call the realm of public pedagogy, are crucial to any notion of politics because they are the sites in which people often learn, unlearn, or simply do not get the knowledge and skills that prepare them to become critical agents, capable not merely of understanding the society and world in which they live but also of being able to assume the mantle of governance.

MG: You have dedicated a great amount of your recent work to what you consider an unfair treatment of the youth in contemporary societies by both public and private institutions (e.g., the government, the educational system, the press, and society in general). What specific role can educators play in countering this trend?

HG: Well, the first thing they can do is to recognize the obligation that adults have to youth, if in fact we are going to take seriously not only the social contract but the very possibility of a democratic future. The second thing that can be done is to try to understand those forces, especially neoliberalism, neoconservatism, militarism, and religious fundamentalism, that view youth either as a commodity or as utterly expendable, especially poor youth and youth of color, and how they can be challenged in every social institution and addressed through policies that truly view youth as a social investment rather than a threat, fodder for the military, or a commodity.

MG: How do you view the introduction of a new academic interdisciplinary subject that aims to develop intercultural competencies, that is, to improve the students' capacity to communicate and interact effectively across cultures, both nationally and internationally? How can educators implement this interdisciplinary and intercultural subject within a critical pedagogy approach? Does this project relate to your claims for a "new language for expressing global solidarity"?

HG: I think that the question of intercultural competencies has to be understood within a broader notion of literacy linked to both the acquisition of agency and the ability to recognize that matters of difference are inextricably tied to issues of respect, tolerance, dialogue, and our responsibility to others. Multicultural literacy as a discursive intervention is an essential step towards not only a broader notion of self-representation but also a more global notion of agency and democracy. Literacy in this sense is not only pluralized and expanded but also becomes the site in which new dialogical practices and social relations are made possible. Literacy as I am using it here does a kind of bridging work necessary to democracy while also offering up modes of translation that challenge strategies of common sense and domination. At the same time, intercultural competencies must be connected to the central dynamics of power as a way of engaging differences and exclusions so as to understand their formations as part of a historical process of struggle and negotiation. In this instance, such competencies further more than understanding and awareness — they also serve as modes of critical understanding in which dialogue and interpretation are connected to interventions in which cultural differences can be viewed as an asset to democracy.

MG: Your writing style is very powerful and idiosyncratic, and you have been both criticized and praised for it. Some of your readers find it too obscure and impregnated with ideology and others find it vibrant, stimulating, and very inspiring. I belong to the latter group, and I would like to ask you to what extent your style is purposeful and what purposes it serves?

HG: I have tried in the last decade to make my writing accessible to a broader public while not compromising its theoretical rigor. This seems to present a lot of problems for those academics whose discourse is largely impenetrable, highly specialized, and plugged into narrow definitions of careerism. Academics, especially on the left in the United States, are generally very bad writers, a problem connected less to matters of skill than to an arcane notion of professionalism. Many live in "theory world" and generally address very specialized audiences. On the one hand, much of their work is indebted to a kind of postmodern irony or cleverness, or is so pedantic that it lacks either any political integrity or passion. On the other hand, the bar has been set so low in the United States around matters of clarity and style that it is always difficult to reach a broader public if conventional matters of style and language are challenged, as they are in my work. Of course, the grumbling about my work is not merely about style; it is also because I often make the political primary to my work in a way that makes the project I am working out of quite clear. The backlash against committed writing, if not engaged politics, is so strong in universities, the media, and other established sites of public pedagogy that asserting the importance of politics as a crucial aspect of everyday life and learning is an incredibly difficult but absolutely necessary fight to wage.

MG: You have been very critical about what the contemporary developed world is providing to the youth, namely more surveillance in schools, the so-called excellence in education translated into more standardized assessment, a commercialized culture, etc. I have no doubt that you are very aware that it is difficult for critical educators, as individual professionals burdened by the demands of the government, the school management, students and parents, and society as a whole, to counter these tendencies on their own. Your writings have undoubtedly inspired and supported their efforts. Do you have any special message for them?

HG: Yes, these are very difficult times, but the stakes are very high, and if we value democracy and have any hope whatsoever for the future, we must continue the struggle for connecting education to democracy, learning to social change, and excellence to equity. The only other option is either cynicism or complicity, and no educator deserves that. I also think it is important to recognize that these struggles are going on all over the world, and that we are not alone and shouldn't be alone in taking on these crucial battles — battles that will determine the fate of global democracy in the twenty-first century.

MG: How do you account for the increasing interest of foreign language/culture educators in your work, despite their traditionally showing little interest in critical theories of schooling and pedagogy?

HG: Of course, one has to recognize that historically there have been a number of foreign language/culture educators who have addressed the connection between language and critical pedagogy, particularly people working in TESOL. I think much of that work was produced far ahead of its time, and only now are the conditions emerging that enable educators to recognize its importance to the current discursive/pedagogical/educational global context. As it becomes clear that you cannot decouple issues concerning language usage from issues of dialogue, communication, culture, and power, matters of politics and pedagogy become crucial to how one understands pedagogy as a political issue and the politics of language as a deeply pedagogical consideration. I have argued for a number of years that language as both an object and subject of mastery, understanding, and engagement is the site in which people negotiate the most fundamental elements of their identities, the relationship between themselves and others, and their relationship to the larger world. I have also made clear that it has become very difficult in light of this understanding to treat language as simply a technical issue. Clearly, its importance lies in recognizing that it is a moral and political practice deeply connected to both matters of critical agency and the unending struggle to expand and deepen democracy itself. Matters of language and culture are crucial to how one is shaped and what one does as an intellectual. Hence, language is the material and cultural foundation for how educators both address and define the meaning and purpose of pedagogy in the formation and acquisition of particular modes of individual and social agency. This is a question that I have been addressing in my work for over 30 years but also one that I have taken up as part of a larger concern with what it means to make the pedagogical more political in its ongoing task of expanding democratic values, relationships, identities, and public spheres.

This is where I think my work seems to resonate in the current historical conjuncture. Learning a foreign language is a largely humanistic endeavor rather than an elite or strictly methodological task, and the force of its importance has to be tied to its relevance as an empowering, emancipatory, and democratic function. My work understands language as a mode of learning and dissent, one that is crucial both to configuring and translating the boundaries between the public and the private and to attending to questions of politics, power, public consciousness, and civic courage. More than ever, language needs to be revitalized as part of a public pedagogy that energizes the imagination, expands the autonomy of the individual, and deepens a viable notion of political agency. Language is part of what Edward Said called a politics of worldliness inextricably tied up to matters of history, power, and a culture of questioning and democratic struggles. Critical pedagogy in my work has always taken the latter concerns seriously, and it just might be that this work is now being rediscovered and used by foreign language/culture educators. I think many people are desperate for a discourse that links critique to hope, knowledge to passion, and pedagogy to justice. I would like to believe my work offers them some hope in dark times.

NOTE

1 This interview was first published in 2006 in the *Language and Intercultural Communication Journal*, 6, (2): 163–175. I am grateful to its editors for allowing the republication of this interview. Manuela Guilherme is a senior researcher at the Center for Social Studies, University of Coimbra in Portugal, where she coordinates two European projects focusing on Intercultural Education. She is author of *Critical*

Citizens for an Intercultural World: Foreign Language Education as Cultural Politics (Multilingual Matters, 2002) and co-editor of *Critical Pedagogy: Political Approaches to Language and Intercultural Communication* (Multilingual Matters, 2004), which includes a chapter by Henry A. Giroux titled "Betraying the Intellectual Tradition: Public Intellectuals and the Crisis of Youth."

Index

181

Dutch cooking

Voor Anne,

Een aanvulling op je verzameling in de hoop dat je hierdoor je Hollandse vrienden blijft herinneren.

Jaap, Riet
Pieter
Susette

en.... Smoky (die van álle sorten eten houdt).

Heleen A. M. Halverhout

DUTCH
COOKING

AMSTERDAM/DE DRIEHOEK

To my american relatives, my canadian and english friends and to all Dutch people who emigrated to various parts of the world.

Copyright ©: De Driehoek, Amsterdam 1972

Third revised edition

Illustraties: G. C. van der Starre

ISBN 90 6030 330 X

Dear friends of our Dutch food

In this book you will find some of our traditional dishes, which you probably liked when dining out or at the home of Dutch friends.

We "Hollanders" as we are mostly called in the States (in England they call us "the Dutch") are great lovers of nice food. And we like to prepare these tasty dishes from the best ingredients. We like to eat them at home in the company of our family, seated at a well-set table, – covered in the Dutch way with a tablecloth of white or colored linen –, under a big lamp ficed in the middle of the ceiling of our diningroom.

Our traditional dishes are mostly based on rather nourishing ingredients, but as you probably know we take only one hot meal a day. The first and the second meal are sandwich-meals.

In my recipes I give the amount 4 Dutch persons would eat. Maybe the amount you would use would be different; that is up to you to decide. There are of course exceptions, because certain dishes or certain baked goods must be made as given

5

in the recipe and I have given you recipes of dishes which are within the scope of the average housewife and made of ingredients you can get at home.

May I give you a suggestion when to make one or more of the following recipes?

When you ask your friends to a party after coming back from your trip to Europe, or

at a church-social, in aid of some good purpose, or when entertaining "Hollanders". They will be delighted with your charming idea, or at so many other occasions, as you will know best.

It has been a very great pleasure to write this book for you. It is always so nice to know that visitors to my country are interested in our "Dutch Fare". I wish you "good cooking" and much fun preparing these typical dishes of the Netherlands.

And to my countrymen and women: I hope you will enjoy these typical Dutch dishes, maybe you will adjust them to your own liking: "As mother used to make it.".

Yours sincerely

HELEEN A. M. HALVERHOUT

Our food habits

The people in the Netherlands have other "food habits" than other people on the continent, in the United Kingdom or the United States of America or Canada. This sounds probably a bit funny for such a small country. But it is a fact and you know the saying: Do in Rome as the Romans do. Freely translated: When in Holland, eat as we do. May I give you a short description of the way we serve our meals?

For breakfast we have bread and butter, or open sandwiches with jam, cheese, "ontbijtkoek" (see recipe page 130). We drink tea with it, or milk, maybe buttermilk. Sometimes we have a boiled egg and children may have a plateful of "pap".

At 11 o'clock ("elevenses") we drink one or more cups of coffee with cream or milk. And treat ourselves to a piece of (buttered) "koek" or some "boterkoek" (see recipe page 121) or cake, for extra festive occasions.

At lunchtime we have another bread and butter meal. Maybe some rolls are put on the table (krentebroodjes, cadetjes, halve maantjes = croissants) and Dutch rusks topped with cheese or jam.

With it we have some meat: liver sausage or ham; maybe a fried egg or two or an omelette. When guests arrive we make a special hot dish: croquettes or macaroni cheese, or ham and cheese savories (see recipe page 31).

Fruits finish off the meal with which we drink coffee, milk, buttermilk or cocoa.

At 4 o'clock it is teatime. A cup of tea and a biscuit is quite usual.
For special occasions we produce fancy cakes, cookies or chocolates.

At 5 o'clock the Dutch drink an icecold "Borrel" or "jenever" (Dutch gin) or sherry, see page 140 for the famous "Bitterballen".

At 6 o'clock it is dinner time. Our first hot meal*. Mainly consisting of:

> a hot entrée (soup)
> or a cold entrée
> meat or fish with vegetables and potatoes,
> sometimes a sweet or fruit to finish.

*) In some parts of the Netherlands the hot meal is served at midday and a bread and butter meal in the evening.

Only on special occasions wine or beer is served.

Coffee may be served after the meal, but is mostly not taken at the dining table.

8 o'clock tea again with biscuits. And maybe people prefer coffee.

Cookies, cake or a more elaborate baked sweet is offered, when we have company (visitors).

Later in the evening some people like to drink beer or wine or Dutch gin (jenever) maybe a liqueur or whisky (bourbon).
You see ... it is different. But you will certainly enjoy it when you are offered these things in the home of a Dutch family.
Mind you, I have nothing against hotels but they do not serve you "real Dutch meals", as you would be served in a typical Dutch home. However there are special restaurants where real Dutch fare is served.

Note

In the recipes you will find either the word Holland or Dutch (officially "the Netherlands"). In America one might mix Dutch = Pensylvanian Dutch, originally German people coming to America speaking Deutsch (German). In England the word Dutch is connected with their overseas neighbours in Holland.

Therefore the same words have not always the same meaning in England or America. Also "cooking ingredients" have not the same meaning.

If in England another word is used, it is put in parentheses e.g. molasses (treacle).

Hints for using this book

Cookery terms

American	*English*
confectioner's sugar	icing sugar.
farina	semolina.
sifted	sieved.
candied cherries	glacé cherries.
preserve	jam.
pudding mold	blanc mange mould.
self-rising flour	self-raising flour.
pancover	saucepan lid.
chili	hot red pepper. Spanish pepper.
casserole	over-proof dish.
platter	serving dish.
pre-cooked	quick boiling.
midmorning "coffee break"	"elevenses".
ground (meat)	minced (meat).
broiler	grill

Oven temperatures

American

gas and electric oven temperatures are given in degrees Fahrenheit

temperature	term
150° F–275° F	very slow oven
300° F–325° F	slow oven
350° F–375° F	moderate oven
400° F–425° F	hot oven
450° F–475° F	very hot oven
500° F–525° F	extremely hot oven

British

gas and electric oven temperatures compared.

gas oven marks	approximate temp. in centre of gas oven	settings	term
¼	240° F (115° C)	200° F (95° C)	cool oven
½	265° F (130° C)	225° F (110° C)	cool oven
1	290° F (145° C)	250° F (120° C)	cool oven
2	310° F (155° C)	275° F (135° C)	very slow oven
3	335° F (170° C)	300° F (150° C)	slow oven
4	355° F (180° C)	325° F (165° C)	very moderate oven
5	380° F (195° C)	350° F (175° C)	very moderate oven
6	400° F (205° C)	375° F (190° C)	moderate oven
7	425° F (220° C)	400° F (205° C)	moderately hot oven
8	445° F (230° C)	425° F (220° C)	hot oven
		450° F (235° C)	hot oven
9	470° F (245° C)	475° F (245° C)	very hot oven
		500° F (260° C)	very hot oven

Temperatures given in both degrees Fahrenheit and degrees Celcius (centigrade) because of the changeover to centrigrade setting in Great Britain.

14

Standard measures and equivalents

American

---

appr. 7   oz (200 grams) one cup (level) sugar, granulated
appr. 5¹/₂oz (155 grams) one cup sugar, brown, demerara
appr. 6   oz (170 grams) one cup butter or margarine
appr. 4   oz (110 grams) one cup all purpose flour (sifted)
appr. 4   oz (110 grams) one cup selfrising (selfraising) flour
appr. 7   oz (200 grams) one cup rice
appr. 5   oz (140 grams) one cup raisins (seedless)

British

---

 8 oz = 230 grammes
 7 oz = 200 grammes
 5 oz = 140 grammes
10 oz = 280 grammes
 6 oz = 165 grammes

Why all this "metric equivalent" business?
As I am sure, you will be using this book when "cooking the Dutch way" you may want to convert your recipes out of your own Dutch cookery book.

Comparison of weights and measures

(All dry measurements are level). With metric equivalents given.

American

cm^3 = css = cubic centimetres
dm^3 = 10 decilitres = litre

(standard cup)	metric equivalent (approximately)
1 cup = 1/2 pint = 8 fluid oz	= 0.237 litres
1 pint = 16 fluid oz	= 0.480 litres
1/4 pint = 4 fluid oz	= 0.120 litres
1 quart = 2 pints	= 0.946 litres
1 fluid ounce	= 29,5 ccs (30 ccs)
1 (dry) ounce	= 28.35 grammes
1 pound = 16 oz	= 453 grammes
1 tablespoon = 0.50 fluid oz	= 150 ccs
1 teaspoon = 0.16 fluid oz	= 5.0 ccs

British

Imperial or British standards	metric equivalent (approximately)
1 cup = 1/2 pint = 10 fluid oz	= 0.28 litres
1 pint = 20 fluids oz	= 0.57 litres
1 gill = 1/4 pint = 5 fluid oz	= 0.14 litres
1 quart = 2 pints	= 1,1 litres
1 fluid ounce	= 0.28 litres
1 (dry) ounce	= 28.34 grammes
1 pound = 16 oz (dry ingredients)	= 453 grammes
1 tablespoon = 0.62 fluid oz	= 17.7 cm^3
1 teaspoon = 0.21 fluid oz	= 5.96 cm^3 (6 cm^3)
1 breakfastcup = 10 fluid oz	= 284 cm^3 (0.3 litres)
1 teacup = 1/3 pint	= 190 cm^3 (0.2 litres)
3 1/2 oz	= 100 grammes
3 1/2 fl. oz = 1 decilitre	= 1/10th litres
2,2 lbs = 1000 grammes	= 1 kilogramme
1 3/4 pints	= 1 litre

Soups / Soepen

Cream soup.

*Cream of tomato soup
with fried breadcubes or croutons.*

Curry soup made of lima beans.

Vermicelli soup with ground meat balls.

Dutch pea soup.

Vegetable soup.

CREAM SOUP

Witte ragoutsoep

2¹/₂ tbsp. butter or margarine
6 tbsp. flour
4 cups brown stock
1 egg yolk
1 tbsp. light cream
some lemon juice.

Add as accompaniment ground meat balls (see recipe of vermicelli soup).

Melt butter, add flour and stir to a smooth paste. Add stock gradually, stirring well. Bring to the boil and simmer for 5 minutes. Then remove from fire. Add some soup to egg yolk diluted with cream. Put mixture back into the soup. Stir well. Add some lemon juice to taste. Add ground meat balls if desired. They must have been cooked separately in a little water in a separate pan. The strained stock can be added to the soup if the soup is thick enough. Otherwise bind the soup with a little cornflour added to the egg yolk mixture.

CREAM OF TOMATO SOUP
with fried bread cubes or croutons

Tomatensoep
met gebakken broodjes

4 cups water
4 large tomatoes
one onion
2 bay leaves
salt
2 tbsp. butter or margarine
1/3 cup flour
parsley
pepper
cream or milk.

Cut the tomatoes in four, put them into the boiling water with the sliced onion, bay leaves and salt. Simmer for 20 minutes and sieve. Melt the butter, add the flour and a little of the soup. When creamy add some more and go on till you have a creamy smooth soup. Add some finely chopped parsley, pepper and the cream or milk. Serve with fried bread cubes. *Fried bread cubes.* 2 slices white bread cut in cubes, crust removed. Butter to fry them into a golden brown. Hand them round separately.

CURRY SOUP
MADE OF LIMA BEANS

Kerriesoep van witte bonen

4 cups of left-over cooking liquid
and some cooked limabeans
2 tbsp. butter or margarine
3 cloves
2 bay leaves
a small chili
3 tbsp. flour
1 tbsp. curry powder
1 onion.

Heat the liquid and the beans. Rub through a coarse sieve. Fry the butter golden brown. Add spices except curry, then the flour and add liquid gradually. Add the curry. Serve with fried bread cubes if wanted. (see recipe cream of tomato soup page 20).

DUTCH PEA SOUP

Erwtensoep

2 cups split green peas
3 qt cold water
1 pig's trotter   1 pig's ear
1 cup bacon squares
4 Frankfurters
1 lb. potatoes   4 tbsp. salt
1 celeriac
1 bunch celery-green
2 leeks   2 onions   salt.

Wash the peas, soak for 12 hours (unless you use quick cooking peas) and boil gently in the water they were soaked in for at least two hours. Cook in this liquid the trotter and the ear and the bacon for one hour. Add the sliced potatoes, salt diced celeriac, cut up leeks and celery leaves and cook until everything is done and the soup is smooth and thick. Add the Frankfurters for the last 10 minutes. The longer the soup simmers the better the taste. Three hours is the usual time in Holland. The soup gets so thick when it cools that it can be cut next day. The next day the soup tastes even better when reheated. That is why it is made in such big quantities.

VEGETABLE SOUP

Groentesoep

4 cups water
3 bouillon cubes or 4 cups white stock (meat or bones)
2 tbsp. quick boiling rice
parsley
1/2 lb. carrots
1/4 cauliflower
a few Brussels sprouts
1 stalk of celery
1 leek
2 tbsp. butter or margarine
2 bay leaves   salt.

Dissolve the cubes into the water. Wash the rice and add it to the water or stock. Cook until tender. Clean and wash all the vegetables. Cut the carrots in rounds, the Brussels sprouts in quarters, the celery in bits, the leek in rounds and the cauliflower in small bits. Sauté the vegetables and the bay leaves for 15 minutes in the butter and add the soup. Simmer for 15 minutes. Before serving, add the very finely chopped parsley. Add salt to taste. Instead of rice you can also take vermicelli. Break it before adding to the stock.

VERMICELLI SOUP
WITH GROUND MEAT BALLS

Vermicellisoep met balletjes

4 cups of white stock (meat or bones)
2 blades of mace or some marjoram
²/₃ cup of vermicelli
¹/₂ cup ground meat (half veal, half pork)
salt, pepper, grated nutmeg
1 egg.

Make a fairly concentrated beef stock and simmer in it the blades of mace or marjoram. Strain and add the broken vermicelli. Prepare some small (the size of a marble) *ground meat balls* by mixing the ground meat with the salt, pepper, a little grated nutmeg and some egg. Roll them in the flour and boil in the soup for the last 15 minutes. The rest of the egg can be added to the soup just before serving, but is not essential. Add salt to taste.

Entrée dishes
or lunch dishes

Dutch Herring
Mixed herring salad
Shrimp croquettes
Meat croquettes
Meat-filled pancake
Ham and cheese savories
Kidney savories
Open egg and meat sandwich

DUTCH HERRING

Hollandse haring

The Dutch herring available in your country is more salty than it is in Holland. This is due to the fact that the preserving salt has gone through a longer permeation process. In Holland the fish is eaten almost as soon as it is brought ashore. In your country it is advisable to soak the herring in milk or water 24 hours before serving, renewing the liquid at intervals and to do this after the fish has been cleaned and skinned. Serve Dutch herring on small toasted canapés as an appetizer, or on ice cubes, with boiled new potatoes and a green salad.

Note that the herring is eaten raw and not cooked.

27

MIXED HERRING-SALAD

Haringsla

1 small cooked beetroot
2 cooking apples
some (pickled) onions and gherkins
8 cold cooked potatoes   2 hard boiled eggs
some lettuce or curly endives
2 tbsp. salad oil   2 tbsp. vinegar
salt   mayonnaise
3 fresh salted herrings.

Soak the herrings as indicated in the previous recipe. Bone the herrings and cut them up in small pieces. Keep a few pieces for decorating. Cut the peeled beetroot and apples in pieces. Chop the onions, gherkins and potatoes and one egg. Wash the lettuce or endives and shred it very finely. Put all these ingredients in a big bowl. Mix it well with salad oil, vinegar and salt. Put the salad on a flat dish and smooth the top with a wet spoon. Coat the salad with mayonnaise and decorate with quarters of egg, pieces of herring and surround it with very small bits of "yellow" lettuce (the inside leaves). Serve it with toast and butter or, if dished up at lunchtime, with bread and butter.

SHRIMP CROQUETTES

Garnalen croquetjes

1 cup cooked shrimps (prawns)
¹/₂ envelope gelatin
2 tbsp. flour   2 tbsp. butter or margarine
¹/₂ cup milk   1 egg yolk   light cream
juice of ¹/₂ lemon   salt, pepper, chopped parsley
2 egg whites   1 tbsp. salad oil   dry bread crumbs
fat or oil for deep frying.

Wash and drain the shrimps. Soak gelatin in some of the cold milk. Make a thick sauce of flour, butter, milk and stock and add shrimps and gelatin. Beat the egg yolk with the cream, add the sauce and return to saucepan for thickening, taking care that it does not boil. Add lemon juice, parsley, salt and pepper. Spread this mixture onto a shallow dish to cool and set.

When set, cut in eight equal parts and form a firm cylinder of each. Roll each in bread crumbs, then in a mixture of beaten egg whites and salad oil, then again in bread crumbs, again in egg white and bread crumbs. Fry in hot deep fat (400° F.) until golden brown and seve hot, garnish with some sprigs of parsley that have been fried crisp (but not brown) in the same deep fat. Serve on a platter on a doyley.

MEAT CROQUETTES

Vleescroquetjes

1/2 lb. lean veal
1 1/2 cups water
seasoning: a small onion, parsley, bay leaf
dry bread crumbs, egg white and fat for frying
1/2 envelope gelatin
2 tbsp. butter or margarine
3 tbsp. flour
1 cup veal stock
salt, pepper
lemon juice
1 egg yolk.

Boil meat in water with seasoning until well done. Cut in very small pieces. Soak gelatin in some of the cold milk. Make a sauce of butter, flour and stock, add the gelatin, pepper and salt, lemon juice to taste and egg yolk. Add the meat. Taste. Spread this mixture onto a shallow dish. Let cool and set. Proceed as given in the previous recipe.

HAM AND CHEESE SAVORIES

Warme ham- en kaassandwiches

8 thin slices of stale bread
4 slices (¹/₄ oz each) Gouda or Edam cheese
4 slices ham (¹/₂ oz each)
butter or margarine, or dripping for frying.

Remove the crust from the bread and cut it in identical slices. Cut the cheese and the ham to the same size. Put 1 slice of ham and 1 slice of cheese between two slices of bread.
Spread the sandwiches on the outside with butter or margarine. Fry them golden brown and crisp and serve this savory either for lunch, or as an entrée, after the soup with a main meal.

MEAT-FILLED PANCAKE

Gevulde pannekoek

For the pancakes:
1 cup flour   1¹/₂ cups milk   2 eggs   salt
butter or margarine for baking.

For the filling:
4 tbsp. butter or margarine
¹/₃ cup flour   2 cups stock or bouillon
salt, pepper, nutmeg, lemon juice to taste
2 cups cooked meat, ground or minced
¹/₂ cup canned mushrooms.

Make a thick brown sauce of butter, flour and stock: add seasoning, keep stirring and mix with meat and mushrooms. Keep hot but take care that it does not boil, or meat will get tough. Filling can be made in advance. Make smooth batter of the pancake ingredients. Heat butter in a 10-inch skillet. Use half of the batter; brown pancake slowly on one side until done. Slide onto platter and keep hot. Make second pancake in same way. Spread meat mixture on light side of first pancake and turn second pancake, brown side up, on top of first. Cut into wedges and serve at once with a green salad. Serve as a diner entrée or for lunch.

KIDNEY SAVORIES

Nierbroodjes

1 large calf's kidney
2 tbsp. chopped onions
1 tbsp. butter or margarine
salt   2 tbsp. flour   ²/₃ cup stock
Worcestershire sauce   pepper
4 slices stale white bread
1 egg, beaten   1 tbsp. milk
¹/₄ cup dry bread crumbs
fat for frying   parsley.

Wash and clean kidney. Parboil in water for one minute. Discard the water. Chop kidney very finely. Sauté onions in the butter, add kidney before onions brown. Add salt and continue frying until light brown. Sprinkle flour over the mixture and gradually add the stock. Cover and allow to simmer very slowly for 15 minutes. Add Worcestershire sauce and pepper. Taste and set aside to cool. Cut slices in half. Heap kidney mixture on bread. Put the egg in a deep plate. Stand the pieces of bread in the plate. Baste thoroughly. Coat with bread crumbs. Have deep fat ready 360°–370° F. (180° C.) and fry the savories until golden brown. Serve on a doyley on a platter. Garnish with fresh parsley sprigs.

OPEN EGG
AND MEAT SANDWICH

Uitsmijter

This is a snack, ordered mostley in a small restaurant, when one is in a hurry but wants to eat something substantial. It consists of 1 or 2 slices of white bread, buttered, topped with a liberal portion of cold, cooked thinly sliced roastbeaf or ham or veal. And on top of this two fried eggs (with one egg it is called a "halve" (half) uitsmijter).

I can recommend you this when you ransack the refrigerator and find eggs and meat. You will certainly find some bread in the bread-bin.

Poultry and game

Stewed rabbit

Curried chicken-fricassee

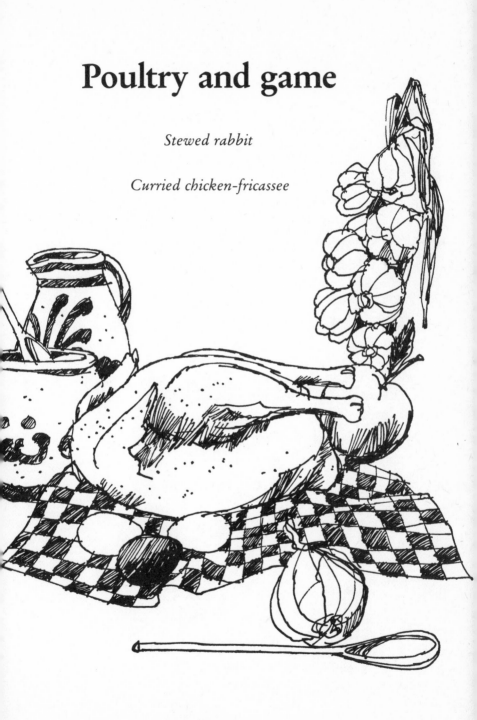

CURRIED CHICKEN-FRICASSEE

Kip met kerriesaus

One cut-up chicken
salt
1/3 cup butter or margarine
1 teaspoon curry or more to taste
1 medium chopped onion
2 cups chicken broth
1 cup fresh mushrooms
3 tbsp. flour
milk.

Salt the chicken parts and fry in butter on all sides in a large skillet or Dutch oven. Add curry and onion 5 minutes before the frying is done and fry to a golden brown. Add the broth, cover and leave to simmer until chicken is cooked. Cook mushrooms no longer than ten minutes in this mixture.
Remove the chicken and the mushrooms. Strain the liquid and thicken it with the flour which has been mixed with some milk beforehand. Replace the chicken and the mushrooms in this sauce and heat. Serve with rice or in centre of a rice ring (rijstrand).

STEWED RABBIT

Gestoofd konijn

One cut-up rabbit
¹/₃ cup butter or margarine   1 large onion, chopped
pepper, salt, bay leaves, thyme, small hot chili, parsley, celery,
carrot, all chopped
1 lemon.

For the sauce:
2 cups stock or bouillon   ¹/₄ cup butter or margarine
3 tbsp. flour   1 tbsp. tomato paste   1 large chopped onion
seasoning and chopped vegetables as for rabbit above.

Rub rabbit pieces with pepper and salt and brown in butter on all sides. Add onion, seasoning, chopped vegetables and some water. Cover and simmer one hour or until half done. Meanwhile make the sauce. Fry onion, bay leaf, thyme and chili in butter. Remove from skillet with skimmer, leaving the butter. Add flour and brown slightly, stirring constantly. Then add stock, tomato paste, pepper and salt and cook for 10 minutes. Pour sauce over rabbit and cook one more hour or until meat falls from bone. Add lemon juice. Serve with rice or mashed potatoes and with a side dish of either tomato salad, cabbage or Brussels sprouts.

38

Potatoes

Boiled potatoes
Dutch mashed potatoes
Home-fried potatoes
Potato salad

BOILED POTATOES

Gekookte aardappelen

The Dutch are very particular about the texture of their boiled potatoes. They eat quite a lot of them with their evening meal. Potatoes must be flaky when dished up.

2 lb. potatoes
1 cup of water
salt.

Peel the potatoes, remove the eyes and put the potatoes at once into cold water. Put ½ inch of water in a saucepan with a tightly fitting lid. Add the potatoes and the salt. Bring quickly to the boil and then turn gas or electric hotplate down, as low as possible just keeping the steam *under* the lid of the pan. Cook for 20 minutes, drain and shake well until dry and flaky.

DUTCH MASHED POTATOES

Aardappelpuree

Always make nice and white mashed potatoes from freshly boiled potatoes. If made from cold boiled potatoes the colour of the mashed potatoes is not white.

2 lb. potatoes
1¹/₂ cup milk
grated nutmeg
¹/₄ cup butter or margarine
salt.

Boil the peeled potatoes. Mash them when still warm with a fork or put them trough a mincer or through a sieve. There must not be any lumps in them. Bring the milk, nutmeg, butter or margarine and salt to the boil. Add the mashed potatoes at once and stir well. Then, with a wooden spoon, whip the mixture well until it is white and creamy, and serve, or put it into a casserole, dot with some butter and brown under the grill or in the oven.

HOME-FRIED POTATOES

Gebakken aardappelen

2 lb. boiled potatoes
¹/₄ cup butter, margarine or cooking fat.

Cut the potatoes in slices and fry in the butter until they are
golden brown. Turn them frequently with a spatula.

POTATO SALAD

Aardappelsla

1 tbsp. mustard powder
1/2 onion
2 tbsp. vinegar
mayonnaise
3 tbsp. chopped parsley
1 cup french dressing
3 cups cold boiled potatoes
salt
pepper.

Mix the mustard with the chopped onion, vinegar, mayonnaise and parsley and dressing in a bowl. Slice the potatoes and stir carefully through the sauce, adding salt and pepper to taste.

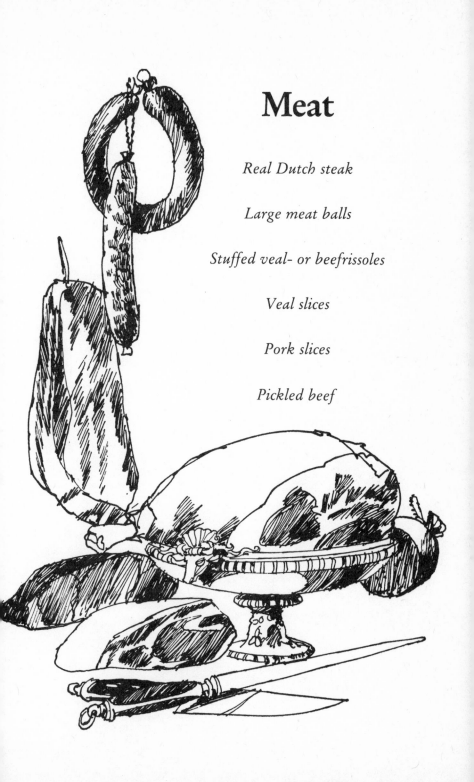

Meat

Real Dutch steak

Large meat balls

Stuffed veal- or beefrissoles

Veal slices

Pork slices

Pickled beef

REAL DUTCH STEAK

Hollandse biefstuk

for 4 people:
one piece of 1 lb very tender lean steak
or 4 small steaks
(filetsteak, tenderloin or rumpsteak)
or 4 pieces of 4 oz each
salt   pepper   milk
butter (no margarine).

Scrape (do not wash) the meat. Rub it with salt and pepper. Melt butter in skillet. Add meat when the "skum" of melting butter disappears and the butter is very hot. Put the meat into the butter, do not use a fork but two spoons (the juice must be sealed into the meat and the prongs of a fork may make holes in the meat out of which the juice will "ooze") and sear the meat on one side, then on the other side. Brown on both sides. Keep moving. The Dutch eat their "biefstuk" very rare, but if you do not like underdone meat, fry it a little longer. Then take the meat out of the pan. Keep it hot. Pour one tbsp. milk in the pan, reheat (dissolve the brown bits in the pan) and let the gravy thicken a little. Pour over meat.
Serve with home-fried potatoes (see recipe page 43) and a salad (lettuce) or with fresh green peas.

LARGE MEAT BALLS

Gehakt

1/2 lb. ground beef
1/2 lb. ground pork
4 slices stale bread
1/2 cup milk
1 tbsp. salt
bread crumbs
1/2 tsp. nutmeg
pinch of pepper
1/2 onion
1/4 cup margarine or fat
1 tsp. tomato-paste or 1 tbsp. tomato juice.

Mix the meat in a large basin. Remove the crusts from the bread and soak in the milk. Fry the chopped onion in some fat. Mix this all together with salt, pepper and nutmeg. Shape into 4 or 8 balls. Roll through flour and fry them until brown in the fat. Add some water and simmer for 15 minutes. Add tomato paste to gravy. Serve with boiled potatoes and boiled vegetables. Serve the gravy seperately in a gravy boat to pour over the potatoes.

STUFFED
VEAL- OR BEEFRISSOLES

Blinde vinken

4 thin slices veal or beef, 2 oz each
2 large slices of bread
some milk
salt
pinch of nutmeg
2 oz ground veal or beef or sausage meat
1 egg
4 thin slices lean bacon
cotton thread or cocktailsticks
1 tsp. cooking oil
bread crumbs or Dutch rusks
butter or margarine.

Crumble the bread and soak it in milk until soft. Make it into a smooth paste with a fork. Add salt, grated nutmeg and ground meat. Work it into a firm mixture in which no lumps of bread may be noticeable. Separate the egg. Brush every slice of meat with a little unbeaten white of egg and coat this side with a slice of bacon and some ground meat-paste. Roll up and secure the meat with some cotton or stick two cock-tailsticks in the part where the meat joins. Put rest of white of egg, the yolk and the cooking oil in a deep plate. Mix it with a fork. Put some bread crumbs or finely ground rusks on a piece of greaseproof paper. Put the "rissoles" through egg, roll them in bread crumbs or rusks crumbs and melt some butter or margarine in a shallow pan or Dutch oven until golden brown. Put the meat into the fat, fry to a golden brown, then add very little water. Cover the pan and simmer for 20 minutes, (beefrissoles for 1 hour). Carefully remove the threads or the cocktailsticks, use the sauce as a gravy over e.g. mashed potatoes (see recipe page 42).

VEAL SLICES

Kalfslapjes

4 thin slices of lean veal
salt
breadcrumbs or Dutch rusks
$^1/_2$ cup butter or margarine
1 lemon.

Wash the meat and season it with salt. Coat it in bread crumbs
or finely ground rusks. Melt the butter or margarine in a frying pan until brown and fry the veal slices in the butter,
browning them on both sides. Cook slowly, without a lid on
the pan for 20 minutes. Turn the slices occasionally. Then
take them out of the frying pan. Keep them hot.
Make the *Dutch gravy* (jus) by adding 3 tbsp. water, stir and
dissolve the brown bits in the pan. Good gravy should be $^1/_3$
fat and $^2/_3$ brown stock.
Serve the veal slices with a slice of lemon on top and serve the
gravy with boiled potatoes.

PORK CHOPS

Varkenscarbonade

4 pork chops
pepper
salt
butter or margarine.

Fry the chops. Cook over low heat 35–40 minutes until tender. Make the Dutch gravy (jus), see recipe on page 51. Serve with potatoes and Brussels sprouts.

PICKLED BEEF

Runderlappen

1¹/₂ lb. lean stewing beef (cut in four steaks)
pepper   salt
6 tbsp. butter or bacon drippings
1 large onion
1¹/₂ tbsp. vinegar
1 tsp. mustard
1 bay leaf
some cloves and peppercorns.

Scrape the meat and rub with pepper and salt. Heat butter or fat in a skillet or Dutch oven until it is real hot and thoroughly brown the meat on both sides. Add the sliced onion at the last moment, fry them very lightly without getting brown. Dissolve the remainder in the pan with some water and pour it over the meat. Add vinegar, mustard and the herbs; cover and allow to simmer very gently for about two to three hours, or until very soft, while turning every half hour.

Serve the meat with mashed potatoes (see recipe page 42). Strain the sauce if desired and pour over the meat. Red cabbage is a favorite vegetable with this dish, or spinach, or chicory.

Casserole dishes

Hunter's stew

Meat and potato casserole

Curried-rice and meat casserole

Savory beef and onion stew

HUNTER'S STEW

Jachtschotel

As much cold meat as available
½ lb. cooking apples
3 medium onions, peeled and sliced very thin
3 tbsp. butter or margarine
12 big boiled potatoes
pepper
salt
1 cup stock or bouillon made from meat cubes.

Slice the meat, peel the apples, slice them. Fry them with the onions until golden brown.

Arrange alternate layers of sliced potatoes, meat, onions and apples in a casserole. Season with pepper and salt. Take care that the last layer will be of potatoes, but do not put it on top yet. Pour the stock over the contents of the dish. Finish off with potatoes. Dot with butter. Put in the oven until thoroughly hot and brown on top.

Serve with spiced red cabbage or with stewed sliced (cooked) beetroots (see page 73) or thick applesauce.

MEAT AND POTATO CASSEROLE

Filosoof
(Lit. Philosopher's dish)

¹/₂ lb. cold meat
1 lb. boiled potatoes
2 tbsp. butter or margarine
1 cup gravy and water or stock
1 small onion
pepper
salt
nutmeg
bread crumbs
butter.

Mince the meat, mash the potatoes, fry the chopped onion in the butter. Mix all these ingredients together and add the gravy or stock until it is as thick as mashed potatoes. Sprinkle in some pepper, salt and nutmeg. Put in a casserole, cover with bread crumbs, and some knobs of butter. Heat and brown in the oven or under the grill.

CURRIED RICE AND MEAT CASSEROLE

Kerrieschoteltje

2 big minced onions
$^1/_2$ tbsp. currypowder
1 cup or more minced leftover pork meat
1 cup uncooked quick boiling or 3 cups cooked rice

salt
2 cups meat stock.

Melt the butter in a skillet, add the onions and curry. Fry to a golden brown. Add meat, rice (always cooked), salt and stock. Heat thoroughly. Serve with a green salad.

SAVORY BEEF
AND ONION STEW

Hachée

2 large thinly sliced onions
¼ cup flour
¼ cup butter or margarine
2 cups stock or stock of meatcubes
3 bay leaves   5 cloves
1 tbsp. vinegar
½ lb. sliced cold or leftover meat, preferably beef
2 tbsp. cornflour
pepper
Worcestershire sauce.

Brown the onions and the flour in the butter in a saucepan. Add stock gradually, stirring all the time. Add bay leaves and cloves and simmer for five minutes with the lid on the pan. Add the vinegar and the diced meat, simmer for another hour. Mix the cornflour with a little water, add this to the stew to thicken the sauce. Simmer for 5 minutes, stirring continuously. Make it to taste with a little pepper and Worcestershire sauce.
Serve with mashed or boiled potatoes and red cabbage (see recipe page 41, 42 and page 75) with this dish.

Fish

Fried fish

Stewed eel

Flounder or sole with shrimps

Cod-fish and rice dish

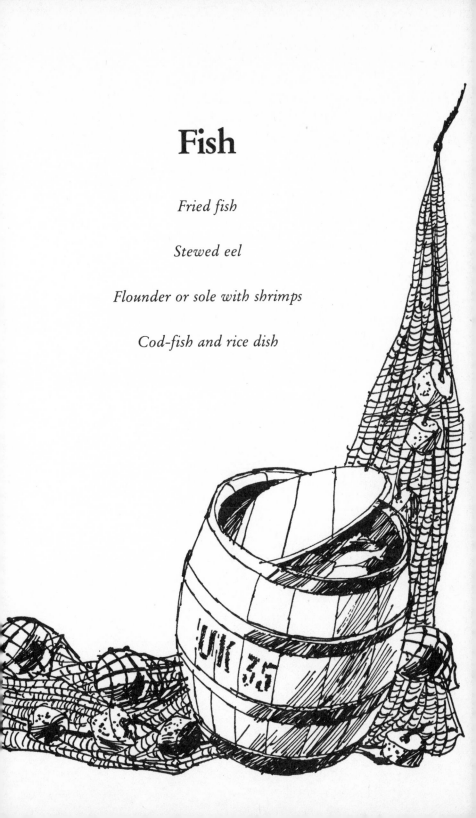

FRIED FISH

Gebakken vis

Fish for frying may be: any fillet
whiting
haddock and the like
cooking oil.

Fry the cleaned and seasoned fish in a skillet with cooking oil
1/8 inch deep. Either dip in flour or in milk. Sprinkle with
lemon when cooked. Serve with home-fried potatoes (see
recipe page 43) and a green salad. Haddock may be served
with stewed beetroots.

STEWED EEL

Gestoofde paling

1¹/₂ lb. eel
¹/₄ cup butter or margarine
salt
water
lemon
bread crumbs.

Cut the skinned eel in slices, clean and wash them, salt the slices and put them in a casserole dish. Add a little water, lemon juice and butter. Sprinkle bread crumbs over the fish, bake in a hot oven, with the lid on, for 15 or 20 minutes. Lower temperature, remove lid and cook for a further 10 minutes. Serve with boiled potatoes and a green salad.

FLOUNDER OR SOLE
WITH SHRIMPS

Tongfilet met garnalen

1 lb. fillets of flounder or sole
salt
3 tbsp. butter or margarine
2 tbsp. flour
1½ cup fish-stock
juice of one lemon or equal quantity of white wine
1 egg yolk
¼ cup of cream or milk
¼ cup washed shrimps
parsley
lemon wedges.

Tie each fillet in a knot. Boil the fish in about two cups of salted water or "court bouillon" (fish-stock to which some white wine is added), until just done but still whole. Make a thick sauce of butter, flour and stock – add lemon juice or wine and then carefully the egg yolk and the cream or milk. Heat the fish and the shrimps in this sauce and sprinkle with parsley.

Decorate with parsley sprigs and lemon wedges.

COD-FISH AND RICE DISH

Stokvisschotel

2 lb. dried salt codfish, soaked, shredded
1 or 1¹/₂ tbsp. salt
1¹/₂ lb. potatoes
3 cups of uncooked (quick-boiling) rice
¹/₂ lb. chopped onions
¹/₂ cup butter or margarine
2¹/₂ tbsp. flour
prepared mustard.

Tie up dried fish in rolls and cook in salted water to cover. Simmer gently to prevent it getting hard. Cooking time 1–1¹/₂ hours. Turn out on serving dish. Peel potatoes and boil in little salted water (30 minutes). Turn out on dish. Boil rice, dry and turn out. Fry onions in some fat until light brown. Prepare mustard sauce from 1¹/₂ cup broth (fish stock), the butter or margarine, the flour, salt and a spoonful of mustard. Serve separately with the other dishes. Eat out of a soup plate. Mix everything in the plate and eat with a dessert or soup spoon. Serve with melted butter.

Casserole dishes

Dutch fish casserole

Fish casserole with mustard sauce

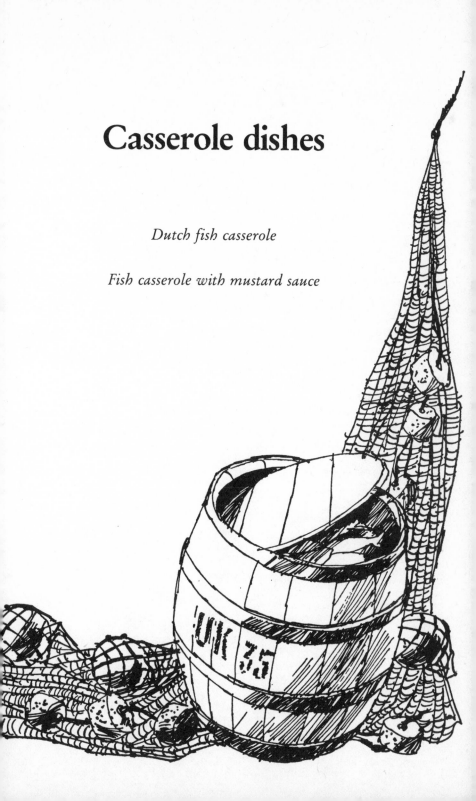

DUTCH FISH CASSEROLE

Panvis

The same ingredients as for the previous recipe. Same preparations but place mixture of all the ingredients in a casserole. If too dry add some water the fish has been boiled in. Sprinkle with bread crumbs, dot with butter. Place in oven to heat and brown. Serve with a salad.

FISH CASSEROLE
WITH MUSTARD SAUCE

Visschotel met mosterdsaus

For the casserole:
2 large sliced onions   2 tbsp. butter or margarine
1 lb. boiled or leftover fish (whiting, cod, plaice or
frozen fish)   lemon juice
leftover Dutch mashed potatoes (see recipe page 42).

For the mustard sauce:
1¹/₂ cup of fish stock (if leftover, otherwise take 1¹/₂ cup
of water and 1 meatcube)
a scant ¹/₂ cup flour   2 tbsp. butter or margarine
prepared mustard. (In Holland we use the Dyon-type.)

Bring the fish stock or water to the boil. Mix the flour with
a little water to a smooth paste and pour into the sauce liquid,
stir until it thickens. Add the butter or margarine and the
mustard. Fry the onions to a golden brown. Put the bits of
fish on the bottom of a casserole. Sprinkle some lemon juice
on them. Alternate with mashed potatoes, onions, fish and
mustard sauce, until all the ingredients are used up and finish
with a layer of mashed potatoes. Put the dish in the oven to
heat and brown on top.

Vegetables

Stewed beetroot

Spiced red cabbage

Spinach with hard boiled eggs

STEWED BEETROOT

Gestoofde bieten

1½ lb. cooked beetroot
1 small onion
salt
1 tsp. sugar
3 cloves
dash of vinegar
knob of butter or margarine
2 tsp. cornflour.

Peel (slip off skins) the beetroots and slice them. Put them in a saucepan with a little water, chopped onion, salt, sugar, cloves, vinegar and butter or margarine. Simmer them for ten minutes (keep the lid on the pan). Bind the liquid at the last moment with a little cornflour, made into a paste of pouring consistency with some cold water.

SPICED RED CABBAGE

Rode kool

One small red cabbage
1/4 cup of butter or margarine
3 cloves
2 cooking apples
1 tbsp. sugar
some vinegar, if liked
salt.

Remove the outer leaves of the cabbage. Cut the cabbage in halves. Remove the core. Wash and shred cabbage very thinly. Put a little butter or margarine in a saucepan and 1 cup of water. Add the red cabbage, the cloves, the peeled, cored and sliced apples and simmer the vegetables with a tight fitting lid on the pan for 3/4 hour. Then add the rest of the butter or margarine, the sugar, some vinegar and simmer for another 5 minutes.

SPINACH
AND HARD-BOILED EGGS

Spinazie met harde eieren

4 lb. spinach
salt
2 tbsp. flour
2 tbsp. butter or margarine
8 fingers of bread
2 eggs
butter to fry bread in.

Pick and wash spinach, add salt and cook without water. Toss spinach after it has boiled a few minutes. Cook for 5 to 10 minutes. Drain, cut or chop up spinach, stir in flour and add butter. Boil up to thicken. Fry fingers of bread in butter and hard-boil the eggs. Decorate spinach with fried bread (standing upright) and eggs cut in eight.

Casserole dishes

Chicory dishes

Cabbage and meat balls casserole

Brown beans and bacon

Hotchpotch

Curly kale and sausages stew

CHICORY OR ENDIVES WITH CHEESE SAUCE

Witlof met kaassaus

2 lb. of chicory
salt.

For the cheese sauce:
3 tbsp. butter or margarine
a scant 1/2 cup flour
1 1/2 cup half milk, half water
or some stock made from
2 meatcubes
1/2 cup grated Gouda cheese
Worcestershire sauce
salt
pepper.

Cut a very thin piece from the bottom of the chicory. Then insert a pointed vegetable knife and remove the core, which is rather bitter. Wash the vegetable and boil it for 20 minutes in salted water, or until tender. Then drain it well, put it in a casserole and cover the chicory with a cheese sauce made as follows:

melt the butter or margarine, add the flour and blend into a smooth paste. Then add the milk, water and meat-cube-stock stirring well. Boil for 5 minutes and add the grated cheese off the fire. Make it to taste with a little Worcestershire sauce and some salt and pepper. Cover the vegetable with it and put in the oven to color to a golden brown.

CHICORY WITH HAM

Witlof met ham

A variation is: boil the chicory heads. Drain and wrap each head in a slice of ham. Put in a casserole. Cover with thick cheese sauce and put into the oven to brown.

CHICORY WITH EGGS

Witlof met eieren

And a second one: cook them, drain well. Hard-boil one egg a head. Peel. Cut into halves (lengthwise). Melt some butter. Serve chicory on a hot plate. Decorate with eggs and hand round the butter and some grated nutmeg separately.

CABBAGE AND MEAT BALLS CASSEROLE

Koolsoorten met gehakt

1 head of cabbage
1 lb. ground beef or pork, prepared for meat loaf
according to preference
mashed potatoes. (See recipe page 42).

Clean and shred the cabbage and boil until almost done (¾ hour). Drain well. Meanwhile roll meat loaf ingredients into balls, brown them in butter in open skillet. Add a little water and simmer until done. Prepare the mashed potatoes. Place half of the cabbage in a casserole, top with the meat balls and cover with the remainder of the cabbage. Pour some of the gravy over the dish. Cover with the mashed potatoes. Dot with butter and brown in hot oven.

BROWN BEANS (Kidney Beans) AND BACON

Bruine bonen met spek

1 cup brown beans
bacon
salt
onions.

Wash beans in ample water, soak overnight and boil in soaking water. Add salt when beans are nearly done. Cooking time 3/4–1 hour. Clean bacon, cut into strips or squares and fry slowly until brown. Clean onions, cut in pieces, fry in bacon dripping. Use dripping as a sauce. Serve with boiled potatoes (see recipe page 41) and thick apple sauce (appelmoes).

HOTCHPOTCH

Hutspot met klapstuk

1 lb. lean boneless chuck (thin flank)
(England: lean brisket)
salt
2/3 lb. onions
4 lb. potatoes
2 lb. carrots
milk
4 tbsp. fat, butter or margarine
pepper.

Wash meat, boil in 2 cups water and salt for about two hours. Scrub and mince carrots. Peel, wash and slice onions and add them to the meat together with peeled and cut potatoes and carrots. Boil until done (about 30 minutes). Remove meat from pan. Mash all the vegetables and add fat, butter or margarine and pepper. If too thick add some milk (but a spoon must stand up in it). Serve with the sliced meat. This dish is eaten as a main meal dish, either with some soup to start, and followed up with fruit, as the dish is very nourishing. This amount serves 4 people in Holland (they have big appetites).

CURLY KALE AND SAUSAGES STEW

Stamppot van boerenkool met worst

2 or 3 lb. curly kale
3 lb. potatoes
milk
salt
about 1 lb. smoked sausage or Frankfurters
4 tbsp. fat, butter or margarine
pepper.

Strip wash and cut the kale very finely. Boil kale in little boiling water with salt, about 40 minutes. Add peeled and cut potatoes and sausage and enough water to prevent burning (cooking time 30 minutes). Remove sausage from pan, mash remainder and stir in boiled milk until smooth. Taste, add some pepper if desired.

"Stamppot" means that the vegetables and potatoes are mixed to a smooth consistency. It is a typical winterdish at home and the Dutch have a saying: never eat curly kale before the frost has got at it.

Pancakes
and other specialities

HOLLAND DROP-SCONES

Drie in de pan

Drie in de pan means: Three-in-the (frying) pan. The Dutch make them mostly of a yeast dough a little thinner than for Dutch doughnuts. But they can also be made of self-rising flour:

2 cups self-rising flour
salt
1¹/₂ cup lukewarm milk
1 egg
1 cup mixed currants and raisins (washed)
butter, margarine or cooking oil for frying
sugar.

Put the flour and the salt into a bowl, make a well in the centre. Put in the egg and 1 cup milk. Mix to a smooth batter. Add rest of milk and fruit. Then melt butter or oil in heavy skillet. Drop three pancakes into the hot fat and fry them on both sides to a golden brown. Turn them when puffed and full of bubbles (as you do griddle cakes or scones). Serve hot with sugar.

CINNAMON TURN-OVERS

Wentelteefjes*

8 slices stale bread
1 tsp. ground cinnamon
sugar
1 egg
1¹/₂ cup milk
pinch of salt
butter or margarine to fry.

Take the crusts off the bread. Stir cinnamon and sugar together. Add the beaten egg and milk, also the salt. Soak the slices in this mixture. Fry them slowly in butter on both sides and sprinkle with sugar before serving.

* American: French toast

REAL HOLLAND PANCAKES

Eierpannekoeken

These pancakes are as big as a dinner plate and formerly even bigger (12" in diameter!). Nowadays you may find such big pancakes on the menu of a restaurant, but at home we make them the dinner plate size. They are either eaten as a savory (with smoked sausage or bacon) or as a sweet (plain with molasses or golden syrup or with apples). Pancakes are best when made with yeast and they should be served piping hot. Use two skillets when available. Keep the pancakes hot on steam, or covered in the oven. Cold pancakes are awful!

The following recipe is a luxury one, for special occasions, as many eggs are used in preparing (in stead of yeast).

For one large pancake: 1 cup flour   salt
2 large eggs or 3 medium (¹/2 cup beaten)   1 cup milk
at least ¹/4 cup butter or margarine.

Put the flour and the salt in a bowl, make a well in the middle and add the beaten eggs. Mix to a smooth batter. Add the rest of the milk. Melt half the butter in a heavy skillet. Pour the batter into it. Turn these pancakes frequently, each time adding some butter. They should then become golden brown and crisp at the sides.

ORDINARY PANCAKES

Gewone pannekoeken

4 cups flour
or 4 cups Aunt Jemina pancake mix
salt
1 cake yeast (²/₃ oz)
4 cups lukewarm milk
butter or margarine.

Put the flour and the salt in a bowl. Make a well in the centre. Add the diluted (with a little milk) yeast. Add 2 cups milk and mix to a smooth batter. Add the rest of the milk. Leave to rise for ³/₄ hour. Heat enough butter in a heavy skillet. Pour in part of the butter and fry the pancake on both sides. (You can toss the pancake in the air for turning, if you like. Otherwise use a spatula). Keep them hot and serve with sugar or molasses, golden syrup or treacle.

APPLE PANCAKES

Appelpannekoeken

The recipe of page 90
and a small tart (cooking) apple
for each pancake
brown sugar
cinnamon.

Make the batter. Core, peel and slice the apples. When baking the pancake put 3 or 4 slices on top and cook them in the batter. Serve with sugar or brown sugar and some cinnamon, if liked.

BACON PANCAKES

Spekpannekoeken

Ordinary pancake recipe (see page 90)
(without butter or margarine)
3 oz bacon rashers.
Serve with brown sugar or molasses,
treacle or golden syrup.

Make the batter. Meanwhile fry the bacon in the skillet until crisp. Divide into as many portions as pancakes required. Also pour dripping out of the pan. Use for frying next pancake. Put the bacon on the bottom of the pan. Pour batter on top. Bake the pancakes until crisp at the sides and golden brown. Toss (turn) once or twice.

DUTCH DOUGHNUTS*

Oliebollen

1 cake yeast (²/₃ oz)
1 cup milk   2¹/₄ cups flour
2 tsp. salt
1 egg
1¹/₂ cups currants and raisins (washed)
1 tart (cooking) apple
oil for deep frying.

First blend the yeast with a little lukewarm milk. Sift the flour and salt. Add milk, mix to a batter with yeast and egg. Add currants, raisins and peeled, minced apple. Leave batter in a warm place to rise to double its size. Heat the fat to 375° F. (190° C). Put two metal spoons into the batter. Shape balls with the two spoons and drop them into the fat. Fry them for 8 minutes until brown. The doughnuts should be soft and should not be grease-soaked inside. If they are fried too slowly the crust becomes hard and tough and the doughnuts become greasy. Drain on absorbent paper. Serve then piled on a dish and cover thickly with sifted confectioner's sugar. Eat them hot, if possible.

"Oliebollen" are a traditional treat on New Year's Eve in Holland.

* makes 20

SNOWBALLS*

Sneeuwballen

¹/₂ cup cold water   salt
¹/₂ cup butter or margarine   10 tbsp. flour, sifted   2 eggs
2 tbsp. washed, dried currants or sultanas or raisins
oil for deep frying
sifted confectioner's sugar.

Mix water, salt and butter and bring to the boil. Remove from heat and stir in flour. Put back on heat. Keep stirring with wooden spoon until mixture leaves the pan and forms a ball. Remove from heat. Cool and then break in the eggs one at a time, beating well until smooth. Add the currants and raisins. Heat fresh oil or fat to 360°–370° F. (180° C.) and with a metal tablespoon (which should be dipped in the hot oil first) take out a spoonful of batter and fry until golden brown on both sides. This takes about ten minutes. These will puff up and become very light. Watch the temperature of the fat. Drain on brown paper and sprinkle with confectioner's sugar.

These "Snowballs" are also a traditional New Year's Eve sweet. They can also be made without the fruit. Then they must be cut open at the side and filled with sweetened whipped cream.

* makes 20

Steamed puddings

Steamed sultana pudding
with molasses or sauce
(golden syrup)

John in the sack

STEAMED SULTANA PUDDING WITH MOLASSES OR TREACLE SAUCE

Ketelkoek met stroopsaus

For the pudding:
2¹/₂ cup self rising flour
1 cup milk
1 egg
salt
¹/₂ cup each currants and raisins, washed
butter or margarine
bread crumbs or ground Dutch rusks.

For the sauce:
1 cup molasses or treacle (Brown treacle, if possible)
3 tbsp. butter or margarine
a dash of cinnamon.

Wash the fruit. Dry it in a towel. Crease a pudding-basin or a tube centre mold. Also grease the lid. Coat both with bread crumbs or ground Dutch rusks. Beat the egg, mix in the flour, the milk, salt and fruit. Mix to a smooth batter. Pour it into the basin (which may be ³/₄ filled only) and close tightly. Lay waxed paper loosely over tube centre mold if used. Cook for two hours in boiling water. When cooked take it out of the basin, turn it on to a big plate and dry it a moment under the grill. Make the molasses or treacle sauce: slowly melt the molasses or treacle and the butter or margarine over a low fire, put it in a gravy boat. Serve the pudding in slices and pour the sauce over it. This pudding, when left over and cold, can be eaten for tea, with butter or margarine and sugar, or spread with butter or margarine and treacle.

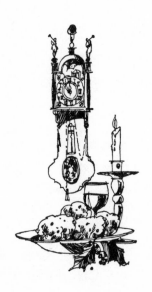

JOHN IN THE SACK
A Dutch steamed pudding like roly-poly

Jan in de zak

1 cake compressed yeast (²/₃ oz)
¹/₄ cup lukewarm water   3 cups sifted flour   1 egg   salt
³/₄ cup milk, scalded and cooled to lukewarm
¹/₃ cup each to raisins and currants (washed)
chopped peel.

Sprinkle yeast into lukewarm water and stir until dissolved. Place flour in bowl, add egg and milk, stir with wooden spoon until flour absorbs liquid. Then add fruit and salt and mix well. Add the yeast-water mixture and blend well with wooden spoon (dough will be sticky). Place dough in bowl, cover and let rise in a warm place for 45 minutes. Meanwhile sprinkle a clean wet cloth with flour. Roll dough into an oblong and tie loosely into cloth, filling two thirds full. Firmly fasten ends, stick safety pin in the middle. Steam 2 to 3 hours. Remove from cloth and serve hot with a molasses (treacle) sauce or with melted butter and brown sugar. Do not cut with a knife, but with a piece of string. If served cold, the next day, sprinkle with sugar and spread with butter.

"John in the sack" derives its odd name from the fact that it used to be made in a clean white pillow case, instead of in a mold. (Nowadays we use a linen cloth).

Desserts (Sweets)

The Hague bluff

Yoghurt cream with fresh fruits

Bread porridge

Hang-up

Dutch rusks with red currant sauce

Farina (semolina) cream with sultanas

Rice with currants

THE HAGUE BLUFF

Haagse bluf

The good citizens of the Hague were often accused by their countrymen – rightly or wrongly so – of bragging or showing off. The following recipe, "The Hague Bluff", is so named because it produces quite a fluffy dessert out of practically nothing. It is a great favourite with Dutch children.

5 tablespoons red currant or raspberry juice
1/2 cup sugar
one egg white.

Put the juice, sugar and the unbeaten white of egg in a deep bowl or in an electric-mixer (blender). Beat by hand ten minutes or more, the idea being that the longer one beats, the more one gets. Serve with a wafer or lady finger.

YOGHURT CREAM
WITH FRESH FRUIT

Yoghurtvla met vruchten

4 cups plain yoghurt
(yoghurt in Holland is rather thin,
like custard. Hence 4 cups of it.)
1 package instant vanilla pie filling
4 cups milk
1/2 lb. fruit in season
sugar to taste.

Wash the fruit and place in a glass bowl and cover with sugar to taste. Leave sugar to permeate for a couple of hours.
Take enough pudding powder to mix with 4 cups of milk and prepare according to indication on package. Chill. Mix well with chilled yoghurt and pour over fruit just before serving. Decorate with some well chosen fruits and serve with wafers or lady fingers.

BREAD PORRIDGE

Broodpap

4 cups milk
4 slices stale bread cut in dice
1/2 cup of brown sugar
2 tbsp. of ground cinnamon
1 tbsp. butter or margarine.

Bring the milk except for a few spoonfuls to the boil. Add the bread. Boil for ten minutes. Mix the sugar with the cinnamon and stir into the milk. Add the butter at the last moment.

HANG-UP*

Hangop

2 quarts buttermilk (8 cups)
sugar to taste   ground cinnamon
1 Dutch rusk per person or some crackers.

Place a clean, wet cloth in a strainer or colander. Pour the buttermilk into the cloth. Leave it there to drip for at least two hours, or until the residue in the cloth is as thick as unwhipped cream. Stir and scrape it off the cloth from time to time in order to allow the whey to drip away freely. Now scoop the stiff cream of the buttermilk off the cloth into a bowl and whip with a whisk until all lumps are removed. Add sugar to taste and chill. Serve in a soup plate with ground cinnamon and coarsely crumbled Dutch rusks, which are sprinkled on top.

This dessert is called Hang up, becauce in former days the buttermilk was poured into a wet linen pillow case and hung up by a string above the sink. The name has stuck and some people still make it that way.

* in Britain it resembles Bonny Clabber

FARINA (semolina) CREAM WITH SULTANAS

Griesmeelpap met rozijnen

4 cups milk
2/3 cup sultanas
a pinch of salt
3 oz. farina
4 tbsp. sugar
1/2 tbsp. butter or margarine.

Bring the milk to the boil with washed sultanas and the salt. Mix sugar and farina thoroughly and stir into the boiling milk. Boil gently 5–20 minutes (the coarser the cereal, the longer the cooking time). Add butter. Eat out of a deep plate.

RICE WITH CURRANTS

Rijst met krenten

1¹/2 cup (quick-boiling) rice
1¹/2 cup currants
4 cups water
¹/2 tsp. salt
lemon rind
butter or margarine
sugar.

Wash the rice and currants well and cook together in the water. Add salt and lemon rind. Serve with butter and sugar.

DUTCH RUSKS
WITH RED CURRANT SAUCE

Beschuit met bessensap

6 tbsp. red currant jelly
1/2 cup boiling water
1 cup water
4 Dutch rusks
1 stick cinnamon
peel of 1 lemon
2 tbsp. cornflour.

Dilute 3 tbsp. of jelly with the boiling water. Put the rusks in a shallow, oblong dish and soak them in the liquid. Bring the rest of the jelly, water, cinnamon and lemon peel to the boil in a covered saucepan and leave to simmer for a while. Mix the cornflour with a little cold water to a pouring consistency. Remove the cinnamon and the peel and thicken the red currant jelly sauce with the cornflour without boiling it. Pour the sauce over the rusks and serve either hot or cold.

Puddings

*Farina (semolina) pudding
with red currant sauce*

Chocolate custard

Black and white custard

Chipolata pudding

FARINA (semolina) PUDDING WITH CURRANT SAUCE

Griesmeelpudding met bessensap

For the pudding:
4 cups milk   vanilla essence to taste   2/3 cup farina
2 tbsp. cornflour   1/4 cup sugar   pinch of salt   1 1/2 tbsp. butter
1 egg yolk beaten and one egg white beaten stiff.

For the sauce:
Jar of red currant jelly   juice of two lemons
1/2 cup boiling water.

Boil the milk with vanilla. Add mixture of farina, cornflour, sugar and salt, stirring vigorously. Turn the heat to low; add butter and then the egg yolk carefully. Then fold in the beaten egg white. Pour pudding into a mould rinsed with cold water and chill.

Place currant jelly in a saucepan. Add lemon and boiling water, bring to a boil and stir until smooth. Chill.

Turn the pudding onto a platter and surround it with part of the sauce. Serve the rest separately in a gravy-boat. The thickness of the "griesmeelpudding" can be adapted to taste by altering the amount of farina given above. In Holland it is generally preferred quite thick.

CHOCOLATE CUSTARD

Chocoladevla

3 cups milk
3 tbsp. cornflour
1 oz or square unsweetened chocolate or 1 oz cocoa
6 tbsp. sugar
a pinch of salt
whipped cream (sweetened).

Bring the milk except for a few spoonfuls, to the boil. Mix the cornflour, chocolate and sugar dry and smooth out the lumbs. Then add the cold milk and blend smoothly. Pour into the boiling milk, add the salt and boil stirring well, for three minutes. Let cool, stir to prevent forming a skin. Pour in a shallow glas dish and top with sweetened cream.

BLACK AND WHITE CUSTARD

Zwart-wit vla
of crème panachée

Vanilla flavoured ready-made custard and chocolate custard of even texture. Holding one pan in your left hand and the other in your right. Pour both custards, evenly into a shallow glass dish. Top with whipped sweetened cream.

Chipolata pudding

¹/₂ oz or 1¹/₂ envelope gelatin
1 oz lady fingers
3 tbsp. Marasquino liqueur or Kirsch or rum
some whipped sweetened cream
2 oz currants
2 oz raisins
4 eggs
¹/₂ cup sugar
1 cup cream
1 cup milk
2 oz candied orange peel
2 oz peeled almonds.

Soften the gelatin in 5 tbsp. cold water. Cut the biscuits in small pieces. Soak them in the Marasquino or Kirsch or rum. Wash the raisins and currants well and cook them for 10 minutes in some water. Drain them. Mix the egg yolks with the sugar. Scald the cream and the milk. Add to the egg yolks and cook in a double boiler until the mixture coats the back of the spoon. Dissolve the gelatin in this mixture. Add currants and raisins and finely chopped orange peel, almonds and liqueur. Stir in this mixture from time to time.

Meanwhile brush a blancmange mold with unbeaten egg white. The leftover egg whites can be used for making a meringue. When the fruit does not sink to the bottom of the mixture any more fill the mold with layers of biscuits and the mixture. But do not start with biscuits or finish with them.

Let the pudding stand in a cool place until quite cold. Unmold it on a glass dish. Garnish the bottom of the pudding with whipped, sweetened cream.

We do not serve a sauce with this pudding. You can serve a vanilla sauce with it if you want.

Cakes and cookies

Salted cookies

Arnhem girls

Jewish buttercake

Buttercake with almond paste

Limburg pies

Spicy St. Nicholas' doll

Peppernuts

Creamy sugar candies

Snow sponge cake

Christmas ring

Dutch spice cake

Christmas cookies

The story is:
late in the month of November, Saint Nicholas comes on a steamboat from far-away Spain to our country. On the fifth December, his birthday, he rides on a white horse over the roofs of the houses and listens at each chimney whether the children have been good. In front of the fireplace, each child puts one of his shoes, for Saint Nicholas sends his moorish servant Peter down the chimney to put something nice in it.

They sing: *Nicholas, l beg you*
Drop into my little shoe
Something sweet or sweeter
Thank you Saint and Peter

SALTED COOKIES*

Zoute bolletjes

1 cup self-rising flour
¹/₂ cup butter or margarine
salt.

Quickly knead sifted self rising flour, softened butter or margarine and ¹/₂ tbsp. salt into a smooth ball. Shape into 50 small balls, ³/₄" in diameter. Place on buttered baking-sheet and bake in 350° F. oven for 15 minutes, or until golden yellow (sandcoloured).
"Zoute bolletjes" are mostly served in Holland as an appetizer with the "borrel" (Dutch gin). See also page 140.

* makes 50

ARNHEM GIRLS

Arnhemse meisjes

1 cup of butter or margarine
1/2 cup flour
a pinch of salt
about 4 tbsp. water
1 egg
sugar for sprinkling.

Make puff pastry in your own manner of the 4 first ingredients. Roll out thinly. Cut out ovals with a cooky cutter of about 2¹/₂". Place on buttered bakingsheet, not too close together. Moisten tops with a mixture of water and beaten egg and sprinkle with sugar. Bake about 10 minutes in a hot oven (450° F.) until done, very crisp and golden brown.

JEWISH BUTTERCAKE*

Joodse boterkoek

2 cups flour
1 cup butter
1 cup sugar (caster)
1 small egg, beaten
salt
3 oz finely chopped candied ginger.

Knead all the ingredients into a smooth paste, keep half the beaten egg for decorating. Butter a pie pan of 1" deep and 8" diameter. Press the dough into it. Brush the rest of the egg on top. Decorate the top in squares with back of a knife. Bake for 30 minutes in a moderate oven (350° F.) until golden brown. While still hot press the middle of the cake down with the back of a spoon. Cool and when firm to the touch turn out on wire rack.

This cake should be soft inside (but done!) and hard at the outside.

* See note on next page.

BUTTERCAKE
WITH ALMOND PASTE*

Gevulde boterkoek

For the dough:
2 cups flour   1 cup butter   1 cup (caster) sugar
1 small egg
pinch of salt.

For the filling:
2 cups blanched almonds
¹/₄ cup sugar
1 small egg
grated peel of half a lemon.

Knead all the ingredients for the dough into a firm ball. Divide the dough in two and press one half into a buttered pie pan of 1" deep and 8" diameter. Make the filling.
Grind the blanched almonds, mix with sugar, beaten egg and lemon peel and grind once more. Place this almond paste on top of the dough layer and press the other half on top of both. Bake in moderate (350° F.) oven until golden brown and done, about one hour. Remove from pan and cool on wire rack. Cut in wedges or diamonds.

* Both these cakes should be made with butter.

LIMBURG PIES

Limburgse vlaaien

For the dough:
a sweet bread dough (or fine bread dough) baked in a 10"
round pan or in 4 individual smaller pans, made of 2 cups
flour (use your own favourite recipe).

For the filling:
any fruit, dried fruit   sugar.

Limburg pies are thin, flat pies made of bread dough. They are made in all sizes from 4 to 20 inches in diameter. For a pie of about 8 inches a dough made of 2 cups flour will suffice. For preparing dough use recipe for sweet bread dough or fine bread dough adding a little butter or margarine. Knead dough, leave it to rise, roll it out thinly, put it in a greased round pan, cover up and leave to rise to double its size.
Pick dough with fork or knife if it has risen too high. Cut e.q. plums into halves, stone them and put them closely together on dough with cut side upwards, or fill pie with stoned cherries or stewed fruit. Bake pie in hot oven (450° F.) for about 30 minutes. Sprinkle fruit with sugar 10 minutes before pie is taken out of oven, sprinkle once more when pie is done. If stewed fruit is used, mix fruit with sugar before filling pie.

ST. NICHOLAS' DOLL

Speculaaspop

3 cups flour
²/₃ cup butter or margarine
¹/₂ cup dark brown sugar*
a pinch each of baking powder and salt
some milk to soften the dough
1 tsp. cinnamon
¹/₂ tsp. nutmeg
¹/₄ tsp. powdered cloves
¹/₂ cup almonds, blanched slivered and some halves
"for decorating".

Knead all ingredients to a soft ball, except the almonds for decorating. Roll out on a floured board to ¹/₄ inch thickness and stamp out shapes with different butterprints or make a "gingerbread doll" or cooky. Bake 25 minutes at 350° F. You can also make them like "Brownies" and cut them into squares (bake longer, 30–35 minutes). You will then call them: "Speculaasjes".

* When too coarse roll with rolling pin.

PEPPERNUTS

Pepernoten

1¹/₄ cup flour
1¹/₄ cup self-rising flour
¹/₂ cup brown sugar (see note previous recipe)
2 tbsp. water   1 egg yolk
¹/₄ tsp. each of cinnamon, nutmeg, powdered cloves
some anise seeds
a pinch of salt.

Knead all ingredients into a soft ball. Butter two baking sheets. Form about ninety marble-sized balls. Divide them over the sheets, so that they are placed at equal distances from one another. Flatten each ball slightly. Bake about 20 minutes in a moderate oven (350° F.) or until done. (They are then very hard.)

On Dec. 5th "Pepernoten" are often thrown through the slightly opened door by a black-gloved hand, representing "Black Peter", St. Nicholas' faithful helpmate. All the children crawl over the floor on which a white sheet is spread and grab what they can, while singing one of the popular St. Nicholas songs. A loud doorbell ringing just before this procedure enhances the excitement.

SNOW SPONGE CAKE

Moskovische tulband

For a metal fluted mold of 8" diameter and one small round fluted tea-cake tin.

4 eggs
1/3 cup sugar
vanilla essence or grated lemon peel
1 cup flour (sifted)
1/3 cup hard butter or margarine
confectioner's sugar.

Butter the big and the small mold. Coat with sifted confectioner's sugar. Separate the eggs. Add sugar and lemon rind to the egg yolks and beat them with a wooden spoon until of a creamy consistency (takes about 20 minutes). Cut the butter into the flour in very small pieces. Then whip the whites until stiff. Put the egg yolks, the flour mixture and the salt on top of the whites. *Do not stir anymore.*

Fold the ingredients into the whites with a metal spoon until all the flour has been taken up. Then immediately fill the molds for 2/3 and bake the cake for 20 minutes in a moderate oven (350° F.). Remove the small cake as soon as it is done.

Take the snow cake out of the oven. Let it stand for 5 minutes. Then turn it out on a wire rack. Leave to cool. When cold, put the little cake on top of the big one and dust with a thick layer of sifted confectioner's sugar.

This cake can be decorated for Christmas, with a sprig of holly and a red ribbon and for Easter with an Easterchicken. The Dutch serve it also as a traditional cake on New Year's Day with morningcoffee.

CHRISTMAS RING

Kerstkrans

Puff-pastry:
1 cup flour
1/2 cup butter or margarine
water to mix   salt.

For the filling:
almond paste: 3/4 cup shelled, blanched and peeled almonds
1/4 cup granulated sugar
1 egg
the peel of 1 lemon   5 candied cherries.

To decorate:
thin lemon icing   apricot preserve
candied cherries, red and green
candied orange peel
candied lemon peel or angelica
a red ribbon   holly.

Make the filling at least one month in advance. Store in jar. Grind the almonds very finely, add the sugar and the egg, also the grated peel. Mix well. Grind again. Store. When necessary knead through and add some water if paste is too stiff. Make the puff-pastry your favorite way. Roll out into a long strip of

1/8" thick, 4" wide. Brush your baking-sheet with water. Take a pancover that will nearly fit the baking-sheet. Put it in the middle and trace the circumference, this will guide you when forming the ring. Shape almond paste into a roll of nearly the same length. Press 10 halved candied cherries at equal intervals into the almonds paste roll. They must not be visible anymore. Now place the almond roll on the dough, a little above the centre. Wet the lower part of the dough with water and wrap it loosely around the almond paste roll. Put it on the baking-sheet: the "ring" will guide you. Seal the join well and turn roll until the join faces down. Form a ring by joining the two ends together with some water. Brush with beaten egg. Allow to stand for 15 minutes in a cool place. Then bake for 20 minutes in a hot oven (450° F.) until golden brown. When done, coat the ring thinly with preserve and when still *hot*, coat with thin icing (with a few drops of lemon juice). Cool. When firm, take from sheet and cool on wire rack. Decorate with halved candied cherries, orange peel and lemon peel cut in leaf shapes. Tie a ribbon round the ring where the two ends meet and decorate with holly.

DUTCH SPICE CAKE

Ontbijtkoek

2 cups self rising flour
1/2 cup dark brown sugar (demerara sugar)
1/3 cup molasses or treacle
1 cup milk
1 tsp. each ground cloves, cinnamon and ginger
1/2 tsp. grated nutmeg
pinch of salt.

Combine all the ingredients to a smooth paste. Butter an oblong 8" x 3" cake tin, fill with dough and bake for about one hour in a slow oven (300° F.). When cooked, allow to cool and keep in a tin or in the bread-bin for 24 hours before serving.

This cake keeps moist when put in the bread-bin with the bread. The Dutch serve it with their "elevenses", buttered or on a slice of bread for breakfast.

CHRISTMAS COOKIES

Kerstkransjes

2 cups flour
2/3 cup butter or margarine
3/4 cup sugar   1tbsp. milk
1 tsp. baking powder
grated peel of 1/2 lemon
salt   1 egg
rock sugar and 1/4 cup shelled almonds.

Knead flour, butter, sugar, milk, baking powder, lemon peel and salt into a soft ball and leave to stand for one hour. Roll out sections of the dough on a floured board to 1/8 inch thickness and cut out circles with a 2 1/2 inch tumbler. Place the cookies on a small round object such as a thimble. Remove centres and use them to make more cookies.

Coat dough "wreaths" with beaten egg and sprinkle them with a mixture of rock sugar and blanched, chopped almonds. Bake about 15–20 minutes in a 350° F. oven until golden brown. Leave to cool on sheet until no longer soft. Remove and cool further on a wire rack.

Pass gaily-coloured ribbons through the holes and hang them on the Christmas tree.

Ina den Hartog

INDONESIAN

COOKING

To anyone who likes to cook –anyone who likes to eat – this volume will bring the flavour of Indonesia into everybody's home.

Indonesia has developed a cuisine of exceptional delicacy and variety. It is a cuisine unlike that of any other country. In this delightful cookbook the exotic and flavourful art of Indonesian cooking is explained.

The essential ingredient in an Indonesian meal is rice and the „rijsttafel" is famous all over the world.

The recipes in this cookbook were gathered by the author during the many years she spent in Indonesia. Though the recipes are colourful and exotic, the dishes are not difficult to prepare.

Each recipe has been adapted to modern kitchens, substituting where necessary for items, which are not available in western countries. The book also contains information for special ingredients and kitchen-ware.

Charming drawings by the author decorate this exciting cookbook.

DE DRIEHOEK / AMSTERDAM, Publishers
Keizersgracht 756

Miscellaneous

Fried rice

Creamy sugar candies

"Kandeel" (a beverage)

"Slemp" (a beverage)

Savory appetizers

FRIED RICE

Nasi goreng

This dish originated in the Dutch East Indies (now Indonesia) and is very much liked by the Dutch. It is eaten out of a soup plate with a large spoon.

Butter, margarine or oil
3 tbsp. very finely chopped onions
some garlic or garlic powder
spices: $1/2$ tsp. coriander, $1/2$ tsp. caraway seed
$1/2$ tsp. finely chopped chili (hot red pepper)
1 cup chopped ham or cooked pork
salt   pepper
$31/2$ cup cold cooked rice
an omelet, made of 3 eggs
if desired 1 cup cut-up shrimps
cucumber salad.

Fry the onions in the butter until light brown. Add the garlic, the spices and the meat. Season with salt and pepper. Fry the meat for a few minutes. Add the very fluffy and dry rice. Keep stirring until the rice browns lightly. If too dry add some meat stock. Add the shrimps if desired.

Now bake an omelet, cut in thin slices. Put the rice-mixture in a shallow dish and garnish with the omelet slices.

This dish may be served with cucumber salad. And one should drink a glass of beer with it. If you want it rather "hot" add some chili powder or very little dried chili.

When available in your neighbourhood serve with "prawn chips" (kroepoek) made of dried shrimps fried in oil. You might be able to get it in a shop where they sell products from Singapore or Indonesia.

CREAMY SUGAR CANDIES

Roomborstplaat

1¹/₂ cup white sugar
1 cup brown sugar
¹/₂ cup light cream
1¹/₄ tbsp. butter and some butter
for brushing the molds
3 tbsp. fruit-flavoured extract
or 4 tbsp. instant coffee or
2 tbsp. cocoa.

Place tin rings or other open molds on a large piece of wax paper. (Lids of tins may substitute them). Brush paper and molds with softened butter. Put sugar, cream, butter and the coffee or cocoa flavouring in a saucepan (if fruit extract is used, it should be added later). Bring slowly to the boil without stirring, until a syrup results; this takes about five minutes. A drop of this syrup dropped into a cup of cold water should form a little ball or pea, or if syrup spins a thread.
Remove pan from heat at once (stir in fruit extract). Stir to cool and pour into the prepared molds when the syrup can hardly be poured any more, to a thickness of about ¹/₄ to ¹/₂ inch; the smaller the molds, the thinner the "borstplaat". Cool in the molds, then remove.

BEVERAGES

Dranken

There are a few typical beverages we make for special occasions. A traditional drink, we offer to our visitors when a baby is born is "Kandeel". It is served in small cups and poured out of a pitcher (jug). In the pitcher a long stick of cinnamon is stuck. And a bow is tied round it; a pink one for a girl, a blue one for a boy.

KANDEEL*

¹/₂ cup water
20 cloves
a cinnamon stick
grated peel of ¹/₂ lemon
6 egg yolks
¹/₂ bottle of Rhine wine
1 cup sugar.

Tie the spices in a piece of cloth. Hang it in the water and simmer for 1 hour (add some water when it evaporates). Cool. Beat the egg yolks with sugar until creamy. Add wine and liquid. Put in double boiler and stir until it thickens.

Another beverage the Hollanders drink after skating is:

* for 6 cups.

SLEMP

spices:
½ tsp. tea, cinnamon stick of 1",
saffron, 2 cloves, mace
4 cups milk
grated peel of ½ lemon
2 tbsp. sugar
salt.

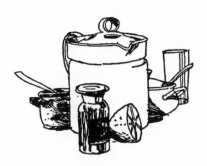

Put the spices in a piece of cloth. Tie with a string. Boil the milk. Hang the spices in the milk (tie the string to the handle of the pan). Add lemon and salt and simmer for one hour. Then remove spice-bag. Add sugar and serve piping hot.

SAVORY APPETIZERS

Bitterballen

1 cup thick white sauce
2 cups chopped cooked meat
(roastbeef or veal or ham or
a mixture of all three)
1 tbsp. minced parsley
pepper   salt
Worchestershire sauce
1 egg
fine dry bread crumbs
oil for deep frying   wooden picks   prepared mustard.

Mix sauce, meat, parsly. Add pepper, salt and sauce to taste. Chill. Shape into balls (1 inch). Roll in bread crumbs. Dry for two hours. Mix egg with 2 tbsp. water. Dip balls in egg, again in bread crumbs.Fry in hot deep fat (400° F.) for 1 to 2 minutes. Drain. Serve piping hot, on a wooden pick. Mustard can be handed round or put on a small dish.
The word "bitter" comes from "gin and bitter" and does not mean the opposite of "sweet".
The people in the Netherlands serve these, when drinking their "Dutch gin", before dinner, called "Borrel". But always serve "jenever" (Dutch gin) icecold. Not "with ice"!

Index (English)

Index (Hollands)